MINISTRY OF JUSTICE THE REP. OF KOREA

VISITOR'S PERMIT.

current for SIX (6) MONTHS or
earlier if holder leaves New Zealand

from -2 MAR 1993 20129

subject to all normal conditions

Immigration Off

Reference
NEW ZEALAND IMMIGRATION ACT 1

DEPARTMENT OF IMMIGRATION
PERMITTED TO ENTER
AUSTRALIA,

24 APR 1986

on

For stay of 12 Month

SYDNEY AIRPORT 54

IMMIGRATION & ETHNIC AFFAIRS

...Person
30 OCT 1989
DEPARTED
AUSTRALIA
SYDNEY 32

THE INSIDER'S GUIDE TO

NEW ZEALAND

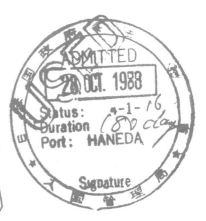

中华人民共和国
广东省公安厅

上陸許可
ADMITTED
15. FEB. 1986
4
Status: 4-1-
Duration: 90 days
NARITA(N)
Immigration Inspector
日本国

ADMITTED
20 OCT. 1988
Status: 4-1-16
Duration 180 days
Port: HANEDA
Signature

№ 011278

THE UNITED STATES
OF AMERICA
NONIMMIGRANT VISA
ISSUED AT

SSED Air Port

U.S. IMMIGRATION
170 HHW 1710

JUL 20 1988

HONG KONG
(1038)
-7 JUN 1987
IMMIGRATION
OFFICER

THE INSIDER'S GUIDES

AUSTRALIA • BALI • CALIFORNIA • CHINA • EASTERN CANADA • FLORIDA • HAWAII •
HONG KONG • INDIA • INDONESIA • JAPAN • KENYA • KOREA • NEPAL • NEW ENGLAND • NEW
ZEALAND • MALAYSIA AND SINGAPORE • MEDITERRANEAN FRANCE • MEXICO • PORTUGAL •
RUSSIA • SPAIN • THAILAND • TURKEY • VIETNAM, LAOS AND CAMBODIA • WESTERN CANADA

The Insider's Guide to New Zealand
First Published 1994
Reprinted 1995

Hunter Publishing Inc
300 Raritan Center Parkway
CN94, Edison, N.J. 08818
published by arrangement with Novo Editions, S.A.
53 rue Beaudouin, 27700 Les Andelys, France
Telefax: (33) 32 54 54 50

© 1994 Novo Editions, S.A.

ISBN: 1-55650-624-4

Created, edited and produced by Novo Editions, S.A.
Edited by: Jude Bond
Editor in Chief: Allan Amsel
Original design concept: Hon Bing-wah
Picture editor and designer: Jude Bond
Text and artwork composed and information updated
using Ventura Publisher software

Printed by Samhwa Printing Company Limited, Seoul, Korea

THE INSIDER'S GUIDE TO

NEW ZEALAND

By Kirsten Ellis

Photographed by Robert Holmes

HUNTER PUBLISHING, INC.
Edison, N.J.

Contents

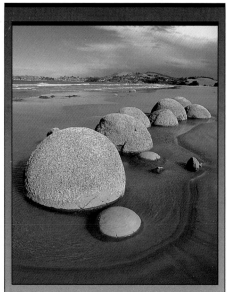

NEW ZEALAND

MALAYSIA

● SINGAPORE

INDONESIA

PAPUA
NEW GUINEA

SOLOMON ISLANDS

NEW HEBRIDES

NEW CALEDONIA

AUSTRALIA

TASMAN

SEA

NEW
ZEALAND

N

150 miles
240 km

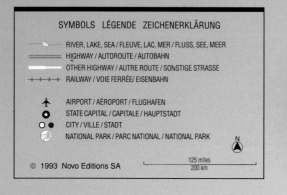

SYMBOLS LÉGENDE ZEICHENERKLÄRUNG

〰 RIVER, LAKE, SEA / FLEUVE, LAC, MER / FLUSS, SEE, MEER
═ HIGHWAY / AUTOROUTE / AUTOBAHN
▬ OTHER HIGHWAY / AUTRE ROUTE / SONSTIGE STRASSE
+++++ RAILWAY / VOIE FERRÉE/ EISENBAHN

✈ AIRPORT / AÉROPORT / FLUGHAFEN
✪ STATE CAPITAL / CAPITALE / HAUPTSTADT
○● CITY / VILLE / STADT
⊕ NATIONAL PARK / PARC NATIONAL / NATIONAL PARK

© 1993 Novo Editions SA

N

125 miles
200 km

L.Map

WESTLAN
N.

Jackson
Bay

Jackson Bay

MT.ASPIRING

Milford
Sound

NATIONAL PARK

La
Wak

Paradise

Wanak

Mitre Peak

Milford Sound

Arrowtown

Glenorchy

Doubtful
Sound

Lake
Te Anau

Queens-
town

Crom-
well

C

FIORDLAND
N.P.

Roxl

Deep Cove

Te Anau

L.Mana-
pouri

Dusky
Sound

Walau R.

Gore

CATLINS
FOREST

Invercargill

Halfmoon Bay

STEWART ISLAND

SOUTH PACIFIC

OCEAN

Cape Reinga
Spirit's Bay
Houhora
Karikari Peninsula
Ninty Mile Beach
Doubtless Bay
Mangonui
Kaitaia
Whangaroa Harbour
Mangamuka
Kerikeri
Matauri Bay
Bay of Islands
Kohukohu
Waimate North
Russell
Rawene
Paihia
Whangarei

LITTLE BARRIER ISLAND
Leigh
GREAT BARRIER ISLAND
Sandspit
Warkworth
KAWAU
Waiwera
Orewa
Cape Colville
Silverdale
Colville
Whangaparaoa
HAURAKI GULF
Coromandel
Bethalls
Tapu
Whitianga
Auckland
Te Puru
Karekare
Manukau
Tairua
Thames
Waihi
Whangamata
Te Aroha
Athenree
Bowentown
WHITE ISLAND
Whakatane
Whanarua Bay
Waihau Bay
Te Araroa
Katikati
Tauranga
Torere
Hamilton
Ruatoria
Te Awamutu
Mt. Ngnongotaha
L. Rotoiti
Ohope
Opotiki
Rotorua
Waitamo Caves
Te Kuiti
Waimangu
UREWARA NATIONAL PARK
Orakei Korako
Waiotapu
Gisborne
Lake Taupo
L. Waika-remona
L. Waika-reiti
Poverty Bay
Taupo
New Plymouth
Tongariro
Turangi
Hawke Bay
EGMONT NATIONAL P.
TONGARIRO N.P.
Napier
Hawera
WHANGANUI N.P.
Hastings
Cape Kidnappers
Te Mata
Wanganui
Havelock North
Palmerston North
Woodville
Levin
Masterton
Castlepoint
Para-paraumu
Upper Hutt
Carter-ton
Riversdale
Paeka-kariki
Lower Hutt
Martinborough
Wellington

TASMAN

SEA

Farewell Spit
Golden Bay
Takaka
Pupu Springs
Karamea
Marlborough Sounds
ABEL TAS-MAN N.P.
Queen Charlotte S.
Nelson
Picton
Cape Foulwind
Westport
Blenheim
Cook Strait
Punakaiki
Charleston
NELSON LAKES
Barrytown
Blackball
NATIONAL PARK
eymouth
Shantytown
Kaikoura
itika
Arahura R.
COOK
Rakaia R.
Christchurch
Lyttelton
Canterbury Plains
Akaroa
o
Fairlie
Timaru
Oarmaru
arch
Otago Peninsula
edin

Welcome to New Zealand

NATURE has always reigned paramount in New Zealand. Nestled deep in the South Pacific, New Zealand lies beneath tumescent mountains of white clouds, a phenomenon that so entranced its early Maori settlers they called it Aotearoa, "the land of the long white cloud." For millennia, New Zealand was its own kind of Garden of Eden. Isolated, its flora and fauna remained largely faithful to the Green Age, the Mesozoic era, that formed it. Amazingly, it has living contemporaries of the dinosaur, in its lushly primeval podocarp forests and the *tuatara*,

the world's oldest living reptile, now found only on a few islands in the Cook Strait and off the east coast of the North Island. For many centuries, New Zealand's forests were the domain of the moa, a colossal flightless bird that grew to be up to four and a half meters (15 ft) tall, until hunted to extinction by the Maoris in the seventeenth century. Its tiny relative, the kiwi, a near-blind, shuffling nocturnal bird, has been adopted as the nation's symbol.

New Zealand is comprised of two main islands — North and South — together 1,600 km (1,000 miles) in length, and is similar in size to Japan or Great Britain. It has a tiny population — only three million people. They are a diverse cultural mixture of Europeans, Maoris and Polynesians and whether they arrived by airplane, boat or — in the far distant past — canoe, all can trace themselves to immigrant stock, often only several generations ago.

Although splintered from the ancient continent of Godwanaland, New Zealand is, in all senses, a young country. It was unknown by the rest of the world until the early sixteenth century, and its documented history is only about 250 years old. With its wild, untrammeled natural beauty, New Zealand seems to stamp its mark on its people too, whose lives easily embrace a certain self-sufficiency and affinity for the open wilds, dense forests and the ocean. Urban populations make up only one third of the nation's total, and Wellington, the capital, has only 350,000 people.

For visitors, New Zealand's most profound lure lies in its natural wildernesses, which offer experiences of tranquility, awesome grandeur or pure scenic beauty. Traveling through the country, you will quickly notice how rapidly dazzlingly different landscapes change within a very short space of time. In the North Island, you can be dabbling your toes from a boat in the Bay of Islands, watching an idyllic sunset across a stepping stone horizon of emerald islets. A few hours away is the bleak remote stretch of Ninety Mile Beach, which curves up to Cape Reinga, the country's furthermost point, where Maoris believe their souls depart for the long journey back to their mythical ancestral land, Hawaiki. Within the central plateau, volcanoes smolder, geysers spurt boiling mud, mist-filled passages reveal limestone caverns, pristine rivers are full of large-sized trout, and peaceful riverside settlements surround maraes (distinctive Maori meeting houses). Over a few days in the less populated, dramatically scenic South Island, you can see glaciers tumbling into subtropical rain forest within the Mt. Cook region on the West Coast; ski in the Southern Alps from Queenstown; explore deep tracts of lush bush, mystical lakes and tumbling waterfalls in Fiordland's Milford Sound region; watch sperm whales surface off the Kaikoura coast or simply laze in the sun at the Banks Peninsula, an hour's drive from the very Anglicized city of Christchurch. Off the coast of the South Island, Stewart Island is the last stop before Antarctica, 1,600 km (960 miles) away, and one of the few places to see the kiwi in the wild.

Perhaps, in the world's eye, New Zealanders have a reputation as jovial ruddy, corrugated-faced farmers, vastly outnumbered by the country's 100 million sheep, living in a rugged nation that breeds world-class rugby players. In fact, it is a country that defies easy labels, a still-young country shaping its identity on the edge of the Pacific Rim. Amongst its luminaries are the writers Katherine

cabbage trees, striated nipa palms, fluffy white *toi-toi*. Up the dusty beaten track, on those lazy summer afternoons, the noisy hum of cicadas would seem to amplify the stillness. It was home, a place to feel the sun on one's face and remember nature.

ON THE RESTLESS PACIFIC RIM

New Zealand lies within the unstable "circum-Pacific mobile belt," the so-called "Ring of Fire," the name given to the struc-

Mansfield, James K. Baxter and Janet Frame, as well as the most famous New Zealander of them all, Sir Edmund Hillary, who conquered Mt. Everest in 1953.

When far away from the country I call home, the New Zealand I recall remains rooted in childhood images. Without having to press a shell to my ear, I can almost hear the whispering of the wild surf, walking barefoot along the black sands of Piha Beach, on Auckland's west coast. Salty mist could be tasted on the tongue, and giant tentacles of seaweed would form fascinating forms amongst shells, seagulls and the shore's lacy froth. Looking up, the headland was reassuringly familiar — yet seen nowhere else in the world — a tangle of spiky

turally restless rim of the Pacific shakily connecting lands as far as Chile and Japan. Earthquakes are common in New Zealand, although major quakes are not nearly as frequent as they are in Japan or many other countries on the Pacific Rim. On average however, one a year reaches Richter magnitude six, but relatively few lives are lost through earthquakes because of precautionary building methods.

New Zealand's islands drifted away from the ancient super continent of Gondwanaland about 100 million years ago, long before the other continents such as Australia

OPPOSITE: The tranquil calm of the Bay of Islands.
ABOVE: A lakeside view in Fiordland, near Queenstown.

and Africa broke off and long before mammals had evolved. This long-term isolation meant that most the country's plant forms are unique in the world. At that time, floral visitors such as bees and butterflies, had not evolved. There was no need for flamboyantly colored flowers, which explains the intense "greenness" of New Zealand's bush.

Until the arrival of humans, the country had no mammals at all except for an indigenous bat. The isolation also explains how New Zealand can be so close to the continent of Australia, renowned for its poisonous spiders, snakes and other deterrents to barefoot bush walking, and yet have none of these except the very rare *katipo* spider. Flightless birds such as the kiwi and the giant moa filled the ecological niches occupied by mammals in other countries until man arrived to destroy their numbers. The animals they brought with them, such as deer, cats, rats, stoats and dogs took their toll on the native inhabitants, both plant and bird. Today all native birds are protected and huge efforts are being made to save those most depleted, such as the kiwi, the kakapo, a large nocturnal parrot, and the takahe, from extinction. Other distinctive New Zealand birds include the flightless weka, the kea, a bold, inquisitive mountain parrot, the kaka, a shy bush forest parrot, and the tui, a bush songbird that lives on nectar, common in gardens and forests throughout the country. Exceptional birds are the yellow-eyed penguin, which can be seen at Taiaroa Head on the Otago Peninsula, and the world's only mainland Royal Albatross colony.

THE HISTORICAL BACKGROUND

EARLY ANCESTORS

The mysterious ancestors of Aotearoa's earliest settlers are thought to have reached the western Pacific some 4,000 years ago, and gradually made their way along the Melanesian chain of islands into the heart of Polynesia. With sails and outriggers to stabilize their canoes in rough weather, they cast themselves eastwards, scattering populations in Fiji, Tonga, the Marquesas and Cook islands, and further still, to Hawaii, Easter Island and New Zealand. The first inhabitants, the Moriois, a Polynesian race, darker than the Maoris and probably of Melanesian extraction, arrived in New Zealand around 750 A.D. Subsisting primarily on fishing and foraging, they also hunted the moa, a huge now-extinct, flightless bird. These early "moa-hunters" settled along the eastern coast of the South Island, and by the time Maori settlers arrived, may have numbered between 10,000 and 20,000. Sometime between the ninth and sixteenth century, the Morioris left New Zealand and settled on the remote Chatham Islands, where cut off by the ocean, their culture evolved apart, and in the eighteenth century declined to just a handful, killed off by Maori invaders and European diseases. The last full-blooded Moriori died there in 1934.

Maori legend has it that the first adventurer to cross the seas to New Zealand was Chief Kupe in the tenth century, who sailed all the way from Hawaiki, (the ancestral home of the Maoris, thought to be in the Society Islands near Tahiti). Kupe allegedly gave directions, passed on over generations to ancestors who came to New Zealand in great ocean-going canoes, named *Tainui, Te Arawa, Aotea, Takitimu, Tokomaru* and many others, arriving in a series of migrations during the fourteenth century. The names of the canoes are all woven into Maori lore, and their landing points, crew and histories all remembered. Today Maoris still trace their ancestry back to the canoes of the great Polynesian migration.

Establishing themselves in their new adopted home, the Maoris evolved one of the world's richest, most complex stone-age cultures. They were able to thrive on forest birds, shell-fish, and fish, also eating the dog and the rat, which they had brought with them in their canoes, and *kumara* (sweet potato), taro and yam. In addition, as Sir Peter Buck, a renowned Polynesian scholar, dryly remarked, "Human flesh was eaten when procurable." Cannibalism was said to have been so popular amongst Maoris living in the Queen Charlotte Sound area, that people lived entirely on "fish, dogs and Enemies." Especially in the North Island, Maoris constructed palisaded, terraced hilltop fortresses, or *pa*, encircled with steep ditches.

Fewer tribes lived in the colder South Island, apart from nomadic moa hunters. The Maoris developed a fiercely tribal warrior culture, in which defeated enemies ended as slaves, (to be eaten later on special occasions), shrunken-head war trophies, or went straight into the pot as part of ritual cannibal feasts.

Although they did not evolve a written language, the Maoris created many complex art forms, especially beautifully carved war canoes; *whare runangas* or "meeting houses;" fine woven cloaks decorated with kiwi, tui, and moa feathers. They adorned themselves with intricate tattoos, on the faces, thighs and buttocks of men, and on the lips and chins of women. They produced exquisite ear rings, and *hei-tiki* or ancestral pendants from carved nephrite jade known locally as greenstone, as well as a formidable array of weapons, including the short spatulate *mere* and *patu*. To acquire it they would risk their lives on arduous journeys across the Southern Alps to reach the West Coast of the South Island, which they called *Te Wai Pounamu*, the Water of Jade.

Over the centuries, the Maoris increased and fanned out across the countryside until the islands were divided up into about 10 main tribes, each tracing its origin to a different canoe, and many lesser ones. Fiercely protective of their tribal identities, they were a people deeply attached to their land, with no concepts of nationhood or race. Not until the arrival of the *paheka* or white man, did warring Maoris concede that each Maori tribe belonged to the same race. So far as it is known they had no name for their race; "*maori*" meant "normal." They used the term to describe themselves only when, for the first time, they encountered another people.

EUROPEAN EXPLORATION

By the early seventeenth century, the boundaries of the African, American and European continents were no longer a mystery. But it was left to a Dutch seaman, Abel Janszoon Tasman, to confirm the existence of *Terra Australis Incognita*, an unknown continent in the Pacific then thought to stretch across the Pacific between South Africa and South America. In 1642, Tasman was sent by the Dutch East India Company to find this leg-

endary land, and anchored at Golden Bay, near Nelson, on December 13. Before they could reach land, four of his crew were butchered by Maoris. Not surprisingly, Tasman named this "Murderer's Bay" and did not attempt to land. Later, the newly-discovered land was renamed Nieuw Zeeland, after the old Dutch province of Zeeland. The next European visitor was Captain James Cook, who first laid anchor in Poverty Bay on the 6th October, 1769. A laborer's son, who rose to become the greatest seaman and navigator of his time, Cook was sent by the

Royal Society and the Admiralty to visit Tahiti in order to observe a transit of Venus, with instructions to afterwards seek out the legendary southern continent. On his first visit in 1769, he established that New Zealand was not part of that mythical land; three years later after touring Australia, he confirmed that it did not in fact exist at all. With him aboard the *Endeavour* were two distinguished botanists, Joseph Banks and Daniel Solander, whose field notes, together with some 360 plant species they collected, contributed greatly to the scientific, botanical and zoological knowledge of this remote world.

Traditional carving adorning a Maori *marae* (meeting place).

Historian Keith Sinclair wrote, "To picture how these undreamed-of strangers must have appeared to the Maoris, we must imagine what our reactions would be if we suffered a Martian invasion. According to one Maori chief, Te Horeta Taniwha, who as a small boy was present when Cook came to Mercury Bay, the Maoris at first thought the white men were goblins and their ship a god. Eighty years later the old man recalled their astonishment when one of the goblins pointed a walking stick at a shag and, amidst thunder and lightening the bird fell down

pelago in detail in his "Journey Around the World," published in 1777, and it was primarily because of these publications that the South Pacific became widely known throughout Europe. Cook noted that he found cannibalism hard to account for in a people "naturally of good disposition," whose "behavior towards us was manly and mild."

Before the end of the century, many other explorers followed Cook. The Frenchman Jean François Marie de Surville arrived two months after Cook and before the Englishman had left. His brutal treatment of Maoris

dead. 'There was one supreme man in that ship. We knew that he was the lord of the whole by his perfect gentlemanly and noble demeanor.' This chief goblin gave the little boy a nail which he long kept with great care as a tool and a god."

In the course of this first and two subsequent voyages—in 1773 and 1776—Cook spent a great deal of time charting New Zealand waters. With him were the Germans Heinrich Zimmermann (who published an account of his travels in Mannheim in 1781), Johann Reinhold and Georg Forster. The last of these was the first to describe the archi-

resulted in the massacre of his countryman, Marion de Fresne, three years later, whose end in the Bay of Islands was particularly lurid. He and 26 of his men made culinary history of sorts when they became the first Europeans to be killed and eaten by Maoris, in an inlet still known as Assassination Cove. In retaliation, the remaining French sailors slaughtered hundreds of Maoris with volleys of gunfire, a massacre that set the stage for decades of misunderstandings, massacres and violence. Other explorers, Duperery, Duplit-Thouars and Dumont d'Urville landed in New Zealand in 1769, 1772 and 1826 respectively.

Trade was to follow close on the heels of exploration.

ABOVE: Two faces of rural New Zealand.
OPPOSITE: New Zealanders grow up with an affinity for most sports and the outdoors.

EUROPEAN SETTLEMENT

When the first Europeans settled in New Zealand, in the late eighteenth and early nineteenth centuries, it was estimated that about 30,000 Maoris lived there. They were whalers and seal-hunters, along with kauri merchants, eager to exploit the rich natural resources Cook had so enthusiastically reported on. So thorough was the slaughter of the seals, that by end the of first decade of the nineteenth century they had almost

hunted them to extinction. From Kororareka (now known as Russell) in the Bay of Islands and many other smaller settlements scattered along New Zealand's coast, notably at Dusky Sound in Fiordland, they relied heavily on Maori assistance, and the Maori in turn were quick to see the advantages of such European commodities as muskets, metal implements, potatoes, fruit trees, pigs and sheep. Yet these seamen earned the hatred of many Maoris by treating Maori conscripts badly, or even kidnaping them as crew. They also infringed Maori spiritual law in *tapu* in innumerable ways, treated their women as prostitutes, stole crops and sacred greenstone items as "souvenirs" and were always embroiled in drunken brawls.

Finally revenge was exacted. In 1809, a Maori who was working his passage back home to Whangaroa in the Bay of Islands aboard the *Boyd* alerted his tribe to the injustices he'd suffered at the hands of the crew. Almost everyone aboard the ship was killed and eaten in retribution. For some time afterwards, shipping vessels were very wary of North Island ports. New Zealand had suddenly become notorious as being one of the most dangerous places in the Pacific.

Dubbed the "St. Augustine of New Zealand," the Reverend Samuel Marsden

founded the country's first mission in 1814 in Kororareka. Renowned as the "priest with the whip," Marsden had previously been active in Sydney where his brutal treatment towards the Aborigines had already caused some scandal. Yet he was the most influential of an early wave of Christian missionaries who sought to "reform" the morals and lifestyles of Maoris and raucous early settlers alike. When Charles Darwin called briefly at the Bay of Islands aboard the *Beagle* in 1835, he could find few redeeming features in Kororareka, but much praise for the newly-created mission house of Waimate North, located inland, which can still be seen perfectly preserved.

This was a time of confusion and disillusionment for many Maoris, who were dying in droves from inter-tribal battles (with newly-introduced muskets) and European diseases, particularly influenza. Keith Sinclair writes: "Above all there was the feeling, openly expressed, that the Maoris were dying out. The *ngarara*, lizard of death, was gnawing at the heart of the people. First of all in the Bay of Islands, then elsewhere, losing faith in their own gods and culture, they turned in hope or despair to the Europeans for guidance." During the 1830's, Christian chiefs put aside their extra wives, gave up tribal massacres and cannibalism, and freed their slaves.

In 1833, the country's first British resident, James Busby, arrived in Kororareka to safeguard the fledgling European settlement. When the British Government later decided in 1840 that they wanted to annex New Zealand, they sent Lieutenant Governor William Hobson to oversee the signing of a treaty with the Maori chiefs before proclaiming British sovereignty.

The bureaucrats, missionaries, traders and hundreds of Maoris who met on the lawns of Busby's Waitangi house on February 5, 1840, probably had in common a desire to sort out matters of difference and come up with a treaty that struck a working relationship, so that trade could prosper. The Treaty of Waitangi was signed by some 50 chiefs after a full day and night of discussions, and later taken around the country to be signed by a further 500 chiefs, although these signatories by no means represented all the tribes of New Zealand. Although regarded as the founding document of the New Zealand nation, whose status became that of a British possession in return for guarantees of certain Maori rights, the treaty's legal standing is dubious and many New Zealanders question whether it has been properly observed. The first visible revolt came when Hone Heke, one of the first chiefs to sign the Waitangi Treaty who later became bitterly disenchanted with its implications, chopped down the British colors atop a flagpole at Russell, the newly-named capital of New Zealand. Three times it was erected again, and each time Heke chopped it down again, the last time as part of his successful campaign to devastate Russell township. A bloody war broke out, led by Heke in the north and Chief Te Rauparaha along Cook Strait, with fierce fighting. But as they hardly had any firearms they were forced to surrender after three years. The ensuing "peace" did not last long, and there was a large scale renewal of warfare which lasted from 1860 to 1881, a period termed the "Land Wars." Maoris gathered around their great war chiefs Wiremi Kingiu, Te Kooti and Maniopoto, and even managed to draft some white men into their ranks. With their traditional guerrilla tactics they terrorized many European settlements in central North Island, and ran a separate political state in "King Country" within the Waitomo District and the central Taranaki region, until they were finally defeated by British forces.

Some pride was restored to the Maori people with the creation of Maori royalty in 1859, with the coronation of Potatau Te Whero Whero (1800–1860) who was crowned the first Maori king amongst much celebration at Ngaruawahia on May 2. His descendants continue the tradition of Maori royalty today.

CHILD OF MOTHER ENGLAND

Meanwhile in the first few decades of settlement, from 1840 to 1870, tens of thousands of immigrants had been making the 90-day voyage out to New Zealand, most of them from Britain. Edward Gibbon Wakefield, together with several other Englishmen, developed the New Zealand Company, and under a policy of selective immigration, set about founding a series of planned settlements, beginning in the Wanganui area, New Plymouth and Wellington, and drawing immigrants largely from Devon and Cornwall. Although not a Wakefield-inspired settlement, Auckland was founded as the nation's capital in 1841 when Governor Hobson decided that the Bay of Islands was not a suitable location. In 1848, Dunedin was founded by settlers sent out by the Lay Association of Scots while two

Studies in contrast. OPPOSITE TOP: New Zealand's rich coastal scenery and BOTTOM the scenic solitude of its rain forests.

years later, the "pilgrims" of the Canterbury Association landed at Lyttelton and struggled over the Port Hills to found Christchurch. By the 1860's, all of New Zealand's major provincial centers had been established.

There was an early striving among New Zealand's settlers to recreate in their new land all the civilizing touches of the culture they had left behind in Britain. They founded libraries and athenaeums, choral, literary and theatrical societies and newspapers. Certainly white New Zealanders are always very quick to point out that their

country was not founded as a penal settlement, like Australia. Another factor in the colony's increased settlement was the Gold Rush during the 1860's, followed by cotton schemes, attracting another 100,000 new immigrants, many of them coming from Scandinavia and Germany as well as Britain. Soon New Zealand was experiencing its first economic boom with the export of frozen meat — thus laying the foundations for its reputation as one of the world's greatest meat exporters.

The liberal regime that took over in 1891 implemented a number of sweeping social reforms. New Zealand's women were granted the vote in 1893, vying with the state of Wyoming and Pitcairn Island, 25 years before Britain or America and some 75 years ahead of Switzerland. Other far-sighted social reforms and pioneering legislation included old-age pensions, minimum wage structures, the establishment of arbitration courts and the introduction of child-health services. By 1907, the country had become a dominion of the British Empire.

The advent of the World War I reinforced the nation's ties to Mother England. Earlier, in 1899, the country sent a total of 6,500 men to fight alongside the Australian and British against the Boers in South Africa, many of them paying their own passage and even supplying their own horses. During World War I, some 40 percent of the male population aged from 25 to 45 years old, saw military action in North Africa and Europe, as part of the Australia-New Zealand Army Corps (ANZAC), with their tragic debacle on the blood-drenched sands of Gallipoli on April 25 1915, when 8,587 soldiers lost their lives and some 25,000 were wounded, a day now commemorated as Anzac Day.

Two generations of New Zealand men traveled as far as any soldiers in the history of war. This participation rate was amongst the highest of all countries and exceeded that of Belgium, where much of the fighting took place. Nearly 17,000 men died in action in World War I, at a time when the entire population of New Zealand was only one million. During World War II, when nearly 200,000 New Zealanders were called to war, more than 12,000 died in battle, many of them under the command of General Douglas MacArthur in the nearby Pacific campaign, others in North Africa, Italy and Crete, where they are still remembered as courageous fighters. Field Marshall Rommel had immense regard for the Maori Battalion, which numbered around 17,000 men, considering them to be some of the world's most formidable warriors. New Zealander, Second Lieutenant (later Captain and Sir) Charles Hazlett Upham was one of only three men in the world to be awarded a bar to his Victoria Cross.

Following the war there was a new wave of immigrants. Aside from British and Irish, these were primarily Dutch, Yugoslavians, Austrians, Swiss and refugees from Eastern Europe and the Baltic States.

In 1947 New Zealand's parliament adopted the Statute of Westminster, in which it became a full partner in the British Commonwealth. The country's government is modeled on the British parliamentary system, with a party approach to politics and an independent judiciary.

MODERN NEW ZEALAND

New Zealanders tend to see their economic development since World War II in two distinct phases: before Britain's entry into the European Economic Community (Common Market) in 1973, and then the aftermath compounded by the Oil Crisis of the same year. The 1950's and 1960's were boom years for the country, when its people were living "high on the sheep's back," as they say, supplying much of the dairy products and meat consumed by "the Motherland." When the changes brought about by Britain's EEC membership all but destroyed it as a market for New Zealand, the latter entered a period of recession. Nonetheless, it remains one of the world's largest exporters of the best quality butter, cheese, wool and meat, and continues to develop and expand new markets in Europe and Asia.

In 1984, David Lange, a former lawyer for dispossessed Maoris in the outer suburbs of Auckland, became at 41, the nation's youngest prime minister. Under the Labor Party, New Zealand proclaimed itself a "nuclear free zone" and crossed swords with the United States by refusing entry to nuclear-powered American submarines to its ports, a stand which resulted in New Zealand being excluded from the ANZUS defense pact, and the subject of on-going debate.

Internationally, New Zealand has a prominence that is nothing less than astonishing when you consider it is a country of only three million people. Regarded as an important Pacific nation, it has taken a strong political stand on anti-nuclear and peace issues. A strong backer of the Green movement, New Zealand has long condemned French nuclear testing at Mururoa Atoll in French Polynesia. In one of the more peculiar twists of international relations, the French retaliated by sending saboteurs to bomb the Greenpeace ship, *Rainbow Warrior*, moored in Auckland while it was preparing for a voyage to the atoll, killing the ship's photographer and putting a frost on relations between the two countries for some time.

The nation has been undergoing rapid economic restructuring, firstly under the Labor government, whose policies of privatization and de-regulation have resulted in what has been termed the "Thatcherization" of New Zealand, while under the new National Party, this has continued at the same time as a dismantling of the long-standing trade union and social welfare systems.

New Zealanders are proud of their record of racial harmony between the white majority and Maori minority, who represent nine percent of the population. There has never been any racial segregation and

inter-marriage is common. Also represented amongst minority groups are immigrants from Samoa, Tonga, Nuie, the Cook islands, China and South East Asia, who together form three percent of the population. Over the past decade, a great deal more official sensitivity has been shown towards Maori issues, notably resulting in a government drive to revive the Maori language and the setting up of the Waitangi Tribunal to arbitrate claims by Maoris over tribal lands.

OPPOSITE: The snow-capped Mt. Ngauruhoe towers above a barren vista in the North Island.
ABOVE: View from Abel Tasman National Park.

Adventuring Forth: The Great Outdoors

NEW ZEALAND'S most profound attraction is its extraordinary amalgam of landscapes, ranging from high volcanic mountains and long, lonely beaches to massive glaciers and quiet, isolated valleys. These vast expanses, often empty of people, offer a wide range of opportunities to action-seekers who thrive on recreational adventure and the exhilaration of a challenge. New Zealanders, with their tough, hearty, pioneer spirit are the ideal people to build an adventurer's Mecca, and they are in the ideal spot to do it.

The country is small, jam-packed with beaches, mountains and rivers and there has been an explosion of recreational resources, so that travelers can tour the North and South Islands, enjoying many totally different outdoor activities without any difficulty. This section of the guide is divided into activity sections that briefly describe the highlights of many old favorites — pastimes like trout-fishing, golf, sailing, skiing and trekking — as well as new ones, like the latest crazy adrenalin pursuit of bungy-jumping, the sport in which you attach yourself to a rubber cord and hurl yourself from a high place. This will give you an idea of the opportunities available throughout the country and the kind of costs involved, although prices quoted in the book may fluctuate seasonally. The best reference guide for tour operators is *New Zealand Outdoor Holidays*, up-dated regularly and available free from most major tourist information centers.

NEW ZEALAND NATIONAL PARKS

In 1887 the Tuwharetoa Maori people made a gift of their ancestral volcanic peaks of Tongariro, Ruapehu and Ngauruhoe in the North Island, to the people of New Zealand, thus creating New Zealand's first, and the world's second, national park. The country has 12 national parks, all natural wildernesses, with mountains, glaciers, fiords, lakes, beaches, rivers, and many with rare and endangered animal life, maintained to preserve their uniqueness.

Crisscrossed with hundreds of kilometers of walking tracks, short and long, and dotted with mountain huts, they are New Zealand's most remarkable asset.

In the North Island, **Urewera National Park** is the largest virgin native forest rich in bird life, with two spectacular lakes, Waikaremoana and Waikareiti. **Tongariro National Park** contains three volcanic peaks, Tongariro, Ruapehu and Ngauruhoe, the latter two occasionally active, and the North Island's most popular ski field. **Egmont National Park**, dominated by the Mt. Fuji-lookalike Mt. Egmont, is set against a lush backdrop of Taranaki farmland. **Whanganui National Park** surrounds the Wanganui River, New Zealand's longest navigable river, with many tramping tracks.

In the South Island, **Abel Tasman National Park**, close to Nelson, has perfect golden beaches, secluded coves and native bush. Mountainous **Nelson Lakes National Park** encloses the beech forest-fringed lakes Rotoiti and Rotoroa. Along the West Coast, the **Paparoa National Park** contains many curious fluted limestone rocks and cave systems, most dramatically the delicately-layered Pancake Rocks at Punakaiki. **Arthur's Pass National Park** straddles the Main Divide of the Southern Alps, with many challenging treks. **Mt. Cook National Park**, which encircles New Zealand's highest mountain, is a popular ski field as well a mountaineering and trekking base. **Westland National Park** has excellent fishing in its lakes Mapourika and Wahapo, while some of the most rewarding walking tracks are found within the far south national parks of **Mt. Aspiring** and **Fiordland**, the latter one of the world's largest nature reserves, with remote valleys of native beech forest.

There are three maritime parks — the **Hauraki Gulf**, **Bay of Islands** and the **Marlborough Sounds** — offering sheltered bays for swimming, boating, diving and fishing, and another 21 forest parks. For information about any of these parks, you can contact the Department of Conservation, P.O. Box 10-420, Wellington.

TREKKING

One of the best ways to appreciate the beauty of New Zealand's landscape is by

Rural splendor on the back road to Lake Wanaka.

foot. Even within a relatively concentrated area you'll discover a seemingly endless variety of scenery. Almost 20 percent of the country falls within some kind of nature reserve, offering vast opportunities for trekking and walking — or "tramping" in Kiwi slang — for people of all ages and fitness levels.

Depending on your stamina, tramping can mean anything from an afternoon enjoying the serenity of the tall kauri forest in Auckland's Waitakere Ranges to "going bush" for days in remote Fiordland, or anything in between. All you need to do is find your own level of challenge, whether you want to be self-reliant and "freedom walk," or join a guided walk.

Within the country's national parks and reserves are an impressive network of over 860 "tramping huts," so that more often than not, a tent is unnecessary. Usually spaced four to five hours walk apart — a comfortable walking distance for averagely fit people — the huts contain bunks with mattresses, cooking facilities (gas or fireplaces and wood), tap water and "long drop" (pit) toilets. You should come prepared with your own billy (a metal container for cooking and boiling water) and food. Fees for use of Department of Conservation (DOC) huts range from $4 to $12 and tickets for the huts can be found at any DOC office.

THE TRACKS

Throughout New Zealand's parks and reserves, short walks of up to a day's length are found everywhere, often marked with a "W" sign. In popular walking areas, tracks are well-formed, easily followed paths; off the beaten track the ways may be less cared for, but you will probably have the scenery all to yourself.

Of all treks the country's most famous is the **Milford Track**, a four day trek (walking up to six hours a day) between the head of Lake Te Anau and the Milford Sound in Fiordland National Park. About 33 km (20 miles) long, the trek is rated among the finest walks in the world. Because it is so

popular, the track hut's accommodation must be pre-booked. The track itself is open from early November to early April, although heavy rain can close it sooner. Costs for a five-day Milford Track "package," which includes all food, accommodation at THC hotels, as well as huts along the track, transport from Te Anau Downs and boat cruises, are $999 for adults and $750 for children under 15 years-old.

Even if you are "freedom walking," it costs an adult $153 and a child $101 for transport services to and from the track, excluding food and accommodation costs along it. All bookings for independent trampers are handled by the THC Te Anau Resort Hotel, P.O. Box 185, Te Anau, ((03) 249-7411, fax: (03) 249-7416.

Other renowned tracks include the **Routeburn-Caples** (three to four days), **Greenstone**, (two to three days), **Hollyford** (five to six days), **Kepler** (three to four days), **Dart-Rees**, (two days), **Dusky Track** (up to eight days), **Heaphy** (four to five days), **Copland Pass** (three to four days) and the **Abel Tasman National Park Coastal Track** (three to four days) in the South Island, and the **Whirinaki Track** (three to four days) and the **Ketetahi** (two to three days) and **Rainbow Mountain** (two days) tracks in the North Island.

All offer both freedom and guided walk options and each have their own character; the Milford Track delves deep into the sanctity of lush native forest; the Greenstone is a mellow river bank track through rolling beech forest; the Abel Tasman follows a golden coastline past many curving bays; the Hollyford walk clings to the tops of the valley, offering majestic views of snow-peaked mountains, while the Whirinaki walk offers glimpses of kauri giants.

For detailed information, contact any DOC office, or write to their head office at P.O. Box 10420, Wellington, which has pamphlets, maps and listings for all guided treks.

GUIDED WALKS

Not everyone feels inclined to launch out into the wilderness as an independent

A view from alpine pasturelands of the spectacular Mt. Cook.

"tramper." Throughout New Zealand there are a number of guided walks available for you to enjoy all the pleasures and challenges of the natural environment without having to fend for yourself. Most of them last from two to five days, with the overall fee covering all equipment, accommodation and food. It also means you can trek without having to carry a heavy back pack, secure in the knowledge that all responsibility for safety, shelter, food, bedding and general organization lies with the walk operator. You need carry only a small day pack with your own personal belongings. Costs for these guided walks vary between about $530 and $1,000. To find out more information on individual tracks, contact the DOC. *Tramping in New Zealand*, by Jim de Fresne, (Lonely Planet Publications), is an excellent reference for serious trekkers, and has detailed descriptions of all major walks in the country. There's also a series of *Shell Guides* on the most popular tracks, widely available at Automobile Association (AA) offices.

When embarking on a trek, even a short one, you'll need a pair of strong walking boots, woolen socks, undershirt, warm jersey, sleeping bag, hat, gloves, a windbreaker with a hood, a small water bottle, insect repellent and extras like sun protection cream, sunglasses and a camera, all of which can fit into a small backpack, which you should line with plastic to keep the rain out. You also need to take high-energy provisions to keep up your strength along the way, all food utensils, and lightweight tent gear if you're not sleeping in a hut. It's often possible to hire boots, raincoats, backpacks and tents from shops and track offices.

MOUNTAINEERING

Mountains run down both islands of New Zealand, with some thirty peaks higher than 3,000 m (9,900 ft), including Mt. Cook, in the glacier-tipped Southern Alps, at 3,764 m (12,349 ft), the highest mountain in Australasia. Although not high by world standards, these mountains still offer considerable challenges for experienced mountaineers.

The unpredictable nature of mountain weather and the sheer difficulty of many ascents make this no activity for unaccompanied, inexperienced amateurs. Instead, it's possible to hire a commercial guide, while local alpine clubs often run mountaineering courses that can be a good way to get started. The normal climbing season extends from November to March, and the best weather for climbing is usually at the end of this season.

While Mt. Cook and Westland National Park contain most of the more renowned ice and mixed rock routes, other areas allow climbers to combine treks in gentle rolling valleys, then tackle mountain adventures above the snow-line. Mt. Aspiring National Park has many challenging alpine climbs, transalpine trips and easy tramping routes within a few kilometers distance of each other. In Fiordland National Park, the Darran Mountains offer sheer granite cliff climbs and plenty of scope to break difficult new ground. Arthur's Pass is an excellent introduction to mountaineering in the Southern Alps, and has professional guidance and advice available from the park headquarters.

For further information, contact the New Zealand Mountain Guides Association, P.O. Box 20, Mt. Cook; or the New Zealand Mountain Safety Council, P.O. Box 6207, Wellington, ((04) 388-7162. Particularly in the Mt. Cook and Canterbury region, there are several guided trips for novice climbers who want an introduction to the Southern Alps, with prices ranging from $600 to $2,500.

SKIING

New Zealand offers enormous potential for winter sports and until recently it has been one of the country's best kept secrets. Most commercial fields have highly qualified ski schools, good supplies of rental equipment, good restaurant facilities and spectacular views of rolling snow-powdered mountains. Daily lift passes range from $30 to $41, rental equipment from $18 to $22 (skis, boots and poles) and lessons from around $22 for half day group classes to $50 for one hour individual tuition. It's always worth checking to see what packages are being offered by the Mt. Cook Group, who often create "bargain" week-long deals with accommodation, ski-hire, lift passes and transport.

The South Island offers the most dramatic skiing. The Southern Lakes ski region, centered on Queenstown and Wanaka, has four fields, which together offer some of the most varied skiable terrain in the world, with breathtaking panoramas over sparkling lakes, green valleys and alpine mountains. Close to Queenstown, Coronet Peak and The Remarkables ski areas have everything a skier could want — accommodation of all types, more than 50 restaurants to choose from and a befuddling array of other non-skiing activities that could exhaust even a hyperactive sportsperson. Near Wanaka are the Treble Cone and Cardrona fields, the first renowned for extensive expert skier territory, peppered with moguls, the second, a laid-back, family-orientated field, especially good for learner skiers. Near Christchurch, within the Canterbury region, the Mt. Hutt field offers the country's longest season (from late May to early November), aided by a $4 million snowmaking system. Nearby Porter Heights offers impressive terrain even for experienced skiers, while further south, Ohau and Dobson have good fields for intermediate/advanced skiers, and **Rainbow Mountain**, tucked away in Marlborough, has only rope-tows, but offers splendid scenery.

In the North Island, the two main ski fields are Whakapapa and Turoa, both located on the slopes of 2,796 m (9,173 ft) Mt. Ruapehu, an active, occasionally smoking volcano whose cone dominates the island's central plateau. Nearby Tukino is a smaller club field, with only rope-tows but some thrilling ski terrain.

The country's only cross-country Nordic field is on the Pisa Range, near Wanaka, which has some 25 km (15 miles) of groomed ski trails with terrain suitable for learners through to advanced telemark skiers. Hire facilities, instructors, guides and overnight ski-touring opportunities are available at the field's center.

Heliskiing has become a phenomenon in New Zealand, where deep powder-snow, comparatively low altitudes and stunning scenery combine for near-perfect conditions. From Wanaka and Queenstown, Harris Mountains Heliski, the second largest heliski operation in the world, and Southern Lakes Heliski, offer more than 400 individual runs in a 2,000 sq km (1,200 sq miles) area of high peak terrain. Here, heliski runs trace the momentous silhouettes of the Tyndall Glacier, with its steep peaks and glacial chutes, and wide treeless fields. At Mt. Cook, Alpine Guides operate ski planes to the spectacular Tasman Glacier, which offers a run of 13 km (eight miles) amidst the magnificent peaks and frozen ice falls of New Zealand's highest alpine region; yet is suitable for intermediate and confident beginner skiers. They also offer more than 60 virgin snow runs to heliskiers, as well as the Fox Glacier run which descends 1,000 m (3,300 ft) to the West Coast.

INTO THE DEEP BLUE

When it comes to messing about in boats, New Zealand's long coastline, pristine waters and many secluded inlets and bays offer almost endless variety. The maritime reserves of the Bay of Islands, Hauraki Gulf and the Marlborough Sounds are among the best areas for exploring afloat. You can take a commercial cruise on a motorized catamaran or launch ranging from a couple of hours to a few days. Yacht and launch charters are found throughout the country, a superb, if exclusively-priced, way of enjoying many remote coastal locations on your own. Bookings are heavier and prices are higher during the popular summer months, November to February.

Other choices include skippered charters, where you'll be guided by a knowledgeable boatsman and have everything done for you, although the captain will probably involve you in navigating, and join in sailing and motor-cruising. Some charters may just tour New Zealand waters, while others sail further afield to the Pacific Islands. Charter costs vary, with the size of the vessel ranging from $80 per day for a two-berth 5.76 m (19 ft) yacht to $600 per day for a three bedroom, two-bathroom, 13.9 m (49 ft) performance cruising yacht. You'll get cheaper rates during the mid-February to Easter and off-peak (Easter to late

October) periods. In the Hauraki Gulf, New Zealand's sole surviving kauri schooner *Te Aroha* makes regular trips to Great Barrier Island, 80 km (50 miles) from Auckland, and the romantic square-rigged sailing ship the *Tucker Thompson*, operates day charters and Pacific Island cruises from the Bay of Islands. The *SV Tradewind*, an authentic Topsail schooner, makes Subantarctic voyages to remote scientific and wildlife stations from Lyttelton harbor, near Christchurch.

You can also "bareboat" hire any vessel appropriate to your level of expertise. All equipment is supplied with the boat, and you skipper as well as organize provisions and your itinerary yourself, or arrange with the operator to provide basic needs.

It's well worth investing in a copy of *Cruising New Zealand Waters — A Guide to Shore Facilities*, by Jane and Michael Burroughs, (1989), Heinemann Reed, Auckland.

Other boating holidays cater for diving, snorkeling and fishing enthusiasts, most having all equipment on board. You can also hire a self-drive houseboat on Lake Rotorangi, deep in the farmland and native bush of Wanganui. Costs vary from $340 to $1,000 for four days on boats with up to eight berths, or you could board a large jetboat for a five day cruise on the Wanganui River.

New Zealand Nature Journeys and Cruises operates journeys to remote areas like the Chatham Islands, the coast of Fiordland, Stewart Island, the Subantarctic Islands, as well as the Hauraki Gulf and the Marlborough Sounds on the research vessel Acheron. Contact them at P.O. Box 22, Waikari, Christchurch, ((03) 374-4393, fax: (03) 374-4393, or freefone (0800-808082.

WHITE WATER RIVER RAFTING

Rafting down white water rapids is an established part of the New Zealand adventure scene, with about 50 established companies involved in leading parties down a whole variety of rivers. Trips can range from a few hours to up to five days. Tour operators will supply all equipment, including helmets, wetsuits, booties and camping equipment. The most popular river rafting period is during the summer months

from October through to May, although you could raft all year round. Prices range from about $50 for a half day up to $1,000 for a five-day trip.

In the North Island, the torrential waters released from Wairoa River near Tauranga are considered an adrenalin-laced highlight of the sport. In Hawke Bay, you can meander along the rugged Mohaka River on a two to five day trip. In the north, the Bay of Island's Motu River stretches for 95 km (59 miles), while in the Coromandel's Kaimanawa Ranges, the Rangiteki River offers a combination of rugged natural beauty and wild white water. On the Rangitaiki River, near Whakatane, you can raft or try the latest fad — white water sledging — swimming rapids, aided by flippers and a molded plastic "boogie" board. At Waitomo, it's possible to go "Black Water Rafting" through eerie limestone caves.

Queenstown is regarded as the white water capital of the South Island, with dozens of day and half-day trips, sometimes combined with helicopter or jet-boat trips, on the turbulent Shotover and Kawarau rivers, which offers up to grade 5 rapids.

Two to three days trips are offered on the Landsborough River which flows 64 km (40 miles) from the Southern Alps past frozen glaciers, velvety tussock covered river flats, dense virgin beech forests through white water to the West Coast. Less well-known, the Buller, Karamea and Mohikinui river trips offer five hour to two day trips through up to grade-5 rapids past dramatic West Coast rainforest. South of Christchurch, the Rangitata River offers some of the most challenging white water rafting in the country, with descriptive rapids like the Pencil Sharpener and The Pinch.

JETBOATING

In Queenstown, you may make the surprising discovery that New Zealand is the home of commercial jetboating. Innovative New Zealander Sir William Hamilton created a revolutionary propulsion jet that allows navigation both up and downstream in shallow or difficult waterways where a normal propeller would be wrecked.

Versions of Hamilton's jet are now used in Tasmania, Canada and on the Grand Canyon.

The main center for jetboating is Queenstown, where half-hour and hour-long trips on the Shotover and Kawarau rivers are operated, and can be combined with helicopter and raft trips.

Other commercial jetboat trips in the country include trips on the ankle-deep, braided channels of the Waimakariri River near Christchurch, while there are also jetboats trips down the pristine Buller and Makarora rivers. In the North Island, the magnificent

commercial trips on offer. In the North Island, the most exciting rapid-filled rivers are the Wairoa, Waikato, and Ngwapurua rivers. The Motu, Rangitaiki, Mohaka, Tongariro and Rangiteki are also very scenic rivers for longer trips of several days, while the Wanganui River offers long idyllic sections, with short rapids to spice up the adventure. The South Island Buller area is tailor-made for kayakers, with its six or seven grade 3 sections easily accessible from Murchison. You can make long five-day trips on the Clarence River in Canterbury,

scenic gorges of the Rangiteki River are superb jetboat country, while a run on the Rangitaiki River in the eastern Bay of Plenty takes you to the bottom of the dramatic 8 m (26 ft) Aniwhenua Falls. On the Wanganui River you can make jetboat trips ranging from half an hour to five days in a huge 7.6 m (25 ft) jetboat. Near Taupo, you can jetboat up the Waikato River and play in the gushing torrents of spectacular Huka Falls.

KAYAKING

For reasonably experienced kayakers, New Zealand's pristine and scenic rivers and waterways offer endless variety, with many

while further south, the Rangitata, Hooker, Shotover and Kawarau rivers are all challenging with some grade-5 rapids. You can also arrive by helicopter for expeditions into the remote wilderness of the Landsborough, Whitcombe and Karamea regions.

Sea kayaking has become very popular, particularly in the clear waters and secluded coves of the Abel Tasman National Park and the Marlborough Sounds. It's possible to hire specialized sea kayaks and one to four day commercial trips are also available.

During Summer the Outdoor Pursuits Centre at Turangi runs five day courses (costing from $340 to $450) in white water kay-

Jet-boat thrill-seekers on the rapids in Queenstown.

aking, and also operates a South Island Kayak School from Murchison near Nelson. For further information, contact the New Zealand Canoe Association, P.O. Box 3768, Wellington.

SURF-RAFTING

Surf-rafting is a brand-new type of adventure recently established in New Zealand, mainly operating at Piha Beach on the West Coast of Auckland and out on the Otago

Peninsula near Dunedin. Fee-paying, life jacket-clad participants are steered in a surf-raft by experienced drivers through crashing breakers for a scenic cruise along the coast, then back through the surf. You get *very* wet.

ABSEILING AND CAVING

Abseiling and caving as well as "black water" rafting are adventurous variations on the more sedate walks past glow-worms, stalagmites and stalactites in the Waitomo

Caves region, some 75 km (46 miles) south of Hamilton. In the most comprehensive two-day abseil option, operators train participants first, then supervise them on a 90 m (297 ft) descent down a limestone shaft into the mist-filled cavern of the Lost World. A caving trip returns them to the surface, passing chambers massed with glow-worms, stalactites and underground waterfalls.

BUNGY-JUMPING AND PARAPENTING

Leaping off high places with a piece of elastic attached to your ankles has become almost a compulsory activity for adventure seekers Down Under. A Vanuatuan (New Hebridean) initiation rite that was modernized by Oxford University's Dangerous Sports Club in 1979, bungy-jumping has entered the big time. Today, New Zealand is the recognized home of the bungy, and a proliferation of commercial operators offer supervised jumps from cranes and bridges throughout the country. The best is A.J Hackett's operation in Queenstown, where you can leap every day of the year except 25th and 26th December, either from the historic bridge 43 m (140 ft) above the Kawarau River, or from the 70 m (230 ft) Skipper's Bridge. Costs range from $65 to $150.

If you prefer to fly rather than leap, try parapenting, which is basically a cross between hang-gliding and parachuting, and easier to learn than either. Running at top speed along a hilltop, you defy gravity as you launch into the air. Being attached to a flimsy rainbow-striped chute can make you feel like an over-sized dragonfly, but makes you feel relaxed and unconcerned about coming down to earth. Landings are generally safe, if ungainly. Half day parapente excursions for first timers include instruction and flights off the 620 m (2,000 ft) Crown Terrace near Queenstown. During winter, The Remarkables Ski Area runs parapente classes taking-off and landing on skis. At Mt. Cook, Alpine Guides run introductory and advanced parapente courses amidst spectacular alpine scenery. Costs range from $65 to $695, November through February.

ABOVE: Another brave plunge off Skipper's Bridge near Queenstown. OPPOSITE: A proud moment for marlin-catchers on Paihia-wharf.

MOUNTAIN BIKING

This is a faster, bouncier and more exciting alternative to tramping for exploring New Zealand's more remote bush and country areas. As yet there is little in the way of city tracks designed for mountain bikes, but the Auckland-based operator Ross Adventures organizes mountain bike and kayak expeditions to explore some of the city's coastal regions and off-shore islands. Gear and instruction are provided — you don't need much more than lunch, hat and sunglasses.

CYCLE TOURING

If you're fit and determined, cycling can be an ideal way to travel about this not-so-large country with its uncrowded highways. If you don't own a bicycle you can hire one, and equipment is easily found in larger centers. Ten-speeds, tandems and mountain bikes can be hired for simple sightseeing in most cities and towns.

Guided cycle tours are an option if you prefer company or need prodding along! Tours vary from six to 18 days. The bonus of going on a tour is that you are unencumbered by a laden bicycle, plus you don't need to start out superfit because you can opt to ride in the accompanying bus when you're tired. The two handbooks *Cycle Touring in the North Island of New Zealand* and *Cycle Tourism in the South Island* are invaluable and can be bought from Southern Cyclist, P.O. Box 5890, Auckland. Contact Pedaltours in Auckland, ℂ (09) 302-0968 for tours in both islands.

HORSERIDING

Operators run half-day, full-day and longer guided treks that cater to all levels of riding ability. Most stables have a selection of horses varying in height and temperament, suitable for just about all riders. All tack is provided, including hard hats, and most trekking packages will include camping equipment.

In the North Island, some of the most scenic places to go horseriding include the long sandy

bays of Pakiri Beach, north of Auckland and through the lush forest alongside the Wanganui River. Down south, horse treks can lead you through the amber-hued tussock backcountry of Queenstown and Arrowtown, while there are wonderful treks to be made around the Banks Peninsula from Akaroa, near Christchurch. If you spend part of your visit on a farm, you may well be able to go horseriding. You should check when you book.

It's interesting to know that New Zealand has an international reputation for breeding horses, producing some of the

world's finest bloodstock. This industry is centered on the rich farmland of the Waikato and Canterbury regions.

FISHING

Long recognized as a freshwater fishing El Dorado, New Zealand offers a range of angling experience probably unrivaled in the world. Fishing buffs can choose to fish deep in the dense bush of Urewera National Park, haul in large marlin from the big game fishing region of the Bay of Islands, or even helicopter into remote regions to cast for wild rainbow trout in far-flung streams. Just about all New Zealand's luxury sporting lodges specialize in trout, if not big game fishing, and licenses are easily available from fishing tackle and sports shops on a daily, weekly, monthly or seasonal basis. A special tourist license ($56.26) is available at any InterCity office or an accredited travel agency and allows visitors to fish all New Zealand for one month.

The summer trout fishing season runs from October to April in most districts. Winter fishing is the highlight of Taupo, Rotorua where April to May and September to October are the best months. Lake Taupo and Lake Tarawera, near Rotorua, are just two of the region's spectacular fishing lakes. The Tongariro and Waikato rivers are also renowned as great trout-fishing territory

Surfcasting and boat-fishing are ruling passions in New Zealand, and equipment and boat charters are easily arranged, especially in Auckland, Tutukaka, the Bay of Islands, Mercury Bay, Tauranga, Whakatane, the Marlborough Sounds and Milford Sound. There's no closed season and you don't even need a fishing license.

New Zealand has a world-wide reputation for its big game fishing, primarily for marlin and shark. Other game fish found in local waters include the broadbill swordfish; Pacific blue, black and striped marlin; mako, thresher and hammerhead sharks; yellowtail and yellowfish tuna. The main centers for big-game fishing are in the Bay of Islands and Whitanga, Mayor Island and Whakatane in the East Cape region. The best months are between January and May and you'll need to charter a big game boat, with a skipper who provides everything necessary for fishing. For any information of fishing, contact F.W. Murphy, President of the New Zealand Professional Fishing Guides Association, P.O. Box 16, Motu, Gisborne, ((06) 863-5822, fax: (06) 863-5822.

HUNTING

If you are a hunting sort of person, New Zealand's wildernesses offer plenty of challenges. Sika stag and red deer are found in the country's beech forests or above the timberline, on the rolling tussock and snowgrass basins of the Southern Alps. Higher up on the craggy peaks, dedicated hunters can pit their wits against the tahr and chamois. On Stewart Island, whitetail deer are hunted in the forests and brush country. In season, New Zealand also offers hunting for various species of duck, pheasant, quail and geese. You need to have a license, and hunting without a registered guide is not recommended. Contact the New Zealand Hunting and Fishing Consultants, 7 Paorahape Street, Taupo, ((07) 378-3714, fax: (07) 378-3714, who arrange trophy hunts or unguided drop camps from $1,266 for three days.

DIVING

New Zealand has an incredibly long coastline, almost 10,000 km (6,200 miles) long,

with pristine waters full of colorful fish and plant life to entice divers. The Leigh Marine Reserve, an hour north of Auckland, offers easy beach diving, superb visibility in six meters (20 ft) of water, and lots of fish, including some very large snapper and cray-fish. Many good diving spots are very accessible, lying just off-shore, particularly in Northland. The Poor Knights Marine Reserve, 20 km (12 miles) offshore, is just one group in a series of islands, most of which are protected wildlife reserves, that offer excellent diving areas, brimming with reef fish. In the summer months, visibility ranges from 20 m (66 ft) to 70 m (231 ft). In the sheltered Bay of Islands, the weather remains temperate all year round. Within the waters of the South Island's Fiordland,

you can see red and black coral in as little as 6 m (11 ft) of water: normally it occurs at over 120 m (396 ft) depth. Diving off Stewart Island offers remarkable giant kelp forests, and huge paua the size of bread plates.

Within New Zealand waters there are also two main diving wreck sites. The *Rainbow Warrior*, the flag-ship of the Greenpeace fleet, holed in 1985 by a bomb planted by the French Secret Service, has been scuttled on the white sandy bottom in the clear blue waters of the Cavalli Islands, off Northland's east coast. Charter boats make regular trips from the Bay of Islands. The Russian ship, *Mikhail Lermontov*, which sank in the Marlborough Sounds in 1986, is a huge,

The majesty of Mitre Peak in Milford Sound.

easily accessible wreck, with well-established marine life. Dive tours can be arranged with local dive stores in the region. You can ask for any more information from the New Zealand Underwater Association, P.O. Box 875, Auckland, ((09) 849-5896, fax: (09) 849-7051.

GOLF

Avid golfers find New Zealand irresistible. Although it is such a small country, it has

400 or more uncrowded golf courses with beautiful scenery, clean air and splendid playing conditions. There are typical Scottish links-type courses along both coasts of each island to courses at the feet of snow-capped mountains overlooking alpine lakes. One of the courses, Wairakei International, near Taupo in the North Island, has been listed by American Golf Digest as being one of the top 25 courses outside the United States.

New Zealand golf clubs are very hospitable and welcome visitors. Green fees range from about $5 in some country areas (where they often have an honesty box for payment)

to $40 at some of the more exclusive city courses. Many courses have clubs and trundlers for hire, resident professionals and increasingly, motorized carts.

The main playing season is during the winter months of May through October, partly because of New Zealand's mild winters. Visitors will find the courses relatively empty during the summer months. Some tour companies specialize in organizing combined golf and sightseeing tours. For further information, write to: The New Zealand Golf Association, P.O. Box 11-842, Wellington.

FLIGHTSEEING

In many ways, the most spectacular way of seeing New Zealand's spectacular scenery is from the air. You can land on a smoking volcano, hover over a glacier's giant chasms of turquoise ice or step straight into powder-snow highlands from a ski plane. Light aircraft, amphibians, floatplanes, skiplanes and helicopters are all commonly used in New Zealand.

From Auckland you can take an amphibian or helicopter ride out to Hauraki Gulf islands, while from Rotorua, you can fly across the region's steaming geothermal valleys, over the magnificent blue and green lakes. Helicopters land on the active offshore volcano, White Island, and on the crater of Mt. Tarawera.

Ski planes were invented in the South Island, and there's very little that can't be done with them. From Mt. Cook village or the townships of Fox and Franz Josef glaciers, you can make flights across Mt. Cook and the tumbling Hochstetter Ice Fall, then land high on the shimmering neves of the Tasman, Fox and Franz Josef glaciers. For skiers the Tasman Glacier is the Southern Hemisphere's longest ski run.

From Queenstown, a flight over Fiordland's massive mountains, cascading waterfalls and rich green native forest out to Milford Sound is one of the highlights of visiting New Zealand. For a different kind of flightseeing, you can clamber aboard a hot-air balloon — they operate out of Hamilton and Rotorua.

ABOVE: A charming display of the natural warmth of New Zealanders. OPPOSITE: Flightseeing in the Bay of Islands.

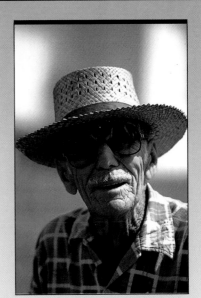

North
Island

AUCKLAND: THE HARBOR CITY

The most unabashedly confident of all New Zealand cities, Auckland is a seductive, laid-back and curious amalgam of Maori, European and Polynesian influences. Over-whelmingly, the city's charms are physical, with its fresh scenery perhaps best appreci-ated during summer when you can prome-nade beneath flaming red archways formed by pohutakawa trees along the seaside **Tamaki Drive**, enjoy the lush solitude of

cones dot the city's narrow isthmus, many of them used by the Maoris as fortified *pa* or villages. One of them is nearby **Rangi-toto Island**, clearly visible from downtown Auckland. The earth pushed the infant volcano up only 750 years ago. It last erupted around 1750 and some say it will again. The trip to the top of any one of these hills, such as **Mt. Eden** or **Mt. Victoria** on the North Shore, offers a spectacular overview.

Certainly Auckland has never exactly lived up to the intriguing name given to it by the Maoris, *"Tamaki Makau Rau"* or

cicada-humming native bush in the nearby **Waitakeri Ranges** or simply laze on one of Auckland's innumerable sandy beaches, enjoying the clear, slightly salty and refresh-ing sea under a full blue sky.

Aucklanders grow up with a natural af-finity with the sea, as the city bridges two magnificent harbors, the **Manukau** and the **Waitemata**, which spill out into the vast **Hauraki Gulf** and its many beautiful off-shore islands. It is rightfully dubbed the "City of Sails:" per capita, more Aucklan-ders own boats than any others in the world, and the yacht-flecked Waitemata Harbour on the annual Regatta is an impressive sight. Auckland could just as easily be called "City of Extinct Volcanoes." No less then 60 hilly

"Battle of a 100 Lovers." This refers not to violent orgies, as the name suggests, but the many bloody tribal wars over Auckland's "loved" location, fought over by many war-ring Maori chiefs, who prized the ease with which they could paddle canoes around its many bays and grow crops in its fertile vol-canic soil. The year 1827 saw the penulti-mate battle when the territory was finally wrested by the fierce Ngati Whatua Maoris, who proved exceptionally able-handed with musketry. During the general up-heaval of the Land Wars, so much of the Maori population in the region was wiped

View of Auckland's skyscrapers from the marina at Westhaven.

out, that two decades later, the British faced little resistance when they offered to buy what is now Auckland's prime land for a song. The transaction amounted to some £50 sterling, with some blankets, axes, tobacco, cooking pots, sugar, flour and clothing thrown in for good measure. On 18th September 1840, the pioneer settlement of Auckland was proclaimed New Zealand's capital by the country's first governor, Captain William Hobson. He named it as a tribute to the Earl of Auckland, then Viceroy of India. Auckland remained capital

until 1865, when the government decided to relocate itself in Wellington, more favorably placed to exert authority over both islands.

Today, Auckland is home to close to a million people, nearly a third of New Zealand's population. The most cosmopolitan and commercialized center in the country, it also has many immigrants from the neighboring Pacific Islands of Samoa, Fiji, Tonga and the Cook Islands, making it the world's largest Polynesian city.

With good reason, Aucklanders consider their city much more progressive than Wellington or any of the other, typically conservative New Zealand cities. Shops and pubs tend to stay open later, and the practice of Saturday shopping was pioneered in Parnell.

You could easily spend a week or two in Auckland, exploring its fine beaches, coastal walks and surrounding countryside, cruising out to Gulf Islands or just sampling the city's convivial cafes, restaurants, shops and nightclubs. But Auckland's greatest asset is its proximity to a vast variety of natural beauty. No matter where you are, within less than an hour you can be enjoying a vista of complete seclusion and tranquility, whether you have left your car at the edge of a forest, or dropped an anchor at an island bay out in the harbor.

ACCESS

The international and domestic airports are located at Mangere, 20 km (12 miles) south of Auckland. The journey into town takes about 40 minutes and the Airporter Bus Service runs every half-hour between both airports and the Downtown Airline Terminal, from 6 am to 9 pm daily, with stops throughout the city including Parnell, the Sheraton Hotel and the railway station. Call (09) 275-7685 for details. The Super Shuttle, ((09) 307-5210 and the Airporter Express, ((09) 275-1234, both provide door-to-door airport transport; the cost varies according to your destination but works out much cheaper than a taxi.

Air New Zealand (((09) 793-7515 or 357-3000, 1 Queen Street) connects Auckland with all major centers in New Zealand, with Ansett New Zealand (((09) 379-6235 or 302-2146, 50 Grafton Road) in close competition. Mt Cook (((09) 309-5395, 105 Queen Street) and local operators like Eagle Air (Freefone ((09) 275-7717, Auckland Domestic Airport) and Great Barrier Airlines (((09) 275-6612, Auckland Domestic Airport) also have flights in and out of Auckland.

The railway station, ((09) 270-5435 or Freefone (0800) 801-070, is situated on Beach Road, and there are only two arrivals and departures each day: the *Silver Fern* departs at 8:30 am and the *Northerner* at 9:15 pm arriving in Wellington at 6:30 pm and 8:30 am respectively.

InterCity buses, (Head Office, Railway Station, Beach Road, ((09) 270-5463) have services from Auckland to just about everywhere in New Zealand. Other companies with services to and from Auckland include Clarks Northliner at the Downtown Airline Terminal, Mt Cook Landline, (((09) 309-5395, Freefone (0800) 800-737, 105 Queen Street) and Newmans, (((09) 309-9738, 69 St George's Bay Road, Parnell.)

GENERAL INFORMATION

The best sources of tourist-related information throughout the country are the Visitor Information offices operated by the New Zealand Tourism Department. The **Auckland Visitors Bureau**, ((09) 366-6888, is on Aotea Square, at 299 Queen Street. It has information on everything you could possibly want to know about Auckland, including such activities as bungy jumping off the Harbour Bridge, horse-riding in the wilds and going hot-air ballooning high above the roofs of the city. You can also try the counters at either the international or domestic airport terminals. The **Touristop Tourist Services**, ((09) 377-5783, is another information office at the Quay Street Downtown Terminal.

Make sure you pick up a free copy of the *Auckland Tourist Times*. The **South Island**

Information and Travel Office, ((09) 303-0473, at Endean Building, 2 Queen Street can answer all queries about traveling in the South Island. Other information services include the **Department of Conservation** (DOC) office, ((09) 307-9279, in the Sheraton complex on the corner of Karangaphape Road and Liverpool Street. They have a copious supply of maps, books and pamphlets on all of New Zealand's National Parks, forests and nature reserves. To find out about walks, tramping tracks and camping grounds in Auckland's ten Regional Parks,

try the **Park Information Service**, ((09) 366-2166, on the corner of Wellesley and Nelson streets, open weekdays.

For information about harbor cruises and ferries, try two offices in the Ferry Building downtown on Quay Street, and pick up the Fullers' *What's On* brochure. **Devonport Ferries**, ((09) 303-3318, runs a catamaran and the 84 year-old *MV Kestrel* to Devonport, every hour on the hour. **Fuller Cruise Centre**, ((09) 377-1771, runs ferry and launch services to islands in the Hauraki Gulf.

ABOVE: The colonial-era shopping village of Parnell. OPPOSITE: Auckland's Ferry Building is a stately echo of the city's colonial past.

WHAT TO SEE

The City Centre

One of best places to start contemplating Auckland's ambience is the waterfront complex at the historic, tan-colored **Ferry Building**, where you can also gather information on making harbor cruises and breakfast at **Cin Cin On Quay**, a stylish brasserie with beautiful morning views across the harbor. Get your bearings with a walk in the inner city. It's not difficult: there's only one main street. From the waterfront, **Queen Street** slices through the city center, lined with reflective-glass high-rise office blocks and shopping centers. Look out for the quaint Victorian arcades of **Queen's Arcade** and **The Strand**. **Vulcan Lane** and **High Street** are Auckland's most fashionable strips with boutiques and street-level cafes.

A five minute hike up the hill reaches **Albert Park**, a manicured green-belt with a floral clock and bandstand. Nearby, **Auckland University** is the largest campus in New Zealand.

City Strolls

If you have a morning or afternoon to spare, **Parnell** and **Ponsonby** are the best places to seek out to get a feel for Auckland's atmosphere. These areas have many interesting shops, with fashion boutiques, galleries and craft workshops as well as many cafes and restaurants. Parnell is the city's oldest and prettiest suburb, with a Victorian revival village with cobbled courtyards, bridges and alleyways that is the city's top boutique and restaurant strip. Dart into the side streets off Parnell Road to see the rows of preserved colonial villas, many being lovingly restored by residents. This is probably the city's most interesting place for up-market shopping, with fashion boutiques, galleries and crafts shops. The **Strand Building**, located off Parnell Rise, is a designer warehouse that houses two leading art galleries.

Parnell has two historic churches, both worth seeking out on your stroll. **St. Mary's Church**, on the corner of Parnell Road and St. Stephen's Avenue was built in the Gothic style, with kauri interiors and stained glass windows. Some ten minutes walk away is **St. Stephen's Chapel**, which overlooks Judge's Bay. Its hilltop grounds make a very tranquil place to picnic in summer, with views across the yacht-flecked Waitemata harbor. From St. Stephen's, you can walk up the slope to the **Rose Gardens** off Gladstone Road, which can be seen at their blossoming best between November and March. Close by, the **Parnell Baths** are wonderful in summer, good for long laps in saltwater and open vistas across the harbor.

Auckland has several other districts with a special atmosphere and interesting character, well worth exploring. **Ponsonby** has many shops, boutiques, restaurants and pretty villas concentrated along Ponsonby Road. Some of the side streets, such as Renall Street and Wood Street, still have a well-preserved colonial feel to them. Close by is **Herne Bay**, an attractive suburb with many secluded beaches and **Karangahape Road**, known affectionately by Aucklanders as "K" Road, which has a Polynesian atmosphere, with colorfully attired women meandering down the street in Samoan dress, and many shops selling Pacific foodstuffs, crafts and fabrics. **Remuera** is Auckland's most exclusive address and nearby **Newmarket** is Auckland's most modern shopping area. Along Tamaki Drive's waterfront, the suburbs of **Mission Bay** and **Kohimarama** are pleasant stops on an afternoon drive. On the North Shore are **Devonport**, a charming harborside settlement, and the meandering coastal suburb of **Takapuna**, both dotted with impressive homes.

Tamaki Drive

Auckland's most spectacular row of bays is encompassed by Tamaki Drive, which meanders unbroken along Judges Bay, Kohimarama, Mission Bay, Okahu Bay and St Helier's Bay. These are all good swimming and wind-surfing beaches, with views out to Rangitoto Island. Every March the **Round the Bays Run** along the 10.5 km (six-and-a-half mile) promenade attracts upwards of eighty thousand New Zealanders and anyone else game to participate. The best lookout points along the drive are at Savage Memorial and Achilles Point. Mission Bay and St Heliers, two of Auckland's exclusive suburbs, are good oases in the sands with ice-cream parlors, cafes and restaurants. At both beaches you can hire bicycles, wind-surfing boards and yachts.

Don't miss a visit to **Kelly Tarlton's Underwater World** at Orakei Wharf, one of Auckland's most impressive attractions, named after its creator who was a renowned diver and treasure-seeker. You step onto a moving walkway through a clear Perspex tunnel that runs for 120 m (394 ft) underwater, and press your face up against giant stingrays, turtles, moray eels, sea-horses and awesome sharks. The beasts are fed by divers at 2 pm. In the foyer, you can admire a family of piranhas and watch a continuous audio-visual show about Tarlton's wreck diving exploits around New Zealand's shores. Afterwards, the best place to muse over your encounter with these creatures of the deep is the Kelly Tarlton Cafe, located right on the pierfront, with delectable coffee and cakes.

Museums, Galleries and the Zoo

It is worth making time to go and see the **War Memorial Museum**, whose giant mausoleum looms above the Domain. Military memorabilia comprises only part of the collection. It has the most extensive display of Maori and Polynesian artifacts and tribal implements you are ever likely to see. Among its highlights are several elaborately carved Maori buildings and the 30 m (98 ft) war canoe, *Te Toki A Tapiri* or "the Axe of Tapiri," which could seat up to 80 warriors and was carved from a single giant *totara* tree during the early nineteenth century. There are free, highly informative 45-minute guided walks around the Maoritanga Hall at 10:30 am and 12:45 pm daily.

The **Auckland City Art Gallery** on Kitchener Street, near Albert Park, has a superb collection of New Zealand art, both colonial and contemporary, housed in an elaborate Victorian building. There are free guided tours at midday Monday to Friday and 2 pm on Sundays. The gallery also stages regular exhibitions of international art and has an excellent specialist book shop and garden terrace cafe. It's open from 10 am to 4:30 pm daily and admission is free. There are many specialist museums and gal-leries in Auckland, and at any time during the year you can probably choose from about 30 exhibitions. Pick up pamphlets at the Art Gallery or scan the *Tourist Times.*

Auckland's Historic Places Trust has restored several colonial homes, full of old-world charm and offering a clear impression of the lifestyle of upper-class European settlers in mid-Victorian New Zealand. In Parnell's Ayr Street there are two historic houses. N° 2, **Kinder House**, once the residence of a nineteenth-century painter, photographer and educationalist, was built in

1857. Its unusual black-colored bricks were hewn from Rangitoto's volcanic rock and its interiors reflect the original owner's eclectic interests. Devonshire teas are served in the leafy garden. N° 14, **Ewelme Cottage** was the home of an early Victorian clergymen with the wonderfully florid name of Vicesimus Lush. It was constructed in 1864 almost entirely from kauri and is crammed with Victorian household paraphernalia. In Mt Albert, **Alberton** at 1 Kerr-Taylor Avenue was the home of the wealthy Kerr-Taylor family whose dances, archery parties and hunts caused social ripples in Victorian Auckland. In Epsom, **Highwick Cottage** at 40 Gillies Avenue, has a grand ballroom and sweeping lawns. Lastly, the **Howick Colonial Village** located 20 minutes drive from town along the Pakuranga Highway on Bells Road near Lloyd Elsmore Park, is an impressive, painstakingly restored pioneer village, complete with furnished cottages,

The Auckland War Memorial Museum in the Domain.

shops, a smithy, courthouse and church. Its interesting feature is an 1847 "fencible" cottage — just one of many military dwellings built by the Royal New Zealand Fencibles to protect against Maori attack.

The **Museum of Transport and Technology** on Great North Road, is a good place for a rainy day. It also has a mock pioneer village, as well as many working displays of vintage vehicles, steam trains, trams, aircraft and machinery. Look out for the aircraft built by New Zealand's earliest aviator, Richard Pearse. There is some evidence that this South Island farmer may actually have made his airborne debut several months before the Wright Brothers attracted world fame, but didn't consider his faltering hops off the ground actually constituted real flight.

You can hop aboard a tram and ride into the adjacent parklands of the **Zoo**, which has more than 1,200 animals, birds, reptiles and fish from around the world. Don't miss New Zealand's indigenous wonders, the tuatara lizards and the nocturnal kiwis. Last admission is 4:15 pm.

Devonport and the North Shore

Half the fun of going to **Devonport** is the 15-minute ferry ride across the harbor, especially aboard the vintage *M. V. Kestrel*, which departs from the Ferry Building every half-hour. Devonport nestles between the twin extinct volcanic peaks of **Mt. Victoria** and **North Head** and is a beach-front haven of attractive villas, craft shops and cafes.

You can walk up to Mt. Victoria, for 700 hundred years the site of a Maori *pa*, or around North Head, which is riddled with tunnels, chambers and gun emplacements from its days as an artillery battery, begun in 1885 and strengthened after successive fears of a Russian naval invasion. A stone plaque on the foreshore between the two hills commemorates the landing of a Maori tribe in the fifteenth century.

Further north lies the beach-front suburb of **Takapuna**. Whilst the beach itself is perfect for swimming, one of the city's loveliest and little-known walks begins at its northern end, past the boat ramp and camping ground. From here a scoria path of black volcanic rock follows the coastline north

with tiny bays, rock pools and contrasting views of grand sea-front homes and magnificent views across Hauraki Gulf. **Milford Beach** and **Mairangi Bay** are particularly lovely. Other Takapuna highlights to seek out are **Lake Pupuke**, and **Killarney Park** situated two blocks from the main shopping area. **The Pumphouse** on the lake, once a vintage water supply station, is now an art gallery.

Cornwall Park and Mt Eden

Not far from the city center, Cornwall Park is an ideal place for rambling walks with grassy pastures and avenues of *pohutakawa* trees. Within the park is **One Tree Hill**, an extinct volcanic cone that was the largest of Auckland's Maori *pa* or fortified village sites. A scenic road winds around the mountain and up to the summit, offering panoramic views across the city, Waitemata and Manukau harbors. At the summit, beneath the lone pine tree, is the tomb of the so-called "father of Auckland," Sir John Logan Campbell, who set up a tent as the city's first store in 1840. With his partner, William Brown, he built **Acacia Cottage**, Auckland's oldest building, at the foot of One Tree Hill. Within Cornwall Park, the **Observatory** nearby is open to the public Tuesday evenings for illustrated talks on astronomy. Call (09) 365-6945 for details.

Not far from Cornwall Park, Mt. Eden and Auckland's highest point, is another extinct volcanic cone and old *pa* site. The view is even more spectacular and blustery than that from One Tree Hill, and you can test your vertigo threshold by leaning over the edge to look 50 m (164 ft) down into its crater. In an old lava pit on the eastern side, **Eden Gardens** is one of the city's loveliest places, with many varieties of camellias, rhododendrons and azaleas amongst native trees and shrubs.

Walks and Parks

Within the city there are two especially pleasant long walks, including the walk along Tamaki Drive, already mentioned. The other is the 13 km (eight miles) long **Coast to Coast Walkway** which takes in much of the city's most spectacular scenery, and encompasses the nature reserves of Albert Park, the Domain, Mt Eden and One Tree Hill. You can pick up an information pamphlet on the walk, with points of interest, cafes and public toilets marked out, from the Auckland Visitor's Bureau.

The **Domain** is the largest and loveliest of all Auckland's inner city parks, a perfect place to have picnics and walk through its many trails. Its 80 hectare (200 acre) grounds are crowned by the **War Memorial Museum**, and encompass many woodland tracks and secluded spots, plus sporting grounds. The Winter Garden has pretty hot-houses and a jungle-like enclosure of native trees.

If you love gardens, don't miss seeing the **Auckland Regional Botanic Gardens**, set in 155 acres (65 hectares) and featuring more than 10,000 plants, some from North America, South Africa, Asia, Australia and Europe. The gardens are readily accessible off the Auckland Motorway on the Manurewa exit, then follow the road to the entrance on Hill Road.

Auckland has a rash of elaborate theme parks, some of which can be quite fun. **Leisureland Funpark**, in Te Atatu North, 15 minutes from the city on the North Western Motorway, has New Zealand's largest rollercoaster and a walkway across an open reserve for lions and tigers. The **Rainbow's End Adventure Park**, located on Great South Road, has an impressive variety of dramatic rides and activities suitable for hyperactive kids. The **Pavilion of New Zealand** on Mongomerie Road, Mangere, is a rather nationalistic open-air showcase, with displays that give you an idea of what the country has to offer, from rugby history to sampling pavlova. For those with a keen sense of humor towards New Zealand's ever-present cultural heritage, **Sheep World**, is a must, not forgetting **Kiwiland** on the Elleslie-Panmure Highway, where you can watch Maori concerts, sheep-shearing, go for supervised horse-rides, watch dogs mustering and other quintessential New Zealand activities.

Harbour Cruises and Tours

You can see the **Auckland Harbour Cruise Company**'s fleet of yachts with their distinctive blue and white-striped sails moored close to the Ferry Building. They offer sedate tours of the harbor aboard lunch, dinner and af-

ternoon cruises. Reservations are essential, contact the Fullers Cruise Centre, ((09) 307-1771. **Te Aroha Cruises** operates an eighty-year schooner on a four-day cruise around the Hauraki Gulf each November through April, and details can be obtained on ((09) 444-9342. The Visitors' Bureau can give you details of other commercial cruise companies which offer cruises aboard racing yachts, luxurious multi-hull launches, commuter ferries and even steam tugs.

Auckland has more than its share of full-day and half-day sightseeing tours. Some

cover the city's main highlights, while others offer specialist tours of historic homes, vineyards and centers of Maori culture. The **United Airlines Explorer Bus** departs daily on the hour from Downtown Airline Terminal between 10 am and 4 pm and visits Victoria Park Market, Kelly Tarlton's Underwater World, China Oriental Market, the Auckland Museum and Parnell Village.

There are three particularly outstanding tours that explore Auckland's landscapes and attractions. **Bush & Beach Tours**, ((09) 473-0189, offers half-day small-group natural history tours to the Waitakere Ranges and West Coast Beaches ($60) and to the Murawai gannet colony ($50). **Old Devonport Ferry & Coach Tours** offers a very enjoyable two-hour tour of Devonport's attractions, departing daily on the hour from the Auckland Ferry Building between 10 am to 3 pm, while **Ross Adventure Tours** explores Devonport on a half day

Solitary landmark on One Tree Hill.

guided tour by mountain bike and sea kayak. Both tours can be booked through Fullers Cruise Centre, ((09) 307-1771 for details.

WHERE TO STAY

The Regent, ((09) 309-8888, fax (09) 379-6445, on Albert Street, is arguably New Zealand's finest hotel, elegant and modern with a polished russet marble lobby, ostentatious bouquets of flowers and relaxed piano lounge bar and fully-equipped business center.

Deluxe

The **Pan Pacific**, ((09) 366-3000, fax (09) 366-0121, on Mayoral Drive, off Wellesley Street is dominated by its impressive soaring atrium with suspended boomerang-shaped sculptures and glass lift. It has a tennis court and business center. The **Sheraton**, ((09) 379-5132, fax: (09) 377-9387, at 83 Symonds Street is located close to "K" Road, the University and city center. Its bar, Grey's, features some of Auckland's best jazz musicians. The **Hyatt Auckland**, ((09) 366-1234, fax (09) 303-2932, at Princess Street opposite the University campus has superb harbor views. The **Parkroyal**, ((09) 377-8920, at the corner of Queen and Custom streets, has a well-acclaimed top-floor restaurant with magnificent harbor views.

Out of town, **Hotel du Vin** ((085) 233-6314, fax (085) 233-6215, on Lyons Road in the Mangatawhiri Valley, some 45 minutes drive from the city center, is a luxurious lodge retreat set within its own vineyard and native bush reserve. Food is the highlight here, with excellent presentation and service. Even if you're not staying here, it's worth making the trip for the excellent Sunday brunch.

Mid-price

There are two Quality Inn hotels, both good choices. The **Quality Inn Anzac Avenue**, ((09) 379-8509, fax (09) 303-8582, at 150 Anzac Avenue, has wonderful views across the Hauraki Gulf, while the **Quality Inn Rose Park**, ((09) 377-3619, fax (09) 303-3716, at 100 Gladstone Road, overlooking the rose gardens, has a swimming pool and an excellent brasserie.

In Takapuna, the **Takapuna Beach Motel**, ((09) 349-7126, fax: (09) 349-8563, on the

Promenade, is a luxurious modern beach-front motel with a restaurant, swimming pool and is just a step away from the sands.

Moderate

Hotel de Brett, ((09) 303-2389, at the corner of High and Shortland Streets, is an Auckland classic. It was built in 1841 and retains its period atmosphere with refurbished thirties style decor, and all its 25 rooms have quirky Art Deco bathrooms. It reduces its rates substantially over the weekend because of the general caterwauling drifting up from the street, the city's main nightclub strip.

There are several other inner-city hotels, all offering comfortable rooms and good facilities. **Park Towers**, ((09) 309-2800, at 3 Scotia Place is very businesslike, while the **Railton Hotel**, ((09) 379-6487, at 411 Queen Street offers bargain rates that include breakfast. **Whitaker Lodge**, ((09) 377-3623, at 21 Whitaker Place, is very close to the University, tucked away on a leafy hillside.

In Parnell, **Ascot**, ((09) 309-9012, at 36 St. Stephens Avenue, is an exceptional Bed and Breakfast establishment in a very pretty colonial home. There are nine rooms, each different and full of welcoming touches.

Equally impressive, the **Devonport Manor**, ((09) 345-2529, at 7 Cambridge Terrace in Devonport, offers much comfortable charm and delicious breakfasts in an 1874 colonial villa with harbor views. The **Esplanade Hotel**, ((09) 345-1291, on the corner of Victoria Road and Queens Parade, is located right on Devonport wharf. It's one of the fading queens of Auckland's pub hotels, and is only 15 minutes from the city center by ferry, the only drawback being noisy revelry and live music in the downstairs bar on Friday and Saturday nights. There are few amenities, but its sea-facing rooms are charming.

Auckland has more than a hundred motels, and consequently standards are kept exceptionally high because of so much competition. Prices usually start from around US$35 for a single to US$45 for a double or twin unit.

Motel Westhaven, ((09) 376-0071, at 26 Hamilton Road, Herne Bay, has microwave ovens and dishwashers in some units, plus a heated swimming pool and children's playground. The lovely beaches of Herne Bay are just a few minutes' walk away. Nearby is the **Harbour Bridge Motel**, ((09) 376-3489, at 6 Tweed Street, converted from a 100-year old homestead with a pretty landscaped courtyard and period furniture. Very secluded and peaceful.

In Parnell, try the **Casa Nova Motor Lodge**, ((09) 377-1463, on the corner of St Stephens Avenue and Parnell Road, or the **James Cook Motor Inn**, ((09) 303-3462, at 320 Parnell Road, the latter right in the heart of Parnell village with an open-air brasserie.

In Remuera, the **Waterfront Motel**, ((09) 520-1196, at 246 Orakei Road, is perched above a secluded inlet. It has bungalow-like units, excellent facilities and full views across Tamaki Drive to the Hauraki Gulf.

Inexpensive
There are a number of very reasonably-priced Bed and Breakfast establishments in Auckland's suburbs which offer more personality and hospitality than a hotel. **Bavaria Guest House**, ((09) 368-9641, at 83 Valley Road, Mt Eden is a slightly eccentric establishment run in the European style, filled to the rafters with alpine memorabilia. German is spoken. **Pentlands**, ((09) 368-7031, at 22 Pentland Avenue, Mt Eden is a friendly homestead with generous breakfasts, lawn tennis, a pool table and mini-gymnasium.

Aachen House, ((09) 520-2329, at 39 Market Road, Remuera is a beautiful Victorian-style family home with seven spacious rooms. Home-cooked dinners and courtesy car available. **Remuera House**, ((09) 524-7794, at 500 Remuera Road is another Victorian guest house.

Backpackers
Downtown Queen Street Backpackers, ((09) 373-3471, at the corner of Fort and Queen streets is a renovated former pub right in the central city. Its well-stocked information board is worth perusing as an up-to-date source of countrywide lodges, tours and attractions. **Downtown Backpackers**, ((09) 303-4768, at 6 Constitution Hill is also central and offers free airport pick-ups. **Georgia Backpackers**, ((09) 339-9560, at the corner of 189 Park and Carlton Gore roads in

Grafton is a very popular Victorian lodge, ideally placed close to the Domain. **Picton Street Backpackers**, ((09) 378-0966, at 34 Picton Street, Freeman's Bay is a brightly-painted colonial house with a very cheerful atmosphere in a pleasant residential street, just around the corner from Ponsonby's lively shops and cafes.

Camping
If you want to feel as much on holiday as possible, apply for a camping permit from the **Auckland Regional Council**, ((09) 379-4420 or (09) 366-2166 and stay in one of the Regional Parks, where you can get back to basics in the great outdoors. Especially recommended are the grounds at Piha and Murawai, on the west coast.

EATING OUT

Auckland offers more scope for culinary hedonism than anywhere else in New Zealand whether you crave a fine restaurant meal or an impromptu snack of smoked mussels or oysters purchased from the back of a roadside trailer. The following recommendations are just a guideline. Serious gourmands should pick up a free copy of the comprehensive *Aucklander Dining Guide* with its listings of more than a 100 restaurants, bars and clubs. Also good is the *Raffles Dining Guide*, found in most Auckland hotels and motels.

Auckland's most elegant restaurants are fully licensed, generally open for lunch and dinner, seven days a week unless stated. Prices vary from $50 to $80 a head and reservations are essential. The **French Cafe**, ((09) 377-1911, 210 Symonds Street, is one of the city's finest restaurants with superb food and stylish interiors. **Harbourside Restaurant**, ((09) 373-3935 at 1st Floor, Ferry Building, 99 Quay Street has superlative food and unrivaled views across the port. On a fine night, request a balcony table.

In Parnell, **La Trattoria**, ((09) 379-5358, at 259 Parnell Road offers innovative Italian cuisine. **Antoine's**, ((09) 379-8756, at 333 Parnell Road prides itself on being Auckland's most elite restaurant, with fine French-influenced cuisine. It's closed on Sunday. Further down is **Clarry's**, ((09) 335-

9902, at The Exchange, 99 Parnell Road. This is currently Auckland's most fashionable lunchtime rendezvous offering Italian influenced dishes. The adjoining **Medusa Bar** is a stylish place to linger, with a lavish, painted ceiling.

On the Tamaki Drive waterfront, there are two outstanding restaurants: **Hammerheads**, ((09) 521-4400, at Orakei, for seafood and further along, **Bistango**, ((09) 355-5210, at 6 St Helier's Bay Road for Mediterranean cuisine.

In Titirangi, there are two exceptional restaurants both with stunning views across the Waitakere Ranges. **Duval's Bar and Brasserie**, ((09) 814-9804, at 473 Scenic Drive has striking, bright blue interiors and an adventurous menu. **Lopdell's Brasserie**, ((09) 817-4218, is above the Waitemata City Art center on Titirangi Road.

There are many less-expensive inner-city restaurants that offer excellent food and a taste of Auckland's lifestyle. Prices rarely fall beneath $35 per head. In Ponsonby, **Prego**, ((09) 376-3095 at 226 Ponsonby Road, serves Italian dishes and has an outdoor courtyard that makes it the most pleasant place to enjoy lunch during summer afternoons. In the city, **Cin Cin On Quay**, ((09) 307-6966 in the Ferry Building on Quay Street overlooks the harbor and seldom closes before 3am. **Rosini's**, ((09) 307-0025, 20 High Street is a slick brasserie-style cafe. **Verandah Bar and Grill**, ((09) 339-6289 at 279 Parnell Road, is open until very late. **Metropole**, ((09) 379-9300, at 223 Parnell Road is an all-day chic street-level bar and brasserie. Sunday nights have a fixed price *tapas* menu at $30 a head, with wild dancing to flamenco music encouraged. **Memphis**, ((09) 379-0355, at 100 Parnell Road, is in a very quirkily restored old house with live music on Thursdays and Saturdays. **Olympic Cafe**, ((09) 524-8997, at 19 Davis Crescent in Newmarket has stylish cooking.

Ramses Bar and Grill, ((09) 522-0619, at 435 Karangahape Road, serves innovative food at very reasonable prices, with no less than four varieties of fresh fish daily. **Guadalupe**, ((09) 373-3076 at 173 Karangahape Road has striking Mexican decor with candles, flowers, fetishes and wooden statues of the Virgin, with South American-influenced cuisine. **L'Escale**, ((09) 309-7408, at 132 Beaumont Street in Westhaven is an all-day cafe inside the marina, much loved by Auckland yachties.

Auckland has a number of all-day cafes. **Rakinos**, on High Street, serves excellent brunches and snacks. **Kerouac**, at 33 Vulcan Lane has a good atmosphere, open all day with brioche baked on the premises. Opposite, **Potter Blair** serves good cappuccinos.

ENTERTAINMENT AND NIGHTLIFE

Not comparable to Sydney's, but by New Zealand standards, Auckland is a bundle of fun for nocturnophiles. For an up-to-date listing of films, theater, concerts and special events, read the entertainment pages in the *Auckland Star,* or scan a copy of the free *Auckland Tourist Times.* The **Aotea Centre** is the country's newest performing arts venue, with performances by the New Zealand Symphony Orchestra and the Royal New Zealand Ballet, and the city has plenty of cinemas and theaters.

When it comes to nightlife, the sedate may prefer cocktails at the Regent, Parkroyal, Pan Pacific or Sheraton hotels, all of which offer sophisticated surroundings and the tinkling music of a resident pianist. Encounter the more raucous side of Auckland at its array of excellent pubs. The **Shakespeare Tavern** at the corner of Albert and Wyndham streets is one of the city's best, famed for its brewed-on-site beers. The **London Bar** in the Civic Tavern, Wellesley Street, is worth seeking out for its two claims to fame: it offers New Zealand's largest international selection of beers — 150 — and is also one of the city's hardiest jazz venues. Jazz is also showcased on Saturday and Sunday afternoons at the **Alexandra Tavern**, 269 Parnell Road, in its outdoor garden. You can hear live poetry readings at the **Albion Pub** on the corner of Wellesley and Hobson streets every Monday night from 7:30 pm. In Ponsonby, the **Gluepot**, in Three Lamps, stages rock Wednesdays through Saturdays. The **Masonic Tavern** in Devonport has live jazz on Thursday evenings. Or you can board the "Jazz Ferry," on Friday evenings, which plies between the Ferry Building wharf and Devonport until midnight.

Auckland's hottest club of the moment is **Don't Tell Mama**, at 340 Queen Street. Spread across several levels, it has a giant dance floor, an assortment of bars and a restaurant. Otherwise, the city's main nightclub zone is centered on High Street, with clubs constantly closing down and being re-opened.

Two predominantly gay clubs are **Alfie's**, a basement disco in Century Arcade, and **Grapes**, on Victoria Street West, though the latter has a rather unattractive suburban atmosphere.

The seedy side of Auckland nightlife is centered on Fort Street, off Queen Street, Auckland's version of Sydney's King's Cross.

SHOPPING

Start with **Victoria Park Market** opposite Victoria Park, an Auckland institution. This renovated turn-of-the-century warehouse has over fifty stalls, cafes and restaurants, free live entertainment on weekends and a tastefully disguised McDonald's. It's open daily from 9 am (10 am on Sundays) until 7 pm (9 pm on Fridays). The **China Oriental Market**, located on the corner of Queen and Britomart streets, is an all-Asian emporium with ethnic food stalls, imported novelty goods, arts and crafts. It's open daily from 9 am to 7 pm. The weekly Saturday morning **Otara Market** (opens at 6 am) is always bustling and colorful, attracting Auckland's Maori and Pacific Island communities.

"K" Road also has a very Polynesian atmosphere. In the arcade leading to Samoa House at N°283, you'll find shops selling tapa cloth, shell crafts, hand-woven bags, coconut soap and many other items from the Pacific Islands.

Auckland has a lot more to offer than sheepskin and greenstone emporia. Specialist craft shops abound both downtown and in Parnell, Remuera and Ponsonby. The city has a strong local fashion industry and several interesting designer shops have international flair. In the inner-city, look out for **Monsoon Menswear** and **Zambesi**, both in Vulcan Lane, **Scotties** at 2 Blake Street, Ponsonby, **Keith Matheson** at 53 High Street and **Bresolini** at 28 Lorne Street. **Fingers** at 2 Kitchener Street, displays the work of many top New Zealand's artisans, while **Handknits** in Queens Arcade has a colorful selection of designer handknits.

Auckland's best, oldest and most interesting antique shop is **Portobello Antiques**, which lies at the corner of St. Georges Bay Road and St. Stevens Avenue, opposite the St. Mary's Cathedral in Parnell. For environmentally-minded shoppers, the **Greenpeace Shop** at the corner of High Street and Vulcan Lane is the only one in the Southern Hemisphere, while **Touchstone** at 6 Lorne Street and **Wild Places** at 28 Lorne Street also specialize in conservation, stocking stationary, T-shirts, art prints and books. Both the **Auckland Art Gallery** and the **Auckland Museum** have excellent shops, the latter great for good-quality artifacts, greenstone carvings and flax-kit bags.

The city's largest indoor mall is the **Downtown Centre** on Custom Street with more than 70 shops and a duty-free section. Opposite, the **Old Customhouse**, the financial heart of Auckland for eighty years, has been renovated into an arts and crafts emporium housing a cinema and cafe. **Tisdalls** at 176 Queen Street specializes in high-quality tramping equipment although it isn't cheap. Good book shops include **Unity Books** at 19 High Street, **Poppies**, at 415 Remuera Road, **Faraway Places**, at 604 Dominion Road, Mt. Eden and **Under Silkwood** at 2279 Parnell Road. **The Polynesian Bookshop** is in Samoa House, Karangahape Road.

AUCKLAND'S ENVIRONS

The Waitakere Ranges and the West Coast

It's almost impossible to really appreciate the magnificence and solitude of Auckland's west coast without your own vehicle. If you can't hire, beg or borrow one, go on the Bush & Beach Tour or ask the Visitor's Centre for advice on bus services or other specialist tours to enable you to reach the more remote tracks and beaches.

One of the most pleasant ways to spend a day in Auckland is to take the **Scenic Drive** through the **Waitakere Ranges** out to the West Coast, located approximately 40 km (25 miles) from town. The Scenic Drive begins just out of Titirangi, and winds through

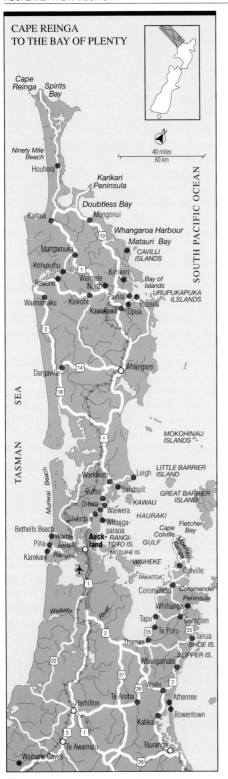

CAPE REINGA
TO THE BAY OF PLENTY

the native forest of the Ranges, which have more than 200 km (124 miles) of walking and tramping tracks and spectacular beaches and cliffs, ranging from dainty 10-minute strolls to overnight expeditions for well-equipped trampers. The **Park Information Centre**, ((09) 817-7134, is at Arataki, about five kilometers (three miles) from Titirangi on the Scenic Drive and is open daily. They can advise you on suitable walks, issue permits for primitive camping sites and inform you of any special events, such as "possum prowls."

The most popular west coast beach, **Piha** is a dramatic black ironsand surf beach, framed by sheer cliffs and dense forests. You can't miss seeing the 100m (330 ft) **Lion's Rock** which juts out into the surf slightly offshore and can be climbed in half an hour. **Kitekite Falls** and **Karekare Falls** are highlights of the many walking tracks that wind across the Waitakere Ranges here, with pathways lined with fluffy *toi-toi*, *nikau* palms, flax, cabbage and pohutakawa trees. From Piha there are several special places to seek out. At the northern end of the beach, the Laird Thompson Track leads across the headland to **White's Beach**, perfect for a picnic or spot of musseling. Further along are the sandy dunes of **Anawhata**. Another walk goes into the lush, primeval atmosphere of the Nikau Grove. At Piha's southern end, take the Tasman Lookout Track to the so-called **Gap**, a crevice pounded out of the headland's hulking granite by the waves. Close by is one of the loveliest places to laze in the sun, a natural lagoon just at the surf's edge, lapped by floating seaweed. Don't forget to sample delicious smoked mussels at the General Store, (opposite the camping ground), and see the village's "Post Office," a tiny shack with a corrugated roof that also doubles as a library. Buses from Auckland service Piha several times weekly.

Across the southern headland lies **Kerekere**, another beautiful, less populated West Coast beach that lies between two rocky escarpments and has a picturesque waterfall and the remains of an old railway. On the northwestern coast, **Bethells Beach** is more exposed to the elements, with wild scenery often thunderous with surf. It's good for windy walks and surfing in complete isolation, while further on, **Whaka-tipu**, offers day-long walks and caves to explore. **Muriwai** beach is incredibly rugged and remote, with open sands sprawling for 48 km (30 miles) backed by rolling dunes. During the week there's hardly a soul about. Walk the Michelson and Maori Bay tracks for spectacular scenery, and see the gannet and tern colonies on the headland above Murawai beach. Finally, a word of warning about the west coast: the surf can be treacherous, despite its immense popularity with surfers. Make sure you stay within patrolled zones because the rip tides are extremely strong and close to the shore.

The Hauraki Gulf

There are fewer nicer ways to spend a day than to take a boat out of one of Auckland's outlying islands. Within the Hauraki Gulf Maritime Park there are some 47 islands — varying dramatically in size, geology, flora and fauna. Below are the ones within reasonable distance of the city, reached either by private boats, regular ferry services or, in some cases, helicopter or amphibious aircraft.

Closest to the city is **Rangitoto**, Auckland's youngest and largest volcano. It's an easy track to the 259 m (854 ft) summit, built by convicts in the thirties, although remember to bring sturdy footwear for the rough scoria is hard on sand shoes. As you walk, it's fascinating to see how vegetation has clung to the primeval black lava rocks. Other well sign-posted walks lead to through *pohutakawa* forests to lava caves and secluded coves. Ferries leave several times a day from the ferry docks in Auckland and arrive at Rangitoto Wharf 45 minutes later. From the wharf you can walk to the summit, four kilometers (two-and-a-half miles), and then down to the other wharf at Islington Bay, or you can follow the track along the island's coast, with its many coves and boathouses perfect for sunbathing and swimming. Whatever way you go, don't miss the last ferry at 5 pm.

Linked to Rangitoto by a narrow strip of land, the verdant island of **Motutapu** makes a pleasant three hour walk from Islington Bay during which you can swim at its beaches and admire its harbor views.

There's a camping ground at Home Bay but you'll need to make prior arrangements with the ranger who is also in charge of Rangitoto. Nearby **Motuihe** has beautiful sheltered swimming beaches, walking tracks into native bush and a shop.

The much larger island of **Waiheke** is a popular weekend haven, and with its many fine beaches, hotels and facilities is virtually considered a quieter-paced suburb of Auckland. Regular car and hourly passenger ferries serve the 4,000 residents of this large island with its delightful sandy beaches, undulating farmland and areas of native bush. Waiheke has a sunnier climate than Auckland, a relaxed atmosphere and is ideal for day trips, weekends or longer holidays. There are plenty of places to stay, as well as restaurants and shops, especially around the main settlements of Oneroa, at the western end of the island, through to lovely Palm Beach and Onetangi in the middle. Beyond this, the eastern part of the island is relatively untouched, with a rough, hilly road.

Waiheke has a great deal to offer — walks, swimming beaches, horse-riding trails — and it also has a thriving community of artists, potters and other crafts people, many of whom have studios open to visitors during the summer months. For a full listing of hotels, backpacker hostels, camping sites, restaurants and activities on the island, refer to the "What's On" newsletter put out by Fullers, available when you buy your ticket at the Ferry Building in Auckland. But some of the above deserve a special recommendation. For stylish, peaceful and inexpensive accommodation, try the **Onetangi Hotel**, ((09) 372-8028, a twenties style hotel complete with double brass beds and a wonderful seafood restaurant. Less expensive, and not quite as stylish, **McGinty's Lodge**, ((09) 372-8118, is on the Strand in Onetangi, close to shops and right on the sea-front. **Punga Lodge**, ((09) 372-6675, at 233 Oceanview Road in Little Oneroa is a more secluded option at similar rates. The island's only resort is **Club Paradise**, ((09) 372-7897, which has moderately priced individual chalets in native bush. Good restaurants include the **Pickle Palace Deli** in Oneroa, the **Fig Tree Cafe**, set on the beach at Blackpool between Surfdale and Oneroa and the more formal **Beaches** restaurant, which appreciates reservations at ((09) 372-5335, in Palm Beach. You can join a small group to tour the island with **Mini-Bus Tours**, ((09) 372-7151.

Of the numerous walks, the most popular leads to the gun emplacements and tunnels at **Stony Batter**; access is via a privately-owned unsealed road. There are two particularly impressive, award-winning vineyards on Waiheke, both offering opportunities to sample and buy, but ring first for an appointment: **Goldwater Estate**, ((09) 372-

Mediterranean olives and English oaks, plus zebras, antelopes and other untethered wild animals. Although these have long disappeared, you will see plenty of wallabies, kookaburras, rosellas and parakeets in the reserve's parkland. The island's many secluded bays and picnic sites are lovely places for a day trip, especially aboard a yacht. There's a very charming place to stay: **Vivian's Bay**, (835 locally, or (09) 422-8835, with furnished chalet accommodation nestled along the secluded beachfront, perfect for a tranquil break and bush walks. Rates are moderate.

7493, at Putiki Bay and **Stonyridge Vineyard**, ((09) 372-8822 at Onetangi.

Other day-trip-distance islands in the Gulf include **Pakatoa**, a small resort island developed into a tourist center for day trippers and holidaymakers, but its over-development is distinctly unappealing.

Kawau is easily the prettiest of the Gulf Islands. It is also the site of **Mansion House**, once the home of New Zealand's early governor, Sir George Grey, which stands on the beachfront and has strutting peacocks on its lawns. Sir George bought Kawau in 1862, and introduced many exotic trees including Brazilian palms, Indian rhododendrons,

Mansion House Ferries, ((09) 425-8006, runs daily services from Sandspit, near Warkworth, about an hour's drive north of Auckland on State Highway One. The **Sea Flight Wavepiercer**, ((09) 366-1421, runs day trips from Auckland to Kawau on Wednesdays, Fridays and Sundays, leaving at 10am and returning at 4pm.

Great Barrier Island is 80 km (50 miles) from Auckland and therefore too far for a day trip With its wild natural beauty, Great Barrier is a better choice for a remote, rugged camping holiday. It has long beaches and pounding surf along its eastern coastline and sheltered anchorages in the west. **Port Fitzroy** to the north, offers some of the best diving and fishing in the country. Stay at

Wharf-side scene at Paihia, Bay of Islands.

The Jetty, (20, in Kaiarara Bay. The island is a noted bird habitat with lots of *kaka*, *kokako*, brown teal ducks and black petrels. Half of the land is a nature reserve, and the 800 residents of the other half have lobbied to keep their roads unsealed and homes powered by generators. Walking tracks and camping grounds enable visitors to appreciate the unspoilt beauty, uncovering old gold, silver and copper mines, whaling stations, kauri dams and hot springs. From the main town of **Tryphena**, you can find a variety of accommodation and transport to hire.

If you have your own boat, you may be interested to stop at **Tiritiri Matangi**, a reserve for endangered species, especially rare birds, while **Little Barrier** has the largest remaining native forest in New Zealand and very beautiful wetlands. For information about these zoological sanctuaries and information about access, contact the Hauraki Gulf Maritime Park Information Centre, ((09) 307-1465.

The Henderson Valley

One of Auckland's great pleasures is touring its picturesque valley vineyards. Many of New Zealand's top vineyards are located within half an hour of downtown Auckland in the Henderson Valley, between the city's outskirts and the foothills of the Waitakeres. At the Visitors Bureau you can pick up a leaflet published by the West Auckland wine-makers that outlines all the vineyards and gives instructions for finding them. Most are open Monday through Saturday, and many offer tastings and restaurant lunches in idyllic settings. The industry has been shaped by generations of Yugoslavian immigrants, so that many of the names, such as Babich, Corban and Delegat have a Serbo-Croat ring to them. Some of the most notable **vineyards** include Cooper's Creek Vineyard, ((09) 412-8560; Selak's Vineyard, Kumeu, ((09) 412-7206; Matua Valley Wines in Waimauku, ((09) 411-8259; and Soljan's Wines, ((09) 836-8365. Alternatively you can join a conducted tour. Information and a wine trail map are obtainable from the Visitors Bureau at Aotea Square.

The Hibiscus Coast

The Hibiscus Coast stretches about 26 km (16 miles) north of Auckland, from Silver-dale to **Puhoi**, a pretty little town with a classic New Zealand pub that is worth a stop at the end of an afternoon. This resort-dotted coastline along the Whangaparoa Harbour has numerous, safe, sheltered beaches. **Orewa** is the largest resort town, with shopping arcades, caravan parks and a golf course. **Waiwera**, a few kilometers north, is a great place to visit during the winter for its hot springs and thermal pools, first discovered, and jealously guarded, by early Maoris, who built a *pa* on the nearby headland. Further along, **Wenderholm** is a nature reserve administered by the Auckland Regional Authority and left as close to a wilderness state as possible. It has lovely beaches and is a perfect place to come for a summer picnic. Even further north are **Sandspit**, where boats leave for Kawau Island, and **Pakiri Beach**, which has dramatic huge dunes and seaside pine forests.

NORTHLAND AND THE BAY OF ISLANDS

Known as the "Winterless North," Northland is a region of unspoilt, natural beauty steeped in early Maori and European history. Northland invariably records temperatures several degrees higher than the rest of the country, and has long hot summers and very mild winters. Within Northland, the Bay of Islands boasts countless sandy beaches and bays, clear water, magnificent scenery and some of the best sailing and fishing in New Zealand. The **Far North** offers 880 km (546 miles) of remote, wild coastline, while the **Kauri Coast** is renowned for beautiful forest sanctuaries, completing the route back to Auckland.

DRIVING UP TO THE BAY OF ISLANDS

It takes about three and a half hours to drive up to **Paihia**, the main Bay of Island's township. After crossing's Auckland's Harbour Bridge, follow State Highway 1 along the Hibiscus Coast and its seaside resorts. It's worth making a detour to **Leigh** to sample super-fresh fish and chips in its pretty wharf setting. Leigh is also the take-off point for dive boats heading out to the **Mokohinau Islands** and the marine reserve around **Goat Island**. Further on, **Warkworth** has riverside cafes and crafts shops. En route, you'll pass through **Whangarei**, Northland's largest city and commercial hub. Although teeming with facilities for visitors, it has few attractions aside from several museums: the eccentric **Clapham Clock Museum** near in the lovely rose gardens of Cafler Park, the nearby **Margie Madden Fernery and Snow Conservatory**, which features 85 varieties of native ferns, and the **Northland Regional Museum** on the city's boundaries. Highlights in the region are **Tutukaka Harbour**, north-east of Whangarei which has excellent rock, line and deep sea fishing as well as diving. It can be used as a base for cruises to the **Poor Knights**, a marine reserve 24 km (15 miles) off the coast, covering an area scattered with early shipwrecks and over 50 diving spots. Within its warm waters you can see many varieties of subtropical and tropical fish, black coral trees, brightly colored sponges and lurid gorgonian fans.

Back on the main highway, turn off for **Kawakawa**, a quintessential New Zealand rural community distinctive for the vintage railway that runs right through the main street. From Kawakawa, you have a choice of entering the Bay of Islands two ways. You can drive north-east to the seaside resort of **Opua**, where you can take a quick car ferry ride across to historic **Russell**, New Zealand's first capital. Or you can take the road that winds directly down to Paihia.

THE BAY OF ISLANDS

Few places in New Zealand are so captivatingly lovely as the Bay of Islands. Located on the eastern coast of the Northland peninsula, some 260 km (161 miles) north of Auckland, the region contains some 150 islands of varying size clustered in pristine turquoise waters. As you sail by, the inviting coves, sheltered beaches and green islets stretch out like stepping stones to the horizon.

If you can manage it, by far the best way to appreciate the Bay of Islands is from the deck of a boat, so that you can explore and

moor at an anchor's whim. Not only can you have a beach to yourself, but often a whole uninhabited island.

For many, the lure to the Bay of Islands lies in its appeal as a big game fishing Mecca with marlin-rich waters and fly-fishing comparable to the Kona Coast of Hawaii. Tales of record fish have abounded here ever since the late nineteenth century whalers made history by rigging nets to successfully trap humpback whales that passed between rocks near Cape Brett. In 1926, the American writer Zane Grey set up a safari-like camp at **Urupukapuka**, the largest island in the bay and wowed locals by catching as many as five marlin in a single day, including a 280 kg (450lb) striped marlin. His Hemmingwayesque eulogy of the

Bay of Islands, *Tales of the Angler's Eldorado*, helped confirm the region's reputation and establish its following.

When not tackling the big game fishing grounds, outdoor enthusiasts can enjoy the Bay of Islands with daytime and evening cruise trips, scenic flights, diving boats (complete with equipment for hire), jet boats for water skiing, sail-yourself yachts, run-abouts and dinghies for hire, fishing trips and bush walks.

Access
Mt Cook Airlines has daily flights to Keri-keri from Auckland and Rotorua, and the closest Air New Zealand flight is to Whan-garei. Great Barrier Airlines flies to Paihia from Auckland during the summer season.

If you're traveling by bus, InterCity op-erates several buses a day from Auckland to the Bay of Islands via Whangarei and Opua, taking about four hours to reach the main center of Paihia. It continues north to Kerik-eri and Kaitaia. Another InterCity bus route goes to Paihia via Dargaville and the Waipoua Forest, making a stop to see Tane Mahuta, the king of the giant kauris. Clarks Northliner and Newmans bus services also connect with the Bay of Islands.

Ferries
Regular passenger ferries operate between Paihia and Russell, taking about 10 minutes either way. The *Bay Belle* runs from Paihia

The sheltered coves of the Bay of Islands.

from 7:20 am to 6:45 pm (10 pm during summer), and from Russell, 7 am to 6:10 pm. If you have a car, you can make the crossing from Opua, where a vehicle ferry service crosses to Okiato Point, 10 minutes' drive from Russell. There are crossings every 10 minutes from 6:40 am to 9:50 pm. If you're caught out late at night or just want some privacy, there a 24-hour water taxi. Contact them at ((09) 403-7123.

Cruises

Even if you don't hire your own boat there

are several day-trip launch cruises from Paihia and Russell that will give you a taste for what lies beyond the Bay's horizon. Fullers run two very popular cruises, both of which stop at Russell and need to be booked at least a day in advance. The three-hour **Cape Brett Cruise** journeys out through game fishing waters to Cape Brett, pierces through an impenetrable-looking gap in Piercy Island, takes a close-up look at the extraordinary colorations of **Cathedral Cove** and stops at **Otehei Bay** on Uru-pukapuka Island, where you can either laze in the sun or climb aboard a submarine viewing vessel. It costs $42 for adults and $19 for children. The **Cream Trip**, so-called because it used to deliver supplies and mail

to dairy farmers on remote stations in return for fresh cream, is a five-hour trip. It continues the tradition, giving the opportunity to meet with locals and cruises at a leisurely pace so that you can see seals, dolphins or even whales. Sometimes however, the pets of island caretakers are the star performers. Among them are McGinty, a golden labrador who swims to the boat to pick up newspapers, and Bremworth, a lamb who trots out to greet the boat at a jetty. The route varies every day according to the pick-ups or deliveries. It costs $45 for adults and $22 for children.

Boat Charters

A slew of charter companies operate out of Paihia, Russell and Opua. You can negotiate a cruise package, covering the costs of being skippered and fully provisioned, or you can "bareboat" hire a fully-equipped surveyed boat, so that you are your own captain and bring your own supplies and fuel. Once aboard you choose your own anchorages and itinerary, free to explore some of the best cruising areas in the Pacific.

Here are some useful contacts:

Rainbow Yacht Charters, ((09) 402-7821, fax: (09) 402-7546, at Opua Wharf, offers the most extensive range of yachts and launches. In Auckland, contact Pier Z, Westhaven Marina, Auckland, ((09) 402-0719, fax: (09) 402-0931.

R. Tucker Thompson, ((09) 402-8430, fax: (09) 402-7221, P.O. Box 193, Paihia, is a beautiful gaff-rigged square topsail schooner, a magnificent sight with its sails billowing on the seas. Its owners run seven-hour day trips around the Bay of Islands, departing Opua at 9.30 am, with a 10 am pick-up at Russell. The trip — with lunch, Devonshire teas and beverages — costs $55, with children under 15 $25 and children under seven free.

The *Triptych*, a 21 m long (66 ft) x 11 m (33 ft) wide trimaran is available for hire. It also operates day cruises. Contact ((09) 402-2355.

Smith's Jet Cruises, ((09) 402-7678 operate daily from Paihia wharf.

Kiwi Cruise, ((09) 402-7730, is an all-day cruise that tours several islands, and stops off for beach volleyball, snorkeling and bush walks. Expect to be treated to a fair amount of droll Kiwi humor. It costs $44 for adults and $25 for children.

Then there is the Bay of Island's equivalent of hiring a car. You can hire self-drive power boats, which have up to six seats. No license is required, although it will be assumed that potential surf racers are competent. Hire prices vary from $30 an hour to $220 for a full day. You also have to pay up to $200 in bond. If you're a beginner, you can learn how to "drive," or be skippered on jet cruises. Contact **Charter Pier**, ((09) 402-7127, at Paihia Wharf.

Northland's most worthwhile attractions. The **Cape Reinga Via Ninety Mile Beach** tour drives up along the mighty Ninety Mile Beach, negotiates the Te Paki Quicksand Stream and, stops for lunch at Cape Reinga and visits the Wagener Museum and the Sullivan's Glow Worm Grotto and Kiwi House. It departs from Paihia at 7:30 am, returning at 6:30 pm, and makes pick-up return stops at Kerikeri, Mangonui and Kaitaia. Adults cost $65 and children $35, with reductions from Kaitaia and Mangonui.

Fishing Expeditions

The period from mid-December to the end of June is renowned for its catches of striped marlin, pacific blue marlin, yellowtail kingfish, yellowfin tuna, broadbill and mako, hammerhead and thresher sharks. From July until mid-December, you can go light tackle fishing for kahawai, yellowtail kingfish and broadbill. You can arrange your own boat, or go along in groups under the guidance of experienced professionals. Contact **Game Fishing Charters**, ((09) 402-7311 at the Maritime Building.

Tours

Fullers has a variety of extremely enjoyable day tours which allow you to see many of

The **Tu-Tu Sand Shark** tour lives up to its name in Maori: "tu-tu" means "to play around." Aboard the Fullers 40-seater six wheel-drive dune machine you cavort across the massive West Coast sandhills, visit kauri fields and negotiate the rocks at Reef Point. There's time for a swim, a barbecue and ball games. The tour departs from Paihia from 7:30 am and returns 6:30 pm, from Kerikeri at 7:50 am, and Kaitaia at 10 am. All pick-up times are confirmed when you book.

Other Fullers tours go to Kerikeri and the Puketi Forest, with mini-tours to Waitangi and Russell.

OPPOSITE: Scene of rural tranquillity in Urupukapuka. ABOVE: Ocean Beach at Whangerei.

PAIHIA

The base for exploring the Bay of Islands, this pierfront township is also where most of the region's fishing fleet is centered. It has pretty, although not secluded beaches, a well-stocked shopping center, umbrella-shaded cafes and a casual, friendly atmosphere. From Paihia you can arrange cruises on every imaginable kind of vessel from a vintage schooner to a modern powerboat for day or week-long trips. There are also scenic launch trips, game fishing boats, jet boats, water taxis and private fishing charters available.

General Information

The **Bay of Islands Information Office**, ((09) 202-7426 is located in the Maritime Building on the wharf in the center of town. Also located here are the **Fuller's Office**, ((09) 402-7421, for booking cruises and tours, a fishing center for booking boats and equipment, the town's bus station and the pierfront where you can catch the ferry to Russell. All offices are open daily from 8 am to 5 pm.

What to See

Set on a magnificent harbor, Paihia's attractions are firmly maritime. Life revolves around the waterfront pier, from which fishing, boating and diving excursions create constant activity. The highlight of the day is the evening's catch, when fishermen haul in huge silvery blue-black marlin, shark and kingfish, whetting the appetites of anyone wanting to try their hand at being a big game fisherman.

Across the Waitangi Bridge is the **Waitangi National Trust Reserve**, a very significant place for New Zealanders, and open daily. At the Visitors Center, bone up on New Zealand history by watching their audio-visual, then walk up through native bush to the **Treaty House**. This gracious colonial mansion was the home of James Busby, British resident in New Zealand from 1832 to 1840, and its rooms have been restored as a museum. Stroll through the beautiful grounds to the impressive **Whare Runanga**, or Maori meeting house, and to the water's edge to see the intricately carved 35 m

(108 ft) Maori war canoe, hauled out each year on Waitangi Day and powered by 80 ceremonially dressed Maoris.

On the other side of the Waitangi Bridge, climb aboard the **Shipwreck Museum**, a three-masted barque which displays treasures and relics salvaged from the some 100 ships which went down in New Zealand waters by the late Kelly Tarlton. It's open daily from 10:30 am to 5:30 pm.

There are some very pleasant walks around Paihia. You can follow a six kilometers (nearly four miles) track from the Waitangi Reserve that takes you to Haruru Falls and up to the summit of Mt. Bledisloe, and crosses a lush mangrove jungle on a wooden boardwalk. There are two other particularly nice short walks close to town: both end up in Opua, three km (two miles) south. One track hugs the coastline, the other goes across the lushly forested headland off School Road and both take about two and a half hours each way.

Another thing to do is to drive to Opua and take the charming vintage train round trip to Kawakawa. It chugs back and forth daily except Fridays and the schedule changes regularly, so call Kawakawa station, call (09) 404-0684 for details.

Where to Stay

Paihia's sea-front is crammed with hotels, lodges and motels. There are three particularly stylish places to stay. The **Paihia Pacific Resort**, ((09) 402-8221, fax: (09) 402-8490, at 27 Kings Road, has a landscaped grotto-like swimming pool, fine restaurant and very plush interiors. Considering the attention to detail and quality here, the moderate rates offer very good value. The other two places are motels, both with luxurious apartment-sized rooms and kitchens, private sun terraces and spa-pools. The **Austria Motel**, ((09) 402-7480, fax: (09) 402-7480, on Selwyn Road is mid-priced, with German, French and Italian spoken. The moderately-priced **Swiss Chalet Lodge**, ((09) 402-7615, fax: (09) 402-7609, at 3 Bayview Road, is charming with light spacious rooms in natural wood, brightened with fresh flowers.

There are several other motels to recommend, all located close to the waterfront with excellent facilities. The mid-priced

Abel Tasman Motel, ((09) 402-7521, fax: (09) 402-7576, is on Marsden Street, while the **Ala-Moana Motel**, ((09) 402-7745, fax: (09) 402-7745, nestled behind the old Stone Church, is moderately-priced. In the same category, you could try the **Seaspray Motor Lodge**, ((09) 402-7935, fax: (09) 402-8436, at 138 Marsden Road or **Cook's Lookout**, ((09) 402-7409, on Causeway Road, five kilometers (three miles) away close to the scenic Hauru Falls with spectacular hilltop views across the harbor and a swimming pool.

The **Alfa Motel**, ((09) 402-7686, on Seaview Road, is a good inexpensive choice, with a secluded location and comfortable furnishings. Backpackers can choose from **Lodge Eleven**, ((09) 402-7487, at the corner of McMurray's and King's roads, which has rooms with their own bathroom facilities, or **Mayfair Lodge**, ((09) 402-7471 at 7 Puketona Road.

Campers will enjoy **The Park**, ((09) 402-7826, fax: (09) 402-8500, at the corner of Seaview and McMurray's Road, with its landscaped grounds, swimming pool and two licensed restaurants. On the main road between Paihia and Opua, **Smith's Holiday Camp**, ((09) 402-7678, has its own private bay and the option of luxurious cabins. The **Twin Pines Tourist Park**, ((09) 402-7322, lies three kilometers (two miles) away at Hauru Falls. It's a peaceful spot with a lodge, cabins and camp sites under leafy trees, with an historic tavern and restaurant nearby.

In Opua, stay at the moderately-priced **Opua Motel**, ((09) 402-7632, on Franklin Street, which overlooks the picturesque harbor. The owners, Sharon and Noel Pasco, also run fishing charters in their catamaran, and are happy to make a package arrangement.

Where to Eat

In and around Paihia there are plenty of memorable places to dine. **Bistro 40**, ((09) 402-7444, on the Marsden Road waterfront has the most romantic atmosphere: a 100 year-old cottage with pretty gardens and jasmine creepers. You can expect superb seafood, poultry and game dishes, while prices are very reasonable. **Esmae's**, ((09) 402-8400, at 41 Williams Road and **La Scala**, ((09) 402-7031, on Selwyn Road, are both

excellent seafood and venison licensed restaurants. **Tides**, ((09) 402-7557, on Williams Road and **The Beachcomber**, ((09) 402-7434, at 1 Seaview Road are good casual choices. **Cafe Over The Bay**, ((09) 402-8147, on the waterfront is an all-day eatery that serves traditional country cooking with an Italian influence. The **Blue Marlin Diner**, ((09) 402-7590, opposite the wharf serves a huge New Zealand-style "all-day breakfast" for $6.95.

In nearby Opua, the **Ferryman's Restaurant and Bar**, ((09) 402-7515, has a wonder-

ful location on the pier, with nautical beams and brass portholes and even a floor window for fish spotting. Its specialties are seafood, crayfish, aged game and lamb dishes. It's open for lunch and dinner.

RUSSELL

Easily visible from Paihia on the other side of the bay, Russell was New Zealand's first capital. With its charming colonial villas tucked along a pretty waterfront lined with pohutakawa trees, there are few traces of its former days as a rowdy whaling port in the

ABOVE: The colonial seafront sweep of Russell township. OVERLEAF: Rolling pastureland near Urquharts Bay.

early 1800s. Then called *Kororareka*, it was dubbed the "Hell hole of the Pacific" for its brawling seamen, runaway convicts, "grog" shops and orgiastic brothels. One early traveler put his viewpoint this way: "Notorious at present for containing, I think, a greater number of rogues than any other spot of equal size in the universe."

General Information
The **Park Headquarters for the Bay of Islands Maritime and Historic Park**, on the Strand has excellent audio-visual and infor-

mation displays on the Bay of Islands, with detailed advice on how to visit the more remote islands and the best walking trails. You can also apply here to stay at the remote lighthouse keeper's house overlooking Cape Brett's rocky outcrop, where you can indulge in isolation for $4 a night. There is room for 14 people. Another idyllic back-to-basics place to stay is the conservation land campsite on Urupukapuka Island. You can make arrangements to be transported to both places by the Fuller's Cape Brett boat.

The **Fuller's Office**, ((09) 403-7866 on The Strand, can help with all information and bookings. There is a bus tour from Russell wharf which takes in panoramic views of the whole of the Bay of Islands, Flagstaff Hill, Tapeka Point, Long Beach, oyster farms and the Russell township.

What to See
Russell has many historic buildings, including New Zealand's oldest surviving church, **Christ Church**, built in 1836, shaded by trees and bordered by a white picket fence, with

graves of whalers and early settlers alongside Maori chiefs and British seamen killed during the Maori uprising in 1845.

Along the narrow, tree-lined waterfront **Strand** is **Pompallier House**, a beautifully restored French Colonial-style Catholic mission house set amongst flowering gardens. One of the few French settlements in new Zealand, it was established in 1841 and originally used as a mission printing press. It's open daily from 10 to 4:30 pm, and displays some of its early Maori bibles. Other buildings to keep an eye out for include the residence of James Clendon, the first United States Consul (appointed in 1838), later used as a schoolhouse. The **Duke of Marlborough Hotel**, known fondly by locals as "the Duke," held the first liquor license in the country. It's no surprise that right next door is the old **Police Station**, (1870), built from solid heart kauri, used at various times as New Zealand's first customs office, courthouse and gaol. The **Captain Cook Memorial Museum**, on York Street, completed for the bicentenary of his landing in the Bay in 1769, has a superb scale model of the *Endeavour* and many related documents to his voyages. It also has many bizarre and fascinating relics of early Kororareka and its inhabitants. There are sperm whale's eardrums, obligatory Moa bones, lead pellets to weigh down Victorian skirts, and a set of fish knives and forks with lobster claws used by Prince Alfred, Duke of Edinburgh at the Worshipful Co. of Fishmonger's banquet during his New Zealand visit in 1869. Within Russell's village, you can browse amongst crafts shops and galleries, stocked with work by local artists and potters.

A social beacon of the town is the building that houses both the tackle shop and the Bay of Islands' **Swordfish Club**. Upstairs in the club's pub, a 462 kg (1,017 lb) blue marlin — about the size of a double bed — dominates the wall, a reminder of what lurks in the waters of the bay.

You can make the short, steep climb to **Maiki Hill**, better known as Flagstaff Hill, for magnificent views across Russell and the open ocean of the Bay of Islands. It was here that the Ngapuhi chief Hone Heke four times chopped down the flagstaff considered to be the symbol of British authority after it was first raised in 1834 as New Zealand's national flag. Twelve days a year, his defiance is commemorated by a flag in the colors of the Maori Confederation of Tribes.

Other places to seek out around Russell include **Tapeka Point** with its two beaches, and **Long Beach**, one of the most delightful mainland beaches in the Bay of Islands.

Slightly further afield, visit the **Pinelands Llama Farm**, which, as well as llamas, has an exotic menagerie of alpacas, Charolais cattle, Angora goats, rabbits and various species of birds. Visit by appointment on ((09) 403-7714.

Where to Stay

The **Duke of Marlborough Hotel**, ((09) 403-7829, fax: (09) 403-7760 on York Street, radiates character and history. Rebuilt four times since whaling days, the hotel's verandah with its umbrella-topped tables is a pleasant place to linger to watch the sunset even if you're not staying here. In the bar the decor leans heavily towards mounted fish and fishing photographs, including one taken in 1956 of Lord and Lady Mountbatten aboard a charter boat with a marlin tied across the stern. There's a traditional pub restaurant. Remember to book sea-facing rooms. Rates: moderate. Just adjacent, slightly more expensive, **Duke's Lodge**, ((09) 403-7899, is an attractive old building with a heated swimming pool and a pretty garden setting. Slightly up the hill, **Mako Motel**, ((09) 403-7770, on Wellington Street (turn left at the sign of the jumping shark) has very luxurious mid-priced rooms. If you have a large family, you might want to stay in the three-bedroom Mako Cottage.

There are several other excellent moderate-price options. **Flagstaff Homestead**, ((09) 403-7862, on Wellington Street, is a small restored pioneer homestead that can take up to six people and has nice sea views. The **Hananui Lodge Motel**, ((09) 403-7875, on The Strand, is right on the water's edge, with spacious, sunny apartment-sized units and a spa pool. Not far from Russell, **Orongo Homestead**, ((09) 403-7527, at R.D.1 is a charming moderately-priced Bed and Breakfast, set within large rounds overlooking peaceful Orongo Bay. Within its huge

grounds it has a a Finnish-style sauna and a small freshwater lake for cold water plunges. **Arcadia Lodge**, ((09) 403-7756, in Florence Avenue offers inexpensive accommodation and has simple rooms, a flowering garden and nice harbor views. In the same category, the **Bay of Islands Lodge**, ((09) 403-8558, at 54 School Road, overlooks Russell from its hilltop location. Campers and backpackers can head for the **Russell Holiday Park**, ((09) 403-7826, on Long Beach Road, located at the top of the hill. It has good facilities and well-stocked tourist cabins.

Russell has several rather select places to stay, and all require advance bookings. You'll notice **Kimberley Lodge**, ((09) 403-7090, fax: (09) 403-7239, on Pitt Street as you enter Russell harbor from Paihia, a grand white colonial-style residence with a large oval window set amongst lush bush. There are four double bedrooms, equipped with every kind of luxury including a CD player and stereo system and spa baths with a special place to put the ice bucket. The lodge serves formal dinners and charges deluxe rates. **Te Maki Villas**, ((09) 403-7046, fax: (09) 403-7537, on Flagstaff Road, are large, luxury self-contained A-frame cottages, moderately-priced. **Okiato Lodge**, ((09) 403-7948, fax: (09) 403-7515, on Old Russell Road, several kilometers away from Russell, is a very exclusive coastal lodge with its own private bay. It charges executive rates that includes all meals and wines and a Kerikeri airport transfer.

OPPOSITE: Christ Church, New Zealand's oldest church. ABOVE: Despite its rowdy history, the old police station in Russell has considerable charm.

Where to Eat

The Gables, ((09) 403-7618, on The Strand, offers stylish dining in an intriguing Victorian building that used to be a nineteenth century brothel and has whalebone stays for its beams. During winter, only dinner is served, with a roaring open fire. In summer, there are lunches and windows are thrown open to the sea. The Orongo Bay Oysters are sublime, and so are the Brandy Snaps with marinated oranges. Reservations are required.

Otherwise, there are several other casual eateries. Try The **Strand Coffee Shop**, which

turns into a BYO in the evening, and the **Verandah Cafe** in York Street. You can get great fish and chips at **Russell Take-aways** on Cass Street.

KERIKERI

In the peaceful, bush-clad setting of the sleepy Kerikeri basin is one of Northland's loveliest settlements. Overlooking the little port, **Kemp House** (1822), the oldest surviving building in the country and the **Stone Store** (1833), are part of the original, well-fortified missionary village and both have quaint museums. Walk through **Rewa's Maori Village**, an authentic replica of a *kainga* or unfortified pre-European Maori village, with elaborately-carved huts and storage pits.

Another site to visit is the **Kororipo Pa**, the fortress of the belligerent Maori chief Hongi Heka, who used to order the decapitated heads of his enemies to be impaled on the fence stakes — to become shrunken heads. Hongi Heka's warriors would assemble here in their gruesome finery before

making rampaging raids on southern tribes. It's reached after a 20 minute bush walk that begins up on the hill just behind the Stone Store tearooms. At the top are views across Kerikeri and the glistening waters of the bay. Other walks in the area include the four kilometers (two-and-a-half miles) **Kerikeri River** Track leading to **Rainbow Falls**, passing the **Fairy Pool** on the way, a very pretty place to stop for a swim and picnic.

Within Kerikeri there are numerous orchards, dripping with summer produce. As you drive, you can stop at wayside stalls and buy bags of mandarins, tangelos, kiwifruit, tamarillos and oranges as well as all sorts of other fruits and vegetables. At the **Orange Centre**, on the Kerikeri crossroad with State Highway 10, you can climb aboard a big fiberglass "Orangemobile" and trundle through the orchards listening to a commentary on the delicate business of raising crops. Uncle Davey's Dream Park, on Wairoa Road, is an outdoor fun adventure park, with bush walks, covered wagon rides, pony rides and treasure hunts.

Many artists and craftspeople live in and around Kerikeri, and at several shops you can see their work in progress, especially pottery. Look out for **Red Barn Pottery** and **The Black Sheep** on Kerikeri Road, and the **Te Awa Pottery** on Waipapa Road. On the nearby State Highway 10, both the **Origin Art and Craft Co-operative** and the **Blue Gum Pottery** shops are worthwhile to visit.

In the area, Doves Bay and Opito Bay are good swimming places, where yachts are often moored.

Where to Stay

Kerikeri has some very special lodges. **Villa del Pescador**, ((09) 407-7178, fax: (09) 407-7178, P.O. Box 283, is highly exclusive, caters only for one group of up to six at a time and does not like its address to be mentioned in print. Daily lease of the mock Spanish Villa costs $2,850, and this includes everything two people could want: transportation, fishing and diving cruises on a 13 m (45 ft) launch, superb meals and wine. **Hau Moana**, ((09) 404-9082, fax: (09) 404-9082, on Kurapari Road is another luxury lodge on the shores of the Kerikeri inlet. Families beware: you can only bring your children if you book the entire lodge! The deluxe rates include sumptuously decorated suites that overlook the shore, all meals, transfers to and from the airport and use of the lodge's extensive facilities. **Riverview Chalet Park Lodge**, ((09) 407-8741, fax: (09) 407-8741, at 28 Landing Road is about the best of them. Nestled in bush with idyllic views of the picturesque yacht harbor, it has luxuriously 3 furnished chalets that feel like small private homes complete with a kitchen, lounge and a sun-deck. It also has a solar-heated swimming pool, private spa and sauna.

go for walks in the surrounding bush and rolling countryside. Write to Maureen Harper, P.O. Box 384, Kerikeri.

UP TO THE CAPE

From Kerikeri, make a detour off State Highway 1 to see the tiny, historic village of **Waimate North**. The first inland European settlement and an early mission station, it radiates unspoilt early colonial charm. The elegant two-storied kauri **Mission House**, (1832) was the home of New Zealand's first

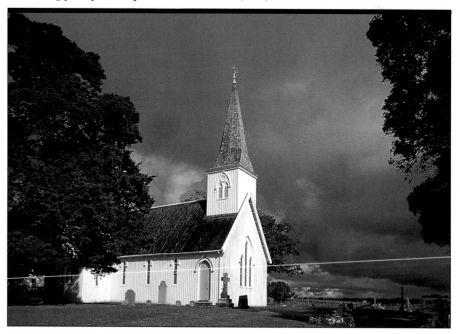

Puriri Park, ((09) 407-9818, on Bulls Road, off State Highway 10, offers inexpensive accommodation at a small orange and kiwifruit orchard, set in beautiful grounds and surrounded by forest. There's a swimming pool and good facilities.

For rock-bottom budget accommodation, try **Hone Heke Lodge,** ((09) 407-8170, on Hone Heke Road, where rooms are only $10.50 a night.

Aranga Holiday Park, ((09) 407-9326, on the Kerikeri Road is an excellent camping site beside the Puketotara Stream. Tucked at some distance from Kerikeri, there's a charming rural place to stay: **Milton Park**, ((09) 405-9628, perfect for a couple, with inexpensive rates. You can horse-ride and

bishop, George Augustus Selwyn. When Charles Darwin visited three years later, he was delighted by this "English farmhouse and its well-dressed fields placed there as if by an enchanter's wand." Within the settlement is **St. John's Church,** (1871) with a sign that asks you to close the door so that sheep won't wander in. Driving into the settlement, you may notice the **Old Waimate Store**, restored and converted into a charming restaurant and crafts shop. During the week they serve sublime Devonshire teas on the

OPPOSITE: The famed schooner, *Tucker Thompson*, in the Bay of Islands. ABOVE: Church of St. John the Baptist, Waimate North. OVERLEAF Seen from above, the emerald and turquoise beauty of the Bay of Islands.

honey-suckle covered verandah. They also serve wonderful pate, quiches, ploughman's lunches and blueberry pie. You can reserve a table for lunch, call (09) 406-8682. They are closed Tuesdays and Wednesdays from Easter until October.

Continue north to **Whangaroa**, which has a quaint colonial-era township and plenty of sleepy, seaside charm. It's famous throughout the region for the big, succulent oysters produced by its harbor farms, so make sure you stop to sample some. By the wharf, the vintage **Marlin Hotel**, ((09) 405-0347, has the town's only restaurant and pub, and also offers cheap accommodation. Secluded in its own private bay and moderately-priced, the **Kingfish Lodge**, ((09) 405-0164, is accessible only by boat and has an excellent seafood restaurant from which to appreciate lushly beautiful views across the harbor.

Whangaroa is a good base for big game fishing, line fishing and dive charters out to the sunken wreck of the bombed *Rainbow Warrior* off **Matauri Bay** and to the beautiful **Cavilli Islands**. You can book cruises through the Marlin Hotel or the Boyd Gallery, ((09) 406-0230, operated by its zestful owners as a dairy, art gallery and informal tourist information office and booking center.

Locals will probably tell you the lurid story of the *Boyd*, whose burnt-out hull lies in the harbor, recounted in *The Historical Legacy*.

Within the region, there are fine beaches at **Tauranga Bay**, **Mahinepua Bay**, **Te Ngahere** and **Matauri Bay**, and bush walks through the breathtaking **Puketi** and **Omahuta** state forests, rich in giant kauri trees.

Further on is **Mangonui**, the main town of **Doubtless Bay** and one of the most picturesque little settlements in New Zealand, and along with Russell and Akaroa on the Banks Peninsula, a much quieter and prettier place to stay than Paihia. It retains many colonial buildings from its historic days as a raucous whaling base, including the **Mangonui Hotel**, ((07) 575-5089, which offers cheap and charming accommodation.

On the wharf, there's an interesting aquarium. You can experience fish another way: the fish and chip shop on the wharf is deservedly famous throughout the Doubtless Bay. If you're only stopping for lunch, try **Cafe Nina** or the **Purple Parrot Cafe**. **The Old Oak** is a vintage pub, full at most times of the day with fishermen pulling each-other's legs with fishy tales.

Along the coastal roads east and west of Mangonui, you can explore the beautiful beaches of **Doubtless Bay**, **Hihi**, **Coopers Beach**, **Cable Bay**, **Taipa** and **Mill Bay** — all attract large numbers of summer holiday makers and have camping grounds, motels and restaurants.

Further north, like a little thumb crooked into the ocean, the **Karikari Peninsula** is one of least developed, most exquisite parts of Northland, indented with sandy bays and coves. Driving around its narrow, rural roads, you'll feel as though you've stumbled on a secret paradise: there are no big resorts or hotels. Just one gorgeous, undisturbed vista after another, always stretching into a sparkling, blue-emerald sea. **Matai Bay** is particularly beautiful, with its sheltered twin bays and steep hillside climb between them. There is also an idyllic conservation land campsite here. The **Reef Lodge**, ((09) 408-7100, at **Rangiputa** is a lovely place to stay, with moderate rates.

THE FAR NORTH

KAITAIA

More a place from which to make the trip to Cape Reinga than a destination in itself, Kaitaia has a cultural mix mainly of Maori and Yugoslavs, the latter descended from Dalmatian gum-diggers who flocked to the region in the nineteenth century. Do stop for the **Far North Regional Museum**, which houses the oldest known European artifact in the country — two anchors left by the St. Jean Baptiste which visited New Zealand in December 1769 under the command of the French explorer Jean de Surville. Also 18 km (11 miles) south-east of Kaitaia, accessible from State Highway 10 and State Highway 1 visit the **Sullivan's Kiwi House**

The Cape Reinga lighthouse at New Zealand's northernmost tip.

and Nocturnal Park on Fairburn Road, which has kiwis and a glow worm cave in a well-landscaped natural setting.

The **Kaitaia Information Office**, ((09) 408-0879 is on South Road, is open from 9:30 am to 10 pm daily.

In the area, stay at **The Park**, ((09) 406-7298, fax: (09) 406-7477, located 18 km (11 miles) from Kaitaia at the Waipapakauri Ramp entrance to Ninety Mile Beach. It's a good place to contemplate the seemingly eternal sands and the last pick-up point for Cape Reinga tours from Kaitaia and Paihia.

driving along its full length — actually 89 km (55 miles) long — recognized as an "open highway," flanked by sand dunes and the scene of the world's biggest surf fishing contest in January each year.

The beach runs from just outside Kaitaia to the top of Northland's peninsula, but it is certainly not a road by conventional standards. There are no sign posts or markings and the "road" is the beach itself, open to all the elements. But it's an open field for an exhilarating zoom along the sands, dipping in and out of the surf line, and

This well-equipped camping ground also has very comfortable, moderately-priced cabins and a simple restaurant.

Cuzzy Leisure Tours, ((09) 408-1853, is the only Maori tour operator in the Far North, named "cuzzy" because it's run by an affable and ample-sized band of cousins.

NINETY MILE BEACH AND CAPE REINGA

Spectacularly lonely and seemingly endless, the beauty of Ninety Mile Beach is not easily forgotten. It's best appreciated by

watching the ocean horizon on one side and mountainous yellow sand dunes fringed with *toi toi* on the other. Colonies of black-backed gulls, terns and godwits look like pebbles from far off and, as you approach, scatter in a forest of flapping wings. Where birds gather, you'll find the sand rich in all kinds of shellfish, such as winkles and *pipies* (a small mussel) and cockels, simply by digging with your hands.

Locals have few qualms about racing up and down the sands on fishing expeditions in whatever kind of transport comes to hand. It certainly looks like a lot of fun, but anyone with a private or hire vehicle would be crazy to subject it to this treatment. Not only will vehicles not be covered by insurance, they

ABOVE: The view from Cape Reinga lighthouse. OPPOSITE: Spirit's Bay, near Cape Reinga, is the mythical departure place for the souls to the spirit world according to Maori lore.

can rust up and easily become stranded in the tide, "white-outs" or stuck in boggy sand which can be as treacherous for humans as it is for cars. The safest and easiest (although not quite as adventurous) option is to take one of the coach tours up the beach to Cape Reinga from Kaitaia, Doubtless Bay or Paihia, which travel up the beach and down an alternative road or vice versa, depending on the tide. Whatever way you travel, Ninety Mile Beach has an eerie, unforgettable beauty. There are many Maori myths attached to it, including the belief that

headland is one of New Zealand's more remote post offices. There are several long, windswept walks you can make, with well-marked tracks, desolately dramatic scenery of giant honey-colored sand headlands clustered with shrubs and vertiginous cliffs towering over blustery deep-blue seas.

As you return to Kaitaia by road, make a stop at **Houhora** to see the **Subritsky/Wagener Homestead** and **Wagener Museum**. Dwarfed by a giant palm tree in its front yard, the nineteenth century cottage was the rural refuge of a Polish emigre family, and

the *taniwha* (ghost) of the sea roams its sand dunes on the night of the full moon.

Cape Reinga is the northernmost accessible point in New Zealand. A lonely white lighthouse stands as a beacon on the storm-battered headland, watching over the spray as the cobalt Pacific Ocean hits the turquoise Tasman Sea. In Maori, Reinga means "place of leaping". Maoris hold that after death, their souls journey to Cape Reinga's **Spirits Bay**, climb down the roots of an ancient pohutakawa tree and plunge into the sea for their departure to the spirit world which is supposed to lie in the direction of Hawaiki. On a clear day, you can see the outline of the **Three Kings Islands**, first recorded by Abel Tasman in 1643. The little store on the

has been left unmodernized since 1900. The eccentric museum has over 50,000 curiosities on display, including Maori artifacts, kauri gum, Victoriana and weapons. It also proudly claims to have the world's largest collection of antique chamber pots (460!) There's a pretty camping spot with good facilities on the seaside inlet.

THE WESTERN ROUTE

Some of the region's most spectacular scenery lies along its isolated western coastline. From Kaitaia, proceed south along State Highway 1 through the Mangamuka Gorge's beautiful native forest and head off southwest at Mangamuka Bridge to **Kohukohu**, on the northern arm of the Hokianga Harbour. A car ferry here crosses to **Rawene**, a seaside settlement that dates back to the 1840's. Stop for a snack at the old Wharf House, which has been converted into a cafe and see **Clendon House**, built in the 1860's by pioneer trader and shipowner James Clendon, the first United States Consul in New Zealand. It still contains many of the family's original possessions. Park your car at North Head and explore its nature trails through a reserve rich in native and exotic breeds of birds.

From Rawene, take State Highway 12 to **Hokianga Habour**, a drive that passes panoramas of rolling farmland and ocean as you wind your way through dusty, unsealed road around the rugged inlets of the fiord-like Hokianga Harbour, which extends for some 80 km (50 miles). A vast mountain of honey-toned sand looms on the other side of the harbor, contrasting vividly against the azure sea and — in summer — an even bluer sky, feathered with cumulus clouds. The landscape is punctuated by pockets of rural communities, with wooden houses and tiny box-like churches decorated only with stark crosses.

At the harbor mouth, the road almost dips into the sea at high tide, lined by silver-dollar trees. Here you'll reach the twin beachfront resorts of **Opononi** and **Omapere**, which are dotted with holiday bachs. During the summer of 1955, a friendly dolphin appeared in the Holianga Harbour and fascinated the nation for the next eight months. Nicknamed "Opo," she frolicked with swimmers, gave children bareback rides and displayed her high IQ by playing with bottles and balls. When Opo was found dead, foul play was suspected. When he was mourning Opo, Wade Doak, New Zealand's whale and dolphin specialist commented of the aftermath that "no other animal has been afforded greater funeral honors." A **statue of Opo** stands outside the Opononi Hotel, and you can see a video of her antics at the **Hokianga Visitors Information Centre and Museum** ((09) 405-8869, open from 9 am to 5 pm weekdays at Omapere.

There are many picnic spots, and two main camping grounds in this area, both right on the sea-front: the **Opononi Beach**

Motor Camp, ((09) 405-8791, has pleasant inexpensive chalet-style cabins and the **Omapere Tourist Hotel**, ((09) 405-8737, next to the Hokianga pier, is also a good choice.

THE KAURI COAST

The special attraction of Northland's West Coast is the **Waipoua Forest Sanctuary** where many magnificent kauri trees escaped the ravages of nineteenth century felling. Encompassing some 9,000 hectares (22,500 acres) it is the largest remnant of the once extensive kauri forests of northern New Zealand and home to many protected bird species. From Omapere, follow the State Highway 12 through **Waimamaku Valley**, a sheltered river village founded in the late nineteenth century. You can stay at the **Solitaire Guest House**, a beautifully restored old kauri homestead set in 12 hectares (30 acres) of farmland on the banks of the Waimamaku river, just south of the village. This is a perfect base for making forays into nearby Waipoua Forest, and your hosts can also arrange pony trail riding, fishing trips and bushwalks. Write to P.O. Box 51, Waimamaku, Hokianga or phone (09) 405-4891. Rates are inexpensive.

State Highway 12 has an unsealed section that cuts through the Waipoua Forest for about 17 km (10.5 miles), so even if you're just driving straight back to Auckland, you'll still have the opportunity to marvel at the beauty and density of the forests. The forest's most famous tree, *tane mahuta*, or "the god of the forest" stands only two minutes walk from the main road, yet the walk to see it is one of the most hauntingly beautiful in the country, dappled with almost subterranean green light and alive with birdsong. Thought to be more than 1,200 years old, Tane Mahuta is over 52 m (171 ft) tall and 13 m (42 ft) in circumference. In Maori mythology it was Tane Mahuta who separated the Sky Father from the Earth Mother and created space for living things to grow, and it's no test of the imagination to see how this tree would have been held in awe when it was first discovered.

There are many well-marked tracks through the forest, ranging from a short two kilometer (one-and-a-quarter mile) walk that continues past Tane Mahuta, to a three-hour walk from the forest summit down-hill to the Forest Information Centre. Other magnificent kauris include *te matua ngahere*, the "father of the forest" and the **Four Sisters**, a quartet of massive trees. Slightly inland from the Waipoua Forest, the **Pioneer Village** at **Kaikohe** has several historic buildings, including a nineteenth century Maori cottage and a courthouse, as well as quite a few relics from the saw-milling days.

There are two camping spots in the region to recommend that allow you to feel

West Coast and not one of New Zealand's most exciting towns. It does have one particularly nice place to stay: the **Kauri House Lodge**, ((09) 439-8082, on Bowen Street, built for a wealthy family in the 1900's, with many curiosity pieces. Bookings are essential and rates are moderate.

Along the main Auckland highway, the **Matakohe Kauri Museum**, 48 km (30 miles) from Dargaville, is worth making a stop for. It is a fascinating temple to the mighty kauri tree and the pioneer days of gum-digging. Among its impressive exhibits are

as close to nature as possible. The closest to the Waipoua Forest is the **Waipoua Forest Camping Ground**, ((09) 439-0605, which lies on the Visitor's Centre Road, off State Highway 12, 23 km (14 miles) north of Kaihu. The **Kauri Coast Motor Camp**, ((09) 439-6621, on Trounson Park Road, lies three kilometers (two miles) off State Highway 12 at Kaihu within the Trounson Kauri Park. It's ideally located for swimming, trout fishing, bush walks, and night walks to glow worm caves in the area. Excursions can be easily made to the beautiful nearby **Kai-Iwi** freshwater lakes, fringed with pines and dotted with white sand beaches.

The return drive to Auckland takes you through **Dargaville**, the hub of Northland's

recreated dioramas with lifelike models of kauri gum diggers and mind-bogglingly huge and varied displays of gum and the uses of its resin, one of those being as an essential ingredient in the manufacture of Victorian false teeth, for example. Its tearooms also serve delicious Devonshire teas.

If you plan to linger in the region, the **Kaipara Harbour** embraces many unspoiled, tranquil bays, perfect settings for fishing, flounder netting, boating or simply relaxing.

Leafy panorama through the branches of the great kauri tree in Northland.

EASTERN AND CENTRAL NORTH ISLAND

THE COROMANDEL PENINSULA

Only a three hour drive from Auckland to the southeast, the Coromandel Peninsula is a thin 100 km (62 miles) long intensely beautiful wilderness area indented with many curving beaches and coves. Although it is one of the most popular holiday regions in the North Island, the peninsula remains completely unspoilt. Off the few main highways, narrow unsealed roads wind through the Coromandel State Forest Park, sparkling streams, craggy volcanic mountains and empty sandy bays. Dividing the waters of the Hauraki Gulf from the Pacific Ocean, the peninsula has a sheltered western shoreline shaded by ancient, gnarled pohutakawa trees that blossom over the road along the glistening water's edge in summertime like endless blood-red clouds.

The peninsula's European history is steeped in gold-mining, logging and gum-digging. Its great *kauri* forests were ruthlessly logged for the ship-building industry, although today you can see some regenerating *kauri* strands amongst the remote inland forests. Scattered throughout are many abandoned mining relics, rusting tramways and shafts from the gold rush in the 1870's. Interest in minerals is still strong today because the peninsula is rich in such semi-precious stones as quartz, amethyst, jasper, chalcedony, agate and carnelian. Hahei on the northeast coast is renowned for its pink-tinged beach, glowing with trillions of crushed colored shells, while to the northwest along Te Mata beach, you will almost certainly find some agate. Recent attempts to revive the gold fields and prospect for other minerals have met with stiff opposition from locals and environmentalists determined to protect the Coromandel region's natural resources from further exploitation.

Access

Air Coromandel offers regular services from Auckland and Hamilton to Thames, Pauanui, Whitianga, Matarangi and Coromandel. Their head office is in Whitianga, ((07) 866-4016.

As everywhere in New Zealand, by far the best way to travel is in your own car. But InterCity has daily services from Auckland, looping up through the peninsula and linking with Coromandel and Tauranga.

Thames and the Pohutakawa Coast

Thames, at the base of the Coromandel Peninsula, is a large, prosperous former gold-mining, timber logging and port town. It was the center of a gold rush bonanza which started in the 1850's that swiftly attracted a population of 18,000 at its peak. Elegant Victorian buildings, the perfectly preserved row of verandahed shops along Pollen Street and remnants of rusting machinery give the town an old-fashioned air. If you've come to the peninsula to get away from civilization then this is probably not the place to stay. But it does have a number of curiosities and attractions, namely the **Historical Museum** on Pollen Street, the **Mineralogical Museum** at the corner of Cochrane and Brown streets and the adjacent **School of the Mines**. The restored **Gold Mine** and **Stamper Battery** at the northern end of town is a working exhibit of gold mining history.

The **Information Centre,** ((07) 868-7284, is on Queen Street. There are excellent Department of Conservation leaflets on forest and coastal walks, and camping in the peninsula.

There are two particularly quirky hotels, both dating from the gold-rush days. The **Brian Boru Hotel,** ((07) 868-6523, fax: (07) 868-9760, at the corner of Richmond and Pollen streets, was built in 1868, and is a fine old colonial two-storied hotel. Rooms are inexpensive. Twice a month, "Agatha Christie weekends" are staged, a phenomenon that has attracted a great deal of national attention. Local fire-fighters and paramedics are often called upon to help recreate convincing "murders." Each of the 35 to 40 guests are suspects and the race is on to guess "whodunit" for a $200 prize. The price of the weekend is $355 and also includes lavish breakfasts, a buffet dinner, and tour of the peninsula. You are asked to bring along your own fantasy costume. Contact the hotel for details. The **Imperial Hotel,** ((07) 868-6200, is also on Pollen Street and inexpensive. On the same street, look out for the **Superior Dairy**, in a pretty colonial villa. It serves morning and afternoon teas on its lawns, and the **Old Thames Licensed Restaurant**, ((07) 868-7207, is a venerable place to dine with excellent venison, scallops, mussels and snapper specialties. Just outside Thames on the main road from Auckland, the **Totara Pa Winery** makes excellent fruit liqueurs and has tastings. Another worthwhile excursion from Thames is to the **Miranda Hot Springs Oasis**, the largest thermal pool in the Southern Hemisphere, with bubbling sauna pools and private spa tubs. Open seven days until 9 pm, it's located six kilometers (nearly four miles) outside Waitakaruru just off the Pokeno/Thames Highway.

As you drive out of Thames up the 32 km (20 miles) Pohutakawa Coast, you'll wind past a string of small settlements and sandy bays. The rocky coastline is ideal for surfcasting, boating and fishing, with abundant mussels clinging to the foreshore's rocks. **Ngairimu** and **Thorntons** bays are wonderful swimming beaches, fringed by Norfolk pines. The Pohutakawa Coast's main settlement is **Te Puru**, while further on **Waiomu** has a large seaside domain, ideal for picnics. Further on, don't miss a detour to the **Square Kauri**, eight kilometers (five miles) up the Tapu-Caroglen Road. Visible from the road, this magnificent tree is thought to be some 2,500 years old, and has a walking track around in the surrounding bush around its base. Close by, the **Ruapara Watergardens** is simply spectacular, with well-established floating gardens of water lilies and cascading waterfalls set within bush grottoes. The gardens are open from October to April, from 10 am to 4 pm. From **Tapu**, the last village on the coast, continue on to **Waikawau**, which has a seaside shantytown of renovated old trams. After **Wilson's Bay**, the road winds into the hills to the town of Coromandel, 30 minutes drive away.

Coromandel

The tiny village of Coromandel has a timewarp atmosphere, its wooden buildings steeped in the nineteenth century gold rush era, and many of its inhabitants are potters and craftspeople still happily living out the alternative values of the seventies. While sitting at the **Star and Garter** on Kaponga Road, enjoying a cappuccino, the only sound I remember hearing in the entire town was the slip-slop of leather thongs on hot asphalt.

Although its name (which derives from the first British ship to use the harbor in 1810) has lent itself to the peninsula, it is one of the least developed settlements in the region.

The **Information Centre**, ((07) 866-5598, on Kaponga Road, has several worthwhile brochures about the region, including the *Coromandel Craft Trail* which tells how to track down many fine crafts workshops, including weavers, potters and basket weavers in the township area. Stop at **Assay Market**, which sells home-made jam and local produce, the **Golconda Tavern** and the **Coro Cafe** for great fish'n'chips, oysters and mussels.

Coromandel Colonial Cottages Motel, ((07) 866-6885, on Rings Road, two kilometers (one-and-a-quarter miles) from town, is a moderately priced Bed and Breakfast with secluded garden setting. Beachfront camping accommodation in the region can be found at **Long Bay Motor Camp**, ((07) 866-8720, situated on the beach front close to the township and **Papa Aroha Holiday Park**, ((07) 866-8818, 12 km (seven-and-a-half miles) away. **Angler's Lodge**, ((07) 866-8584 at Amodeo Bay, located 18 km (11 miles) north of Coromandel also has moderately-priced motel rooms. Backpackers can head for **Tui Lodge**, ((07) 866-8237, surrounded by bush about two kilometers (one-and-a-quarter miles) from town. Call for a free pick-up.

The Cape Colville Loop

Beyond the township of **Colville**, 45 minutes drive from Coromandel, the road that hugs the western side of the peninsula up to Cape Colville is unsealed, but very scenic. Colville was formerly known as Cabbage Bay, named by Captain Cook who insisted that his crew eat the leaves of the native cabbage trees here to guard against scurvy. It looks out across the **Watcherman**, and **Little and Great Barrier Islands**. At the top western tip, **Port Jackson** is a long spacious beach popular for camping and fishing. **Fletcher Bay**, at the northeastern tip of the peninsula, is rich in shipwrecks and mariner's tales and is the starting point for the three-hour **Coromandel Walkway to Stony Bay**. There are Department of Conservation campsites at each of these places, with toilets and barbecue areas. The rugged **Moehau Range**, which means "Sleeping Wind" in Maori, overlooks this remote part of the peninsula.

There is no direct sealed route along the eastern coast to **Whitianga**, a holiday resort and deep-sea fishing base, unless you go all the way back to Thames. The Highway 309 is the shortest route from Coromandel to

Whitianga. This unsealed but beautiful winding road passes a waterfall, a kauri grove, goes through a scenic reserve and offers access to **Castle Rock** — a walk with magnificent views from the summit of the entire Coromandel Peninsula. Look out for **The Falls**, ((07) 866-8683, a restaurant in a pretty colonial building. It's open Thursday to Saturday for dinner from 6 pm, with fresh oysters, bacon-wrapped mussels and delicious home-made cheese cake among its specialities. You can stop for Devonshire teas on its lawns during the weekends between 11am to 4 pm. **309 Honey Cottage**, ((07) 866-5151, is an old kauri cottage set on a river that offers accommodation to families, backpackers, campers or groups for $12 a night, although they ask you to bring your own bedding.

WHITIANGA AND COOK'S COAST

Whitianga, on the east coast, is a popular holiday resort and base for big game fishermen for catches of marlin, kingfish and

shark. *Whitianga* means "the crossing place" in Maori. It was here that Kupe, the legendary Polynesian chief and explorer, is thought to have landed around 950 AD. It was nearby too, that Captain Cook landed in the *Endeavour* to watch the passage of the planet Mercury across the sun in 1769, thus establishing New Zealand's exact longitude. Overlooking **Mercury Bay**, the giant **Whitianga Rock** dominates the seaside township, one of the most ancient headland Maori pa sites with sheer drops to the ocean and magnificent views. Fringed by the sheltered expanse of **Buffalo Beach**, Whitianga has a regular passenger boat across the bay to nearby **Ferry Landing**, on the opposite side of the headland, which has an old stone wharf (1837) and is a good base for exploring **Cook's Bay**, **Hahei** and **Hot Water Beach**.

General Information
The **Whitianga Information Centre**, ((07) 866-5555, at 35 Albert Street can help with all inquires about accommodation, swimming beaches, fishing, boat charters and scuba tours. Make sure you pick up a copy of their useful *Mercury Bay District Craft Trail*.

What to See and Do
In Whitianga township, aside from lazing on the beach and climbing Whitianga Rock, make sure you visit the **Mercury Bay District Museum**, with its detailed relics of Maori and European settlement, opposite the wharf.

The eastern coast is dubbed Cook's Coast because of its many associations with Captain Cook, who closely surveyed it. From Ferry Landing, **Front Beach**, **Flaxmill Bay** and **Cook's Beach** are all beautiful beaches with clear crystal waters and an abundance of crayfish and fish. **Shakespeare's Cliff**, in Flaxmill Bay, was named by Captain Cook, who saw the playwright's profile in the rock outline, while Cook's Beach is where, on November 5, 1769, the explorer planted the English flag and declared New Zealand the possession of King George III. **Lonely Bay** is a small bay cut off by cliffs and is totally unspoilt being accessible only from the Cook Memorial via a short steep walking track.

Further on, **Hahei Beach** is a miraculous sight, with its pink-tinged one-and-a-half kilometers (nearly a mile) beach and drifts of shells, shaded by sloping pohutakawa trees. One of the country's loveliest walks continues along Hahei Beach across the bluff to Cathedral Cave, a gigantic sea-formed cavern about 20 m (66 ft) long which you can walk beneath. From all angles it is an impressive and unusual sight.

The best-loved beach along Cook's Coast is **Hot Water Beach**, which is as good as its name. You can dig yourself a wonderful soak hole from the sand at low tide, warmed by underground hot mineral pools. You'll find the "hottest" water close to the rocks and also where you see steam rising from vents in the sand.

Tours

Kingfisher Tours, ((07) 866-4095, offers a tour that encompasses many of the Coromandel Peninsula's highlights, from Port Jackson to Hot Water Beach.

M.V. Marie, ((07) 866-4446, runs two-hour cruises along Cook's Coast, with a complimentary morning tea at Mahurangi Island. Adults are $18, children $10.

Mercury Star Scenic Cruises, ((07) 866-5472, operates cruises and charters at reasonable rates.

The Riverland Cruising Company, ((07) 866-5922, offers enjoyable one hour cruises up the Purangi Estuary, stopping for wine-tasting at Purangi Winery and at Coroglen.

The River Experience, ((07) 866-5879, offers a scenic flatboat tour of the Purangi Estuary. French spoken. You can also arrange to stay at the rustic **Te Ana Homestead**, on Upper Harbour.

Rangihau Ranch, located near Coroglen, has pony treks through the Coromandel Ranges, ranging from beginner's treks to one, two, three hours and overnight. Book through the Information Centre.

Aotearoa Adventures, ((07) 866-3808, based in Coroglen, run rafting, scenic 4WD trips to gold mines, beaches, bush and spectacular vantage points. They can pick you up at Auckland or Rotorua.

Where to Stay

The **Homestead Park Resort**, ((07) 866-5595, at Flaxmill Beach, Ferry Landing, is one of the loveliest places to stay in the Coro-

mandel Peninsula. Located right on the beach, the homestead nestles in the lee of Shakespeare's Cliff and offers fully self-contained accommodation set in blossoming gardens. There are dinghies for guest's use, while five adjacent bays, including Cook's, Hahei and Hot Water Beach are wonderful places for walks, swimming, fishing and diving. There's also an indoor spa, solarium and outdoor badminton court. Rates are moderate.

In Whitianga township, **Esplanade 21**, ((07) 866-5209, fax: (07) 866-5760, at 21 The

Esplanade, comes well-recommended. It is a lovely bougainvillea-swathed two-storied colonial-style villa overlooking the harbor with large comfortable rooms and inexpensive rates. With similar views, **Embassy Lodge**, ((07) 866-5867, at 8 The Esplanade, offers inexpensive accommodation. The **Cosy Cat Cottage**, ((07) 866-4488, at 41 South Highway, offers very comfortable inexpensive accommodation in a villa with pretty gardens to laze about in. This feline-friendly establishment cooks marvelous breakfasts, has a characterful collection of cat memorabilia and will even arrange to look after your pet cat or dog by prior arrangement. The **Mercury Bay Beachfront Resort**, ((07) 866-5637, offers moderate-priced accommodation right on the beach, and can rent out sailboats, fishing and golfing equipment.

The **Coromandel Backpackers Lodge**, ((07) 866-5380, is located opposite the beach, and hires out kayaks.

OPPOSITE: The decadent appeal of Hot Water Beach, Coromandel. ABOVE: Rare rock formation at Cook's Cove in Coromandel.

Close to Hahei Beach, the **Hay-Lyn Park Lodge**, ((07) 866-3888, on Christine Terrace off Pa Road is set in tranquil bush and offers private and peaceful moderately priced fully-equipped cottages that overlook the beach and Mercury Bay. They also have a spa pool and rooms that can sleep families.

There are several excellent camping areas in the Whitianga region. The **Buffalo Beach Tourist Park**, ((07) 866-5854, at Eye Street, is set within a large parkland close to the beach, and has a full range of accommodation from tent sites to motel rooms.

Within the region's surrounding bays, **Cook's Beach Motor Camp**, ((07) 866-5469, on R.D.1, **Hahei Holiday Tourist Park**, ((07) 866-3889, and **Hot Water Beach Motor Camp**, ((07) 866-3735, are all good choices.

Where to Eat

Whitianga is a fairly casual place and this is reflected in its eateries, which are wonderful for fresh, unpretentious seafood specialities. For a night out, try **Cook's Cove**, ((07) 866-4883, on The Esplanade, a fully licensed seafood restaurant. Otherwise, **Rick's Place** on Monk Street is the only pizza parlor in town, while **Snapper Jack's Restaurant and Takeaways** at the corner of Monk and Albert streets is a BYO indoor and outdoor restaurant that has a fresh seafood bazaar for selecting takeaways.

En route to Cook's Beach on Purangi Road, R.D.1, the **Purangi Winery**, ((07) 866-3724, has a country-style kitchen with very delicious wholesome food. You can also sample their fruit wines and browse in their craft shop. It's open from 9 am to 9 pm every day. You can arrange for free transport from Ferry Landing with the Information Centre.

DOWN THE COAST

Along the 42 km (26 miles) highway from Whitianga to Tairua, you'll pass **Coroglen**, an inland rural township nestled within glorious scenery with many walking and riding trails. There are two places to stay: **Aotearoa Lodge**, ((07) 866-3808, fax; (07) 866-4530, which has a friendly atmosphere and home-cooked meals. **The Redwood**, ((07) 866-3742, is a genuine log cabin which offers accommodation and also has a riverside cafe. They

can also arrange horse-riding, fishing and hunting trips, as well as scenic bush treks. Look out for the orchards around here. Roadside signs say PYO, which means in true New Zealand tradition, that you can "pick your own" fruit. One of the region's best orchards is **Wilderland**, between Whitianga and Coroglen, much-loved by holidaying families for its creamy organic honey, figs, and apples.

Right on the coast, the small settlement of **Tairua** is another popular resort with a beautiful harbor and soft-sanded beaches along The Esplanade. There is a lovely walkway up **Paku Summit**, an old *pa* site, now dotted with precariously perched houses, and absolutely superb views. Nearby is **Shoe and Slipper Island**, whose shape gives it its curious name. Stop at the **Cowshed Shop**, ((07) 864-8039, New Zealand's most rustic information center in a renovated milking shed. It's run by Norm and Cath, who can also rustle up tea and shortcake. In Tairua, stay at the **Pacific Highway Motel**, ((07) 864-8581, with modern Polynesian-style moderately-priced bungalows or the **Pine Lea Motor Camp**, ((07) 864-8561.

On the opposite side of Tairua Harbour, but 22 km (13 miles) away via Hakuai is **Pauanui**, a resort settlement along a pristine white beach strewn with pine trees. Tucked away in a large private estate of native bush, **Puka Park Lodge**, ((07) 864-8188, is an exclusive hideaway lodge. It has 32 luxury chalets, each carefully secluded, which overlook the estuary, ocean and surrounding bush and is renowned for its superb cuisine. It has a large heated pool and a heli-pad.

But you don't have to pay executive rates to enjoy Pauanui. **Pauanui Pacific**, ((07) 864-8933, rents houses for as little as $50 a night, while **The Glade**, ((07) 864-8559, has motel cabins, caravan and tent sites right next to the Tairua Estuary.

Pauanui is also the base for **Doug Johansen's Scenic Tours and Treks** ((07) 864-8731, 864-8859. This incredibly energetic, knowledgeable man runs a variety of unique adventure tours through the mountains, gold mines and old gold towns, and beautiful coastal scenery, with discourses on everything from Maori medicines to botany.

Back on Highway 25, the next main town is **Whangamata**, with its pretty harbor, giant beach much celebrated by surfers and many tranquil bush walks into the nearby foothills of the Coromandel Ranges.

Further along, **Waihi** is a charming former goldmining town with many relics from that era in the area, including the **Pump House**. It also has a vintage railway that runs for eight kilometers (five miles) and operates daily between December 27 and January 31, and only on the fourth Sunday of each month from then on. In Waihi, the colonial-era **Rob Roy Hotel,** ((07) 863-7025, on the corner of Seddon and Rosemont roads, is an inexpensive place to stay.

Make sure you drive the 11 km (seven miles) out to Waihi's magnificent six kilometers (nearly four miles) surf beach, and see the picturesque rural settlement of **Athenree** up on the pohutakawa forested headland near **Bowentown**. Athenree's quaint old-fashioned tearooms are a nice place to break your journey, and afterwards you can stroll along the beach. On Waihi Beach, stay at the inexpensive **Waihi Beach Hotel,** ((07) 863-5402, on Wilson Road. At the southern end, **Athenree Motor Camp,** (07) 863-5600, is a secluded, peaceful place to stay.

If you want to know more about gold mining in the area, join the **Martha Hill Gold Mine Tour** for a free explanation of the mine that has unearthed the largest gold deposit in the province, or **Waihi Goldfield Treks and Tours,** ((07) 863-7699. The **Karangahake Gorge Historic Walkway** is a very scenic trail that encompasses many of the gold mining ruins. The **Information Centre,** ((07) 863-8386, is on Kenny Street and is also a museum and art gallery. They are wonderfully helpful with booking local accommodation.

Lastly, as you loop back to Auckland or to the Bay of Plenty, make sure you stop at **Te Aroha**, the hill station of Coromandel Peninsula. The **Te Aroha Thermal Spa** has seven hot mineral soak pools and an unusual soda water geyser.

BAY OF PLENTY

Rich in both Maori and European history, the Bay of Plenty region offers sunny coastal stretches dotted with fertile orchards and lush forests. The area includes the stunning **Urewera National Park**. Whether you want to go trekking, river-rafting, deep-sea or lake fishing, or simply take in the scenery, this part of the country offers all sorts of potential to be at one with the elements.

DRIVING DOWN TO THE BAY

From the Coromandel Peninsula, the main route to Tauranga follows State Highway 2. One place to stop is **Katikati**, a tiny settlement founded by Irish immigrants last century. Within its environs, the **Morton Estate Vineyard** produces what is arguably New Zealand's best sparkling and Chardonnay white wines. Their Spanish-style **Vineyard Restaurant** is renowned, set in its own pretty garden. The **Fantail Lodge,** ((07) 549-1581, fax: (07) 549-0313, on Rea Road, is a luxurious, Tudor-style mid-priced hideaway in the heart of the Bay of Plenty's kiwifruit producing country. It can accommodate up to four guests and requires advance booking. Another lovely, very rustic place to stay is **Jacaranda Cottage,** ((07) 549-0616, up Thompson's Track, a Bed and Breakfast farmhouse that offers friendly hospitality, wholesome meals and magnificent views in every direction. There are lots of walks and farm activities, and rates are inexpensive. **Sapphire Springs Holiday Park,** ((07) 549-0768, Hot Springs Road, is an idyllic place to camp, within 31.2 hectares (78 acres) of native bush and hot thermal pools. The **Katikati Bird Gardens** have peaceful walkways, interesting flowers, and birds everywhere including in aviaries.

TAURANGA

Tauranga is the main commercial center of the Bay of Plenty, The town's picturesque seaport is one of the busiest in the country, shipping pulp, paper and kiwifruit overseas. Meaning "Anchorage for canoes" in Maori, Tauranga has a beautiful natural harbor, kilometers of fabulous surfing beaches and bush-clad ranges that protect many orchards and gardens. Despite creeping industrialization, Tauranga is an attractive holiday resort, renowned as a base for big-game fishing and all kinds of water-sports, especially at nearby Mt. Maunganui, an imposing 232 m (765 ft) forested mountain at the end of an isthmus. It overlooks the wide-rimmed, golden-sanded Ocean Beach, lined with Monkey Puzzle trees and extending for 15 km (9 miles), including the more secluded sand dunes of Papamoa area, which attract surf-casting anglers and pipi-gatherers.

General Information
The **Visitor's Information Centre**, ((07) 578-8103, is on The Strand, while the **Mt. Maunganui Information Centre**, ((07) 575-5099, is at Salisbury Avenue. They can both advise on all kinds of water-activities, as well as arrange fishing or boat charters. Hopefully, you will not need to call **Surf Rescue**, ((07) 575-7899.

What to See
After a stroll down The Strand's seafront, make your way to **The Elms**, a colonial cottage built in 1847 as part of the Te Papa Mission Station, one of New Zealand's earliest. Located on Mission Street, this historic home opens its library, gardens and tiny chapel to visitors from 2 pm daily except Sundays. Try to catch the 2 pm tour, conducted by Mr. Maxwell, whose tales of the hardships and triumphs of the early missionaries here helps bring The Elms alive. Close to the Mission House, up on Cliff Road, is the **Monmouth Redoubt**, the only survivor of several British military forts built in the Tauranga region during the time of the Land Wars. **The Tauranga Historic Village Museum**, at Seventeenth Avenue West, is a mocked-up early settler's village complete with cobble-stoned streets and vintage transport rides.

There are two wonderful walks to make. A steep trail leads up to the summit of Mt. Maunganui, offering views across to Mayor's Island, the base of Tauranga Game Fishing Lodge, and White's Island on a clear day. Mt. Maunganui village and wharf is quite a pleasant place to linger. You can buy fish and chips wrapped in newspaper and throw what you don't want to hungry seagulls. Back on the seafront, you can stroll along Ocean Beach as far as your legs can carry you.

Preston's Kiwifruit Winery, ((07) 571-0926, on Belk Road, is an attraction in itself, especially if you have discovered how

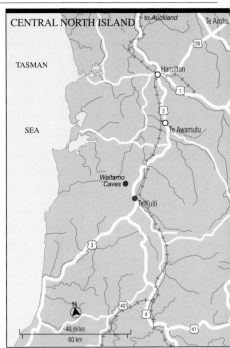

partial you are the New Zealand's ubiquitous furry fruit. You can come here for a free tasting of Kiwifruit wines and liqueurs. If you still aren't sated, you'll enjoy **Te Puke**, 26 km (15 miles) from Tauranga, on the main Tauranga to Rotorua highway, which calls itself the Kiwifruit Capital of the World, but is also rich in avocado, *nashi* pears, persimmons, mandarins, *fejoias*, *tamarillo* and all kinds of other delicious fruits. **Kiwifruit Country** is a theme park dedicated to the fruit, with orchard tours in "Kiwi-Karts," and free sampling of fruit, wine and recipes. Also at Te Puke, **Windrest Cottage** has a beautiful private garden open for Devonshire teas.

Where to Stay
Tauranga has two "grand" hotels, both moderately priced. The **Otumoetai Trust Hotel**, ((07) 576-2221, fax: (07) 576-1226, is on Bureta Road, while the **Willow Park Motor Lodge**, ((07) 577-9198, fax: (07) 577-9198, is at the corner of Willow and Park streets. Less plush, but with a superb location is **Hotel Oceanside**, ((07) 575-3149, at 1 Marine Parade, Mt. Maunganui. From its windows you can watch dawn or dusk settle across the beach, which beckons for walks, jogs and swims.

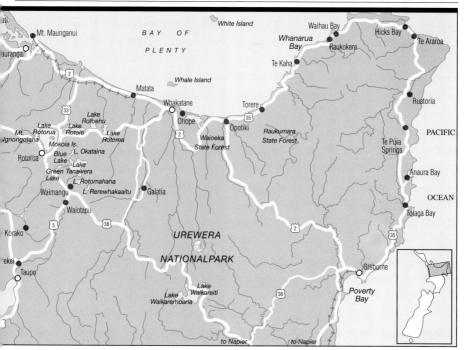

There's a glass-fronted restaurant and a small garden, while rates are inexpensive.

Along Tauranga's harborside isthmus, there are many suburban-style motels. Here are two nice choices, both with inexpensive rates. The **Blue Water Family Motel**, ((07) 578-5420, at 59 Turret Road, has a scenic, secluded location and a thermal swimming pool, and guests can use dinghies and canoes. With similar surroundings and facilities, **Shoalhaven Motel**, ((07) 578-6910, is at 67 Turret Road. **Tauranga Backpackers**, ((07) 578-2382, at 44 Botanical Road, has a secluded bush setting in the middle of town, with nice harbor views.

Campers and caravanners can stay at the **Silver Birch Motor Park**, ((07) 578-4603, at 1010 Turret Road, which has a hot spa and swimming pool, or at the **Mt. Maunganui Domain Motor Camp**, ((07) 575-4471, at 1 Adams Avenue, located at the foot of the mountain and adjacent to the Mt. Maunganui Hot Salt Water Pools.

Where to Eat

First recommendations go to the stylish **Cook's Cove**, ((07) 578-8127, at the pastel-painted colonial-era Hotel St. Amand on The Strand seafront. It serves bountiful

lunches and dinners, and the adjacent **Scotty's Bar** is an open-late cafe with live music.

Oceanside Restaurant, ((07) 578-3149, 1 Marine Parade, Mt. Maunganui, matches superb views of the rolling ocean with seafood specialities. For good hearty, traditional eating, locals will usually direct you to **Becky's**, ((07) 578-7036, at 75 Elizabeth Street and **Bella Mia**, ((07) 578-4996, at 73A Devonport Road, which serves Italian pasta and pizzas. Another Tauranga favorite is **Eastcoasters**, ((07) 578-9928, 77 Devonport Road, an open-late cafe with a varied menu of Mexican, American and vegetarian dishes. On the Strand pierfront, the **Captain's Table Cafe**, is a good place to have breakfast, write postcards or just enjoy the marina. They're open from 7 am to 3:30 pm.

WHAKATANE

About 100 km (62 miles) from Tauranga, Whakatane is the other main coastal settlement in the Bay of Plenty. It lies in the center of an area rich in natural beauty, with many lovely bush walks, some of which start within the town's boundaries, and an undulating golden coastline which curves around the headland to **Ohope**, a popular resort, with the nearby tranquil **Ohiwa Harbour**. Within easy driving distance is the **Urewera National Park**, the largest unspoilt natural wilderness in the North Island, rich in lonely lakes and pristine trout-filled rivers. Whakatane is also the starting point for trips to spectacular **White Island**, a volatile, constantly simmering volcano, just 60 km (36 miles) from the coast. Divers and big game anglers will love Whakatane, whose waters offer up to 50 m (165 ft) visibility and thrive with year-round fishing activity.

An interesting story lies behind Whakatane's name. Maori legend recounts the arrival here of the Mataatua Canoe from Hawaiki. In their desire to reach land, the men leaped ashore, momentarily leaving the women in the canoe, which was suddenly swept out to sea. Although it was strictly forbidden for women to touch paddles, the chief's daughter, Wairaka, grabbed her father's paddle and cried, *"Kia whaka-tane au i ahau!"* ("I will act like a man!') Following her lead, the women managed to maneuver themselves back to shore. Later, Wairaka's refusal to marry the man chosen for her, in order to win the man she really loved, has also endeared her to posterity in Maori lore. Her statue stands like a sprite with her hair flowing, surrounded by sea on a rock close to where the canoe is thought to have landed.

General Information

The **Information Centre**, ((07) 308-6058, on Boon Street, can arrange all kinds of water sports, diving, fishing, river-rafting; horsetrek, hunting and mountain safari trips are available, and they have many detailed pamphlets on the numerous coastal walks in the area. There are at least six boats registered with the center for diving, reef fishing and big game fishing, some specializing in overnight trips.

What to See

Directly above the town, the forested headland is thought to be the oldest Maori pa site in New Zealand, established by the Polynesian explorer, Toi in 1150 A.D. There are several exceptionally beautiful tracks through its dense bush, ranging from 10 minutes from the headland top up to the Puketapu Lookout and three hours to Ohope Beach.

From Whakatane you can join a helicopter trip out to **White Island**, for a guided walk along the crater's rim, which constantly splutters ash, smoke and steam, and past long-abandoned sulfur mines. The volcano is considered New Zealand's "safety valve," and as long as it continues smoking, scientists believe there is unlikely to be an eruption in the North Island. But its bilious, billowing plumes across the sea's horizon certainly make a compelling, if slightly alarming, sight. On the return flight, you can see the country's largest gannet colony, and sometimes schools of porpoises — even whales. Scheduling of the trips depend on the volcano's "condition." Nearby, **Whale Island**, named for its similarity to a whale's hump, can be visited by boat.

Where to Stay

Whakatane makes a useful base for making early fishing trips, but Ohope, six kilometers (nearly four miles) away, is a much more spectacular location to stay, with its rolling sands and surf beach lined by pohutakawa trees and languid palms. In Whakatane, there are two very plush though nonetheless moderately-priced hotels. **Chatswood Manor**, ((07) 307-0600, fax: (07) 307-0603, at 34 Domain Road, has fully equipped kitchens, a swimming pool and a restaurant. **Tourist Court Hotel**, ((07) 308-7099, fax: (07) 307-0821, is at 50 Landing Road.

At Ohope, all accommodation is right on the beach. The most luxurious place to stay is **Ohope Beach Resort**, ((07) 312-4692, fax: (07) 312-4692, at 5 West End, with its moderately-priced rooms, restaurant, bar and swimming pool. The **West End Motel**, ((07) 312-4665, at 24 West End, is right on the beach, and has inexpensive rates. Close by, the **Ohope Beach Backpackers Inn**, ((07) 312-5173, is another good choice, similarly priced. The **Surf'n'Sand Holiday Park**, ((07) 312-4884, at 211 Pohutakawa Avenue, has motel units, tourist flats, caravan and tent sites. It certainly lives up to its name.

Where to Eat

Perched where the Whakatane River flows into the sea, **The Reef**, ((07) 307-0472, on Murawai Drive, is a delightful place to eat,

The ever-present volcanic specter of White Island off the Bay of Plenty.

with large windows open to the surf. It opens at 10 am for brunch, serves delicious Devonshire teas and also serves excellent meals, with fresh crayfish, scallops and tuna specialities and a good selection of New Zealand wines. Closed Tuesday evenings from 4 pm.

Tours
White Island Tours, ((07) 308-4188, at Whakatane Airport, runs the helicopter flights to White Island. Pick-ups are also arranged at **Opotiki,** ((07) 315-8443.

UREWERA NATIONAL PARK

The river valley of Urewera National Park is easily the largest tract of virgin wilderness left in the North Island, with lakes **Waikare-iti** and the larger **Waikaremoana** ("Lake of the Small Waves") surrounded by towering beech and *tawa-podocarp* forest. Sumptuously beautiful, yet exceedingly remote, the reserve is only partially reached by winding, narrow, unsealed roads, and is a sanctuary for deer and native birds. Rich in Maori legend, it is the original home of the Tuhoe tribe, "The Children of the Mist," who lived in harmony with the dense forest for many centuries.

Spanning 214,000 hectares (535,000 acres), the park is reached by State Highway 38, which passes through Taneatua, Murupara and Waikaremoana, and all have Ranger Stations. Wairoa, in Hawke Bay, also has direct road access into the park. The closest **Ranger Station** to Whakatane is at Taneatua, ((07) 312-9260, eight kilometers (five miles) away. The park's main **Visitor's Centre** is at Waikaremoana, ((06) 837-3803, more easily reached from Rotorua, 160 km (99 miles) away. At all centers, you can see an audio visual on the park that is the best briefing on its treasures. Hunting for deer and wild pigs is encouraged — permits must be obtained. Fishing for rainbow trout in the rivers and lakes is excellent — again permits can be obtained at the Ranger Stations, which also have details about treks, which range from half an hour to 10 days, following ancient Maori trails. One of the most beautiful walks is the four day trail around Lake Waikare-

moana. Or you can walk the Whirinaki Track in neighboring **Whirinaki Forest,** where you can see mighty podocarp forest, a contemporary of the dinosaur, a survivor from the old forests of Godwanaland. If all this wilderness seems too daunting to tackle on your own, join up with local operators of tours and safaris, including Maori guides who retrace their ancestor's footsteps, notably Mohaka Tours. You can get details from the ranger's stations.

Within the park, you can stay at the **Urewera Lodge,** ((07) 366-4556, at **Galatea,** on the shores of Lake Aniwhenua, 64 km (40 miles) south of Whakatane. On the shores of Lake Waikaremoana, you can stay at the **Waikaremoana Motor Camp,** ((06) 837-3826, which has chalets, motel rooms and camping sites. The camp shop sells basic supplies and petrol. During summer, the **Waikaremoana Launch Service,** ((06) 837-3871, operates from the motor camp, with boat trips for sightseers, fishing, and transport around the lake.

ROTORUA

Nicknamed "Sulfur City," Rotorua is one of the few places in the world that can be smelt before it is seen. As your nostrils adjust to the pervasive rotten egg whiff of hydrogen sulfide, you'll notice other idiosyncrasies: steam rising from cracks in the tarmac, boiling-hot puddles and faint, flatulent sounds of bubbling mud. This otherwise placid, suburban town sits on an active fault line beside a massive lake of the same name, surrounded by a countryside filled with geothermal valleys, picturesque lakes, forests of pine and Californian redwood, and slumbering volcanoes.

Since Rotorua's first tourism boom as a spa town in the 1840's, visitors have been fascinated by the region's bizarre, curiously beautiful and sometimes frightening natural wonders. Craters of boiling mud and hot springs, explosive geysers and multicolored terraces of sulfur and silica deposits are considered commonplace phenomena by locals. Yet outside the Rotorua–Taupo region, geysers occur only in southwest Iceland and Yellowstone National Park in the United

States. ("I was pleased to get so close to Hades and be able to return, " said playwright George Bernard Shaw in 1934.) They've also enjoyed the therapeutic benefits of its mineral waters, renowned for relieving many ailments from rheumatism to skin problems. Steam heat, piped from beneath Rotorua's thin crust, heats homes, hotels and mineral hot spas. Needless to say, you will never be without hot water in a Rotorua bathroom!

Rotorua is also deeply rooted in Maori tradition. For centuries the Arawa Maoris lived beside Rotorua's boiling hot pools, believed in utu (revenge) and killed their enemies with jade war clubs and sweet potato digging sticks. Home to one-third of New Zealand's Maori population, Rotorua has a much stronger sense of Maori community and pride than is discernible in other parts of New Zealand. Wood, bone and greenstone carving, as well as weaving skills are being revived, while traditional *hangi* — meals steamed by an underground oven — and so-called Maori "action" dance concerts are the town's only night-time attractions. At these, visitors are welcomed with the traditional Maori greeting — the *hongi*, a pressing and rubbing of noses — and then presented with the spectacle of the *haka*, a men's war dance with fierce tongue flashing, blood-curdling cries and brandishing of weapons. The women follow with a *haka poi*, a string and ball dance accompanied by melodious songs.

Within the city's environs, you can also enjoy lakes Rotorua and Rotoiti for trout-fishing and cruises while bush walks and an almost bewildering array of "action-adventure" attractions, such as whitewater river rafting, scenic flights, hot-air balloons and horse-riding are devised by canny local operators.

The surrounding region is astonishingly beautiful. Dense virgin forests rise up like green cathedrals and secluded lakes have surfaces as moody as moonstones, offering some of the world's best trout fishing. Make sure you explore the tranquillity of the landscape as well as the numerous thermal reserves, no matter whether you prefer the many trekking or riding trails, donning fishing waders or simply having a lakeside picnic.

ACCESS

Three airline companies — Air New Zealand, Ansett NZ and Mount Cook Airlines — link Rotorua with daily direct flights to Auckland, Taupo, the Bay of Islands, Tauranga, Wellington, Christchurch, Queenstown, Mt. Cook and Wanaka. By road, InterCity, Mt. Cook and Newmans buses provide a comprehensive link-up with most of the important cities, centers and minor hubs in the North Island.

GENERAL INFORMATION

The **Visitor's Information Office,** ((07) 348-5179 is at 67 Fenton Street in the town center. This is the place to book all accommodation and sightseeing tours and tickets, as well as ongoing arrangements. They also have a resident fishing expert who can offer free advice to visiting anglers and provide up-to-date details. Another useful local source is the **Department of Conservation Forest Visitors Centre,** ((07) 346-1155 on Long Mile Road, for detailed tramping maps and information on the area's recreational re-

ABOVE: Proud Rotorua citizen.

serves, camping and huts. They also issue hunting permits and fishing licenses. Their Outdoor Guide is an excellent reference for exploring Rotorua's environs. The AA, ((07) 348-3069, is on the corner of Hinemoa and Hinemaru streets. Otherwise, the *Gateway to Geyserland* map, readily found in Rotorua, is a good guide to local attractions.

WHAT TO SEE

The best place to begin your morning's sightseeing is the **Whakarewarewa Thermal Reserve**, at the southern end of Fenton Street, a five minute drive from the town center. Whakarewarewa has been occupied and fought over by warmth-seeking Maoris for centuries and is one of New Zealand's most active geothermal regions. Within the thermal reserve, the showpiece is the Pohutu ("splashing ") geyser, which erupts to 18 m (59 ft) — and sometimes as high as 30 m (99 ft). However *pohutu*'s eruptions are unpredictable and you might have to wait for an hour before being rewarded. This is no place to stray from the beaten track: steam hisses from path fissures, huge vat-like mud pools splutter concentric rings of boiling mud, geysers spurt at unexpected intervals and the whole place has the eerie, primeval atmosphere of a Sci-Fi film set. Not marked on the reserve's tourist map is the silica pit nicknamed "Brain Pot," where according to locals, the Arawa tribe boiled the heads of their enemies.

Also within the complex is an original Maori village, dating from the turn of the century and restored to give visitors an accurate impression of how Maoris lived at that time and earlier. A replica colonial village lies at the end of a pathway lined with *tekoteko*, small human-like carved figures of Te Arawa ancestors. Nearby, Maori residents live in wood-frame houses, bathe in communal hot pools and cook food in outdoor steam ovens. You'll notice the raised graves sealed in concrete to prevent corpses from also being given the hangi treatment in Rotorua's steaming soil. Also in "Whaka" is the **New Zealand Maori Arts and Crafts Institute**, where you can see apprentice carvers and weavers being trained.

Back in Rotorua, explore the pretty lakefront, which has a wide variety of booking offices for all sorts of activities. Take your pick from a few hours' trout fishing, a cruise on a hover-shuttle or on the *Lakeland Queen* vintage paddle steamer, which leaves four times daily.

Mokoia Island, in the middle of Lake Rotorua, is intimately connected with Arawa history and legend, and the site of Maoridom's best-known love story. The story goes that Hinemoa, the daughter of a lake-shore chief, was attracted to Tutanekai,

a young man deemed unsuitable for her by protective elders. One night, Hinemoa heard the sound of Tutanekai's flute serenading her from Mokoia and could stand their separation no longer. Removing her flax cloak and supporting herself with floating gourds, she swam naked from the mainland to the island where he lived, hiding in a hot pool until he found her. Once the union was consummated, the elders conceded defeat and the pair were able to live "happily ever after." You can reach Mokoia Island on the launch Ngaroto which makes several trips daily. Ashore, a walkway leads to an

OPPOSITE and ABOVE: The explosive geysers of Rotorua.

image of *Matua Tonga*, the "Kumara God" and the **Arawa Wishing Rock**, where Tutanekai is said to have played his flute. Apparently, it will grant your wish if you place your palms against the stone. Beyond the rock is **Hinemoa's Pool**, where the lovers found each other. Still warm and inviting, this is a perfect place to soak up to your shoulders while resting your head amongst palm fronds. Less romantically, Mokoia Island was also the home of New Zealand's loudest man, Tutourangi, whose voice could be heard from the island, from the shore at

Rotorua, six kilometers (nearly four miles) away.

Back on shore, a few hundred yards from the booking offices, see **Ohinemutu**, an historic Arawa village and the town's main Maori settlement. Its name means "the place of the killed girl" and refers to a chief's daughter who met the ghastly fate of being tossed into a boiling mud pool. By the lake is the tiny Tudor-style church of **St. Faiths** (1910) which has an etched glass window that depicts Christ wearing a Maori cloak and walking on Lake Rotorua, and outside is a quirky statue of Queen Victoria.

Each night, the Ohinemutu cultural group performs for visitors in the large *whare runanga* or meeting house here.

From here, stroll back to the town center to the manicured **Government Gardens**, dominated by the **Tudor Towers**, a German-style timbered structure with verandahs and turrets that served as a spa in the early 1900's. These days it houses an art and history museum, with exhibits devoted to the 1886 eruption of Mt. Tarawera, a nearby

dormant volcanic mountain. Not only did this eruption totally rearrange the region's landscape but it also destroyed one of New Zealand's most extraordinary natural attractions, the world-famous **Pink and White Terraces**, two vast silica formations which rose 250 m (820 ft) from the shores of Lake Rotomahana, 20 km (12 miles) from Rotorua, once considered one of the world's most outstanding natural wonders. The closest equivalent to be seen now is at Pamukkale in Turkey, near Izimir.

From here, follow your nose through the gardens to **Sulfur Point** where the lake waters are stained white by sulfur from the springs. Close by, the **Orchid Gardens** are worth a visit, with an optional entry to the adjoining **Water Organ**, which has about 800 water jets that sway-swoosh under a light display like fireworks to stirring classical music. Rotorua has two other idiosyncratic attractions: New Zealand's only **Rugby Museum** at 16 Eruera Street and the **Arikapakapa Golf Course** with its boiling mud pool "hazards."

Along with Queenstown in the South Island, Rotorua has quickly realized its potential for reaping big dollars from its many tourists. At nearby **Mt. Ngongotaha**, 12 km (nearly seven-and-a-half miles) west of Rotorua, **Skyline Skyride**, a gondola takes you to the spectacular lookout point above the lakeside township, from which you can clamber aboard a luge and ricochet all the way down a concrete track. Rotorua has several theme parks, of which the **Agrodome**, which boasts a kind of sheep cabaret show is the most popular. **Rainbow Springs** is the most enjoyable of these commercial enterprises to visit. Its natural pools and springs are virtually crammed with thousands of rainbow, brown and brook trout who come here to spawn.

Hot Pools

Whatever else you do in Rotorua, have a hot-pool dip. Most hotels and many private homes have pools which are tapped straight from the underground source. The **Polynesian Pools** are the best public pools, built around one of the town's most famous hot springs, the **Priest's Bath**. A nineteenth century Catholic priest claimed the waters cured his rheumatism — Rotorua's first hot water miracle. "The patients emerging from this bath," wrote a bather from the same period, "look like boiled lobsters." They still do: the temperature on the wooden handrail reads 42°C (108°F) Remember not to wear silver jewelry when taking a dip in a sulfur pool: it turns black. More importantly, as a precaution against amoebic meningitis, don't put your head underwater.

As well as Hinemoa's pool on Mokoia Island, there are three other particularly special, very rustic hot springs to seek out within easy reach of Rotorua, better known to locals. To lie on soft-ash sand in one of these hot perfectly clear streams, surrounded by open sky, trees and meadows is one of life's memorable pleasures. You may have to pay a small donation to local Maoris, who provide wooden changing sheds. **Soda Springs** is a 20 minute drive sign-posted off State Highway 30 to the north between lakes Rotoehu and Rotoma. **Hakereteke Stream**, referred to as Kerosene Creek is located a similar distance to the south on State Highway 5 and has an absolutely blissful hot spring right next to a waterfall within a forest grotto. Finally, the more developed **Hamurana Springs** complex lies on the northern shore of Lake Rotorua and has peacocks on surrounding lawns and a teahouse.

WHERE TO STAY

Being one of New Zealand's top destinations, Rotorua is crammed with every kind of accommodation, most with hot mineral pools. The **Geyserland Resort, (** (07) 348-2039, fax: (07) 348-2033, Fenton Street, would be my first choice. Not only is it friendly and comfortable but it directly overlooks the Whakarewarewa's dramatic furnaces of geysers and bubbling mud pools. Make sure you get a room facing the views, not the road! A resident masseuse is available for all guests. Rates are moderate.

There are two top hotels, the **Kingsgate Rotorua, (** (07) 347-1234 and fax:(07) 348-1234, on Eruera Street and the **Sheraton Rotorua Hotel (** (07) 348-7139, fax: (07) 348-8378, which is the nicer of the two and has a wonderful health club and individual "grotto" spas. Both are in the mid-price range.

Less stylish, but well-kept are the moderately-priced **Quality Inn, (** (07) 348-0199, fax: (07) 346-1973 on Fenton Street and the **Rotorua Travelodge, (** (07) 348-1174, at the lake end of Eruera Street. In the same price range, the **Prince's Gate Hotel, (** (07) 348-1179, at 1 Arawa Street, is a refurbished colonial building with pretty verandahs and a pleasant restaurant, as well as a street-level cafe open from breakfast to supper.

Muiaroha, ((07) 346-1220, fax: (07) 346-1338, at 411 Old Taupo Road, is a tranquil colonial-style retreat set in beautiful gar-

dens, charging executive rates that include all meals.

Fenton Street, which stretches from the town center all the way up to Whakarewarewa, is a suburban highway of competitive hotels and motels, all of a high standard and constantly upgrading their facilities, adding jacuzzis, satellite TV or Swiss-style fencing to up the stakes. Most fall within the moderate price range. The **Hylton Motel, (** (07) 348-5056, at 287, has enormous rooms, while **Links Motel, (** (07) 348-9179, fax: (07) 346-3474, at 418, is another good choice.

Added to this, there are many opportunities to stay on farms or private homes around Rotorua. The Visitors Information Office can recommend and make bookings. A cozy guest house option is **Eaton Hall**, **(** (07) 347-0366, fax: (07) 347-8558, at 39 Hinemaru Street, which serves excellent breakfasts.

OPPOSITE: The Polynesian Pools at Rotorua, perfect for a thermal soak. ABOVE: Traditional Maori action dances at Rotorua.

Backpackers accommodation is available at the **Rotorua Youth Hostel**, ℂ (07) 347-6810, on the corner of Eruera and Hinemaru streets; the **Ivanhoe Lodge**, ℂ (07) 348-6985 at 54 Haupapa Street and **Thermal Lodge**, ℂ (07) 347-0931, at 60 Tarewa Road. The **YMCA**, ℂ (07) 348-5445, is on Te Ngae Road.

For those with camper vans or tents, there are several camp sites to recommend, all with peaceful grounds, hot pools and excellent amenities. Both the **Lakeside Motor Camp**, ℂ (07) 348-1693, at 54 Whittaker Road and the **Rotorua Thermal Holiday Park**, ℂ (07) 346-3140, fax: (07) 346-1324, on Old Taupo Road are excellent options. At some distance from Rotorua are two camps in pristine wooded settings, close to lakeside shores. The **Holden's Bay Holiday Park**, ℂ (07) 345-9925, fax: (07) 345-9925, at 21 Robinson Avenue, lies almost seven kilometers (just over four miles) away. The **Blue Lake Holiday Park**, ℂ (07) 362-8120, is 11 km (nearly seven miles) away, situated right on the beautiful Blue Lake, with cheap bungalows as well as camp sites, horse treks, hire canoes and ski boats.

WHERE TO EAT

Aside from its much-advertised *hangi* concert meals, Rotorua has a number of fine restaurants. The **Lakeside Bar and Grill**, ℂ (07) 348-3700, overlooking Lake Rotorua on Memorial Drive is chic and very reasonably priced. It has such innovative dishes as venison livers, rabbit sauteed with cashewnuts and pecan nuts, smoked salmon pikelets served with sour cream and salmon caviar, and marinated wild boar. **Poppy's Villa**, ℂ (07) 347-1700, at 4 Marguerita Street, has a romantic setting in a restored Edwardian villa and serves excellent New Zealand cuisine and seafood specialities. **Lewishams**, ℂ (07) 349-1786, at 115 Tutanekai Street, has a cozy, colonial atmosphere with two fireplaces blazing in winter and a small back garden for summer lunches. They serve traditional New Zealand cuisine, with excellent lamb and seafood dishes. **Aorangi Peak**, ℂ (07) 347-0046, on Mountain Road, Mt Ngongotaha, has vertiginous views overlooking the lake city and superb venison, lamb and salmon dishes. At the Hyatt

Kingsgate, **Laura's**, ℂ (07) 347-1234, offers fairly expensive formal dining with excellent cuisine and service.

The Landmark, ℂ (07) 348-9376, 1 Meade Street, is another restored Edwardian villa, with a charming atmosphere and reasonably-priced New Zealand specialities. More casual places to dine include the **Cobb & Co Restaurant and Bar**, ℂ (07) 348-2089, at the corner of Hinemoa and Fenton street, which serves hearty colonial-era food, finishing with mouthwatering hot apple pies and brandy snaps. **Heritage Restaurant**, ℂ (07) 347-7686, on Fenton Street, offers similar fare while **Zanelli's**, ℂ (07) 348-4908, at 23 Amohia Street, is good for Italian food.

TRIPS FROM ROTORUA

Outside Rotorua, the landscape is dotted with thermal reserves, tranquil lakes and scenic forest drives. You can plan to see at least one, if not all of the main thermal reserves — **Waimangu**, **Waiotapu** and **Orakei Korako** — as you drive out along the main highway south to Taupo.

In the meantime, the most pleasant way to explore surrounding lakes and sights is by taking a variety of scenic routes. Just off the circular road, on the Rotorua—Whakatane highway is **Hell's Gate** at Tikitere, six kilometers (nearly four miles) from Rotorua, a thermal area noted for its weird landscapes and containing **Kakahi Falls**, the biggest scalding-hot waterfall in the Southern Hemisphere. In Maori, this place is called *"Taku tiki i tere nei,"* which translates "my daughter died in these waters." It commemorates the demise of Huritini, a Maori maiden who threw herself into the boiling falls because her husband had an affair with another woman.

From here, you can branch up to see **Okere Falls**, and wind through corridors of dense native bush to see the lakes **Rotoiti**, **Rotoehu** and **Rotoma**, each seeming more tranquil and beautiful than the other. Trout fishing is a highlight here, and there are many walking trails.

The luxury sporting retreat, **Moose Lodge**, ℂ (07) 362-7823, is located on the southern shores of Lake Rotoiti, along State Highway 30 on the main Rotorua—Whakatane highway. Its deluxe rates cover the lodge's superb meals and cruises on a choice of boats. The **Okawa Bay Lake Resort**, ((07) 362-4599, also on the shores of Lake Rotoiti, is another luxury lodge, with mid-price rates.

One of the loveliest places to visit in this region is **Lake Okataina**, which lies off the tourist track and offers perfect solitude. It's the only lake to be completely surrounded by native forest. You can stay here at one of New Zealand's best-kept secrets, **Lake Okataina Lodge**, which lies seven kilometers (just over four miles) down a narrow, unsealed one-way road that feels like driving through a dappled green tunnel so dense is the surrounding bush. There's no telephone, TV or radio. Just pristine lakeside bungalow-style accommodation, so peaceful you can hear warblers and fan-tails that seem to have lungs as loud as opera singers. The dining room has a changing menu featuring plenty of fresh trout and there's an good wine list. Rates are mid-priced and you'll need to book in writing.

For another excursion, take the Tarawera Road from Rotorua through the district of the **Blue and Green Lakes**, named for their striking iridescent algal surfaces. The first, called *tikitapu* in Maori, has many beautiful lakeside tracks. The second, much larger lake is called *rotokakahi*, a sacred, Maori-owned lake, said to contain *taniwha* (water monsters) and trespassers are not allowed.

The road continues on towards **Te Wairoa**, known as the "buried village." Te Wairoa was once a small Maori-European settlement established by a European missionary in 1852. On the night of June 10, 1886, it was buried when Mt. Tarawera, coughing fireballs and red-hot stones, erupted in a spectacular explosion — "the sky is on fire" — that killed over a hundred Maoris and a few Europeans. Rising steam from the lakes mixed with dirt, ash and lake bed already blown into the air, creating a killer mud that rained down on the countryside, burying Te Wairoa. The village has been partially excavated and its history documented in a small museum which contains artifacts found in the mud. There's a pretty walk to a little waterfall within the nearby forest. From the nearby **Tarawera Landing**, you can join a cruise of several hours that takes in Lake Tarawera, Lake Rotomahana and the Waimangu Thermal Valley. Scheduled trips on the *Reremoana* depart at 10 am, 11:30 am, 12:15 pm and 3:30 pm every Tuesday, Thursday, Saturday and Sunday, until Boxing Day and then daily until the Tuesday after Easter. Until the destruction of the Pink and White Terraces, Victorian visitors, many of whom had traveled from Europe and America, would set out in huge dugout canoes paddled by local Maoris.

Another excellent launch service is run by Craig and Caroline Armstrong, an enterprising, charming young couple who have restored a vintage ferry and launch to gleaming condition. They run 45-minute cruises leaving daily on the hour and a special 11 am two-hour cruise for $25. They will also drop campers off at nearby **Hot Water Beach camping ground**, with its unusual thermal-heated shoreline similar to the one in the Coromandel Peninsula, though only accessible by boat. Call the Armstrongs, ((07) 362-8595, or 362-8590 for details.

If you're driving, the climbing of **Mt. Tarawera**, is best begun from the other side, with a road leading off from **Lake Rerewhakaaitu**. The mountain's name means "burnt bird spears," commemorating the accidental burning of a chief's favorite bird-hunting weapons. It is a desolate mountaintop, which can be reached only by four-wheel drive vehicles and is promoted in Rotorua tourist brochures as the most awe-inspiring landscape outside of Hell. Certainly its vast crater, a six kilometers (nearly four miles) long, 250 m (825 ft) deep chasm created by the volcanic explosion which split the mountain in half, is an awesome sight. Within this enormous wound, shale, scoria and loose rock glisten in many colors ranging from aubergine to gray. Atop Mt. Tarawera, there are spectacular views across to the smoking plumes of distant **White Island** in the Bay of Plenty and the brooding snow-capped mountain-tops of **Tongariro National Park** near Lake Taupo.

Solitaire Lodge, ((07) 362-8208, fax: (07) 362-8445, is one of the country's premier luxury retreats, tucked within a densely forested headland on R.D.5 not far from Tarawera Landing. Guests stay in exquisite, plushly-furnished cottages with large panoramic windows which open out to lovely views across the lake. The deluxe rates include all sorts of activities, such as trout fishing cruises, yachting, trips to nearby Hot Water Beach and haute cuisine meals. Although extremely stylish, the lodge encourages a casual atmosphere amongst its guests and is not at all stuffy. Breakfasts and lunches are held in an open kitchen, where you can chat to the chef or whip something up yourself.

The Thermal Reserves

On the Taupo road are three areas of thermal

which rises and falls some 10 m (33 ft) each month. **Warbrick Terrace** is a steaming, suppurating silica flow dappled with gluggy green, brown, red and white algae capable of tolerating the hot sulfurs waters. It's named for a daredevil Rotorua guide who crossed Frying Pan Lake on a boat, despite the ever-present risk of its spluttering explosions, and survived to tell the tale, although his brother lost his life the same way in another attempt. From here, the walk down to the boat jetty on **Lake Rotomahana** is very beautiful, fringed by native flax bushes. A

activity, each in a totally different setting. First up is **Waimangu Thermal Valley**, 26 km (16 miles) from Rotorua. It lies across from Mt. Tarawera, whose giant eruption formed this eerie valley of boiling lakes and mystical, changeable silica terraces, steaming fumeroles, and numerous boiling springs. A visit to this very volatile area is definitely one of New Zealand's highlights. From the tearooms, the well-marked walk takes about an hour. Special features to watch out for include **Frying Pan Lake**, the largest boiling hot spring in the world, the astoundingly-hued blue **Inferno Crater**,

Two views of Rotorua's dramatic landscape. LEFT: Lady Knox Geyser and RIGHT eerie silica terraces at Waiotapu.

full-day round trip to Waimangu leaves Rotorua at 8:45 pm. Ask at the Information Centre for details.

Closer to the main highway is **Waiotapu**, 29 km (18 miles) from Rotorua. This is one of the most colorful geothermal areas in the world, where you can walk freely around the rims of large thermal craters, many of which have boiling springs and colorful sulfur deposits. Waiotapu is also the home to the ever faithful **Lady Knox Geyser** which erupts daily at 10:15 am, (with the help of some soap) sometimes for up to an hour. Other features of Waiotapu live up to their luridly descriptive names, such as "Paddle-wheel Blowhole", "Bridal Veil Falls", "Devil's Ink Pots" and the orange and green-hued

"Champagne Pool," 60 m (198 ft) deep, which bubbles and steams continuously, with a surface encrusted with silica formations.

The "hidden valley" of **Orakei Korako**, lies 75 km (46.5 miles) south of Rotorua and 40 km (25 miles) northwest of Taupo. This thermal valley lies at the edge of Lake Ohakuri and is reached by jet boat. Once you alight, you can wonder at its large silica terraces, active geysers and mirror-like pools, which give the valley its name, "place of adorning." The fern-fringed **Ruatapu Cave**, with a path that leads down to an underground hot pool, has a preternatural beauty. It's the sort of place you can imagine tribal Maoris guarding down to that last shrunken skull.

Tours

Taylor's Tours, ((07) 346-1333, offers twice-daily half-day tours of Rotorua's main sights. The morning tour includes Hell's Gate, the Buried Village, Blue and Green lakes and the Redwood Forest while the afternoon tour visits the thermal reserves of Waimangu and Waiotapu, and Rainbow Mountain. Both cost $37.

Kiwi Outback, ((07) 332-3629, is a farm 30 km (19 miles) away from Rotorua. Your guide on tramping tours into virgin forest is a New Zealand bushman, farmer and poet. There are two huts set up as bush camps and your stay includes a visit to glow-worm caves at night.

The Farmhouse, ((07) 332-3771, at Sunnex Road, R.D.2, Ngongotaha, caters especially to children on its typical New Zealand sheep and cattle farm. They also have a stable of nearly 90 horses, which can be hired out from one hour to a full day (five hours riding). If you are traveling with children who are keen to learn how to ride this is a great place to learn. You can be picked up from Rotorua.

The Rainbow Mountain Track, ((07) 349-0804, is a guided two-day walk that encompasses the Waimangu Thermal Valley, Waiotapu Thermal Reserve, Kerosene Creek and the Dacite Cone of Rainbow Mountain.

Mt. Tarawera Tours, ((07) 348-0632, offers a half-day tour in a 4 wheel drive van right up to the edge of Mt. Tarawera's summit, looking down into its 250 m (825 ft) deep, six kilometers (four miles) long crater. Adults cost $38 and children $18.

TAUPO

Lake Taupo, from which the town of Taupo takes its name, is New Zealand's largest lake, covering an area of 626 sq km (241 sq miles). An abbreviation of *Taupo-nui-Tia* or "the great shoulder cloak of Tia," Taupo takes its name from the Maori Arawa canoe explorer who discovered the great lake. It is framed by white pumice beaches, yellow-flowered kowhai trees and the distant snow-capped mountain peaks of **Tongariro**, **Ngauruhoe** and **Ruapehu**, all active volcanoes in nearby **Tongariro National Park**, which in the winter boast two large, well-serviced ski-fields. In summer the park attracts energetic mountaineers, nature strollers and chairlift-riding sightseers.

Though peaceful and tranquil now, the lake's 600 sq km (232 sq miles) basin is the crater of an ancient volcano whose last eruption, around AD 130, was one of the most violent in history, six times as violent as Krakatoa in 1883, creating miraculous red skies recorded by contemporary Chinese and Roman scribes. Evidence of the massive blast lies all around the volcanic plateau — in the pumice soil, cliffs and beaches, and in the charred remains of trees protruding from banks on the Desert Road.

Almost perfectly at the center of the North Island, the lake itself is Taupo's star attraction. Its tranquil waters are perfect for swimming, sailing and all kinds of water sports. Or you can drive right around its 195 km (121 miles) circumference. The lake is part of the thermal belt which stretches south from Rotorua, and there are numerous hot pools. The brown and rainbow trout that cluster within the lake and its tributaries have a special place in angling folklore: even by New Zealand standards they are monsters, with rainbow trout up to 9 kg (20 lbs). If you've ever even been tempted to fly-fish, take advantage of the many professional fishing guides here who can share their expertise and show you the best trout spots. The enthusiasm for catching fish is certainly infectious. At times, from the afternoon to sunset, it seems as though the whole community has "gone fishing," leaving Taupo curiously empty.

ACCESS

Air New Zealand has direct daily flights to Taupo from Auckland, Wellington and Wanganui. Mt. Cook Airlines also operates flights to Taupo, with direct flights to Christchurch, Wellington and Rotorua.

Located almost exactly halfway between Auckland and Wellington, Taupo is a major

Taupo Coast Guard Service is ((07) 377-0400.

LAKE CRUISES AND A WALK

You can cruise all around Lake Taupo on the tiny vintage steam ferry *Ernest Kemp* or the *Barbary*, a 60-year old wooden yacht once owned by Errol Flynn, who described his South Pacific sailing escapades as his "years of poverty and vagabondage." Both cruises last for about two hours and visit a modern Maori rock carving beside the lakes, and cost

bus hub, serviced by InterCity, Mt. Cook, and Newmans.

GENERAL INFORMATION

The **Taupo Information Centre**, ((07) 378-9000, is on Tongariro Street and can advise on every kind of lake and river activity, fishing and hunting licenses, skiing, as well as scenic flights by floatplane from the lakefront or by aircraft and helicopters across Tongariro National Park. They have detailed descriptions of the many walking and tramping trails in the surrounding **Puerora** and **Kaimanawa** forest parks. If you're planning a day's fishing and need to know about weather conditions, the

$20 and $15 respectively. The *Taupo Cat* offers a slightly longer cruise and costs $42. If you want to hire a boat to go fishing, it is possible to halve the costs by sharing it with others of a similar persuasion. The average cost for hiring a boat is $125 for three hours. Contact the Information Center for details. At the end of Taupo's Three Mile Bay, **Lion's Walk** follows a line of pumice beaches for about a kilometer. On the way back, you might be tempted to sample fresh fish and chips at **Cafe a la Cart**, near the car-park.

WHAT TO SEE

Within the Taupo area, there are several places of great natural beauty to seek out with other man-made attractions dotted along the way.

As you continue along State Highway 1 towards Wairakei, you'll see the turnoff for **Huka Village Estate** on Huka Falls Road. This collection of restored colonial buildings showcases the life of New Zealand's early settlers, and has craft shops and a village restaurant. Nearby, within the Waikato River, **Cherry Island** is a wildlife park with trout pools.

Further up, five kilometers (three miles) from Taupo, are 11 m (36 ft) **Huka Falls**, a

magnificent vision of surging turquoise, quartz-like water which flows like liquid blue ice from Lake Taupo all the way out to the Tasman Sea, 300 km (186 miles), south-west of Auckland. There are different platforms from which to view. A very beautiful seven kilometer (just over four mile) walk skirts the river through surrounding native forest to the **Aratiatia Rapids**, where the dam floodgates are opened daily at 10 am to 11:30 am and 2:30 pm to 4 pm, unleashing powerful floods. You can cruise the Aratiatia Rapids up to Huka Falls aboard the *M.V. Wairaka*, a vintage riverboat built in 1908 that departs Wairakei Park Wharf daily at 10 am and 2 pm, and costs $15 for adults and $5 for children. The 12 noon lunch cruise

costs $25. Taupo's closest thermal valley is enclosed within **Wairakei Tourist Park**, eight kilometers (five miles) from the township. Its highlights include the **Craters of the Moon** park, with its weird steaming lunar landscapes and multicolored boiling mud pools, and the **Wairakei Geothermal Power Station**, which has an information center open daily between 9 am and 12 noon and 1 pm and 4:30 pm. Just off the main highway on Poihipi Road near Wairakei is the **Honey Village**, which has glassed-off viewing hives, educational videos and a host of honey products to sample.

Back in Taupo, laze and recuperate at either the **A.C. Thermal Baths** or **De Bretts Thermal Pools**, both open daily.

Useful Contacts:
Taupo Lakeside Services, ((07) 378-5596, arranges skippered trout fishing cruises, share trips, self-drive run-arounds, water skiing, jet boats and cruises.

Lake Taupo Yacht Charters, ((07) 378-3444, after hours (07) 373-8146, offers cruises, basic sail tuition, trout fishing introduction and sightseeing, with daily sails at 10:30 am and 2 pm, and 6 pm in summer, $20 each.

M.V. Waimarie, ((07) 377-0345, is a 10 m (36 ft) luxury cruiser can accommodate up to 10 guests for fishing and overnight trips.

Fishing and Water-Skiing Charters, ((07) 378-2736, 378-3444, 378-9002.

Chris Jolly Boats, ((07) 378-0632, fax: (07) 378-9458, offers complete (all equipment provided) fishing charters on any one of his four fishing and cruising boats and also offers guided hunting.

Huka Horse Hire, ((07) 378-0356, offers horse-riding treks at $15 an hour, with full-day wilderness treks on Mondays, Wednesdays and Fridays.

WHERE TO STAY

Within the Taupo region, the most elegant place to stay is **Huka Lodge**, ((07) 378-5791, fax: (07) 378-0427, on the Huka Falls Road, renowned as New Zealand's first and top sporting lodge. Set in its own lush estate on

The mellow stillness of trout-fishing on Lake Taupo.

the banks of the Waikato River, the lodge's standards are flawless. It charges $350 a night for two which includes a full breakfast and a superb five course dinner.

Sixty years ago, Alan Pye, a young Irishman with a zest for trout fishing built the original lodge, and soon attracted anglers from all over the world. British military officers came on furlough from India, wealthy Americans brought up on New York's Catskill streams made annual pilgrimages. Among its early enthusiastic guests was Charles Lindbergh, the aviator,

lodge's boat or fly over remote back country by helicopter.

In Taupo, staying in a hotel with a lakeside view is all-important, and Lake Terrace is lined with all kinds of accommodation. **Lanecove Motor Inn**, ((07) 378-7599, is rather glossy with a reflective glass exterior, with well-equipped, mid-priced suites and a restaurant. **Cascades Motor Lodge**, ((07) 378-3774, fax: (07) 378-0372, is more modest, but much more stylish, set right on the lake with balconies for optimum appreciation of the view, fully-equipped kitchens with mi-

while authors Zane Grey and James A. Michener both spent angling sabbaticals here, the latter writing part of his book, *Return to Paradise*, here.

An eclectic blend of European and New Zealand styles are the hallmark of the lodge. Guests have their own private river-facing cottages, beautifully furnished. Bathrooms have the lovely feature of a glass ceiling, through which you can see towering redwoods. Activities can be sedate — golf, river-side picnics and long walks — or you can trout-fish, horse-trek, cruise aboard the

crowaves and very cozy furnishings. It's moderately-priced and has a heated swimming pool. The **Cottage Mews**, ((07) 378-3004, is another excellent value luxury motel, with private whirlpools and private balconies in its colonial-style cottages, attractively landscaped. **Acacia Bay Lodge**, ((07) 378-6830, at 868 Acacia Bay Road, offers moderately-priced spacious timber cottages, located five kilometers (three miles) from Taupo.

Inexpensive options include **Bradshaw's Travel Hotel**, ((07) 378-8288, at 130 Heuheu Street, the **Sunseeker Motel**, ((07) 378-9020 on the lakefront at Taharepa Road and **De Brett's Thermal Leisure Park**, ((07) 378-8559, fax: (07) 378-8559, on the Taupo/Napier

ABOVE: The surging turquoise waters of Huka Falls, near Taupo. OPPOSITE: Scenic lakeside setting of Lake Taupo.

highway, which offers motel, tourist flats, cabins and sheltered camping sites. Backpackers can head for **Rainbow Lodge**, ((07) 378-5754, 99 Titiraupenga Street, which has heated bunk rooms, a sauna and games area, and will hire out bikes, fishing gear and canoes. **Sunset Lodge**, ((07) 378-5962, at 5 Tremaine Avenue, Two Mile Bay, is another good choice.

WHERE TO EAT

Taupo is one place in the world where you

in a colonial villa with beautiful views. Reservations are required.

More casual eateries in town include the **Cafe Renoir**, ((07) 378-0777, at 77 Spa Road, with a daily changing menu and scrumptiously decadent desserts. **Echo Cliff**, ((07) 378-8539, on the corner of Lake Terrace and Tongariro Street, is a good seafood and steak restaurant, while **Margarita's**, ((07) 378-9909, on Heuheu Street, serves Mexican food. **Blair's**, ((07) 378-3803, in the Suncourt Shopping Centre on Tamamutu Street, is open from 8:30 am and serves wonderful

could say, Marie Antoinette-style "Let them eat trout." Fishing mania breaks down all barriers, and chefs of most hotels and even restaurants will generally enjoy chatting about the size of your day's efforts and cook it according to your taste. They do appreciate at least a day's notice.

There are several rather good restaurants. The **Huka Village Homestead Restaurant**, ((07) 378-5326, serve traditional country-style meals, with home-made soups and breads. **Pepper's Brasserie**, ((07) 378-5110, in Manuel's Motor Inn on Lake Terrace, serves creative New Zealand cuisine, with plenty of fresh seafood dishes. In a similar category, **Truffles**, ((07) 378-7856, also on Lake Terrace, has a pleasant setting

breakfasts. Their fluffy cappuccinos are awe-inspiring. Throughout the day, this is a good place to stop off for a snack of freshly baked muffins or cakes, or to have a sandwich or a salad.

TURANGI

At the south end of Taupo Lake, lies Turangi, a much smaller town also devoted to fishing. You can go boating and swimming in the lake, bird-watching in the nearby vast marshy Tongariro delta which attracts all kinds of waterfowl, and tramping or hunting in the nearby mountain wilderness of the **Kaimanawa Forest Park**.

The Tongariro River surges through Turangi, attracting anglers and whitewater rafters who can follow its tumultuous, maze-like course through many rapids, surrounded on both sides by deep green, moss-carpeted beech forests. The river springs from two sources: the melted snow from Mt. Ruapehu's slopes and the waterfalls in the Waipakihi Valley in the Kaimanawa mountains. At the **Tongariro National Trout Centre**, three kilometers (nearly two miles) south of Turangi, you can inspect the trout hatchery, where young fish are reared in their tens of thousands. The on-site visitor's center contains informative displays on the history, tackle and sport of trout fishing. Another magnet for anglers within easy driving distance is **Tokaanu**, also on the Tongariro River, which also has pleasant thermal baths.

In town, the **Turangi Information Centre**, ((07) 386-8999, is at Ngawaka Place. The **Tongariro Lodge**, ((07) 386-7946, fax: (07) 386-8860, on the bank of Tongariro River, is very luxurious, with deluxe rates, a plush restaurant, and offers hunting and fishing guides. Two special lodges, both with peaceful riverside locations and moderate prices are the **Braxmere Fishing Lodge**, ((07) 386-8011, fax: (07) 386-8011, a good angler's choice nearby at Little Waihi, and **Creel Lodge** ((07) 386-7929, fax: (07) 386-7929, on Taupehi Road. Two good inexpensively-priced choices are the **Tongariro Outdoor Centre**, ((07) 386-7492, on Chuanga Road and **Turangi Holiday Park**, ((07) 386-8754, with cabins, and caravan and camp sites. Both have plenty of hot water and drying facilities for hikers, trampers and skiers. Backpackers' accommodation is provided at **Angler's Paradise Resort Motel**, ((07) 386-8980, at the corner of State Highway 41 and Chuanga Road in park reserve, where rooms are $20 a night.

THE EAST CAPE

Between Opotiki and Gisborne, the isolated 334 km (207 miles) East Cape coastline is full of rugged beauty. It has sheltered coves and irresistible beaches, lined with pohutakawa trees and strewn with curious-shaped driftwood, constantly threaded by a ribbon horizon of deep blue sea. It's also a region

that has remained true to its Maori roots. Driving along its winding, remote roads, you see Maori children confidently galloping across farmland on horses, while the small settlements have a very Maori atmosphere. Sometimes you may catch a glimpse of a Maori ceremony, such as a *tangi* or funeral, being carried out at a local marae, a moving sight with elders wearing the traditional *moko* tattoo intoning songs of mourning. Some of the finest Maori carving can be seen at the marae in this region. You could drive right around the East Cape in a day, just for the sheer pleasure of its wild beauty. Or you can linger, ideally savoring its natural beauty by camping under the stars.

OPOTIKI

The main township of the East Cape, Opotiki is a good place to stop, if not to stay. Stop first at the **Opotiki Enterprise Agency Information Centre**, ((07) 315-8484, to pick up their useful *Opotiki and East Coast Guide*, which details everything worth knowing and seeing in the region, as well their pamphlets on the Maori myths of the region. They can also organize white-water rafting on Opotiki's two rivers, hunting, fishing, helicopter and flying trips to White Island, marae visits and farmstays.

There are all sorts of treks through nearby **Waioeka Gorge Scenic Reserve** and **Raukumara State Forest Park**.

In town, see **St. Stephens Church** (1864), built by the fervent German missionary, Reverend Carl Volkner, who was lynched in 1865 by Maori followers of the Hau Hau cult, who tried to expel Europeans by means they justified with a mixture of Old Testament morality and primitive Maori belief, encouraging at the same time a revival of cannibalism. Opposite, the **Opotiki Museum** is an eccentric collection of hundreds of gloriously obsolete items of the kind people have always brought from stores and then thrown in the attic, whence their grandchildren have rescued and brought them to be exhibited in museums such as this. Another curiosity is the old **"4 Square"** shop, with its sloping wooden floors, counter service, copper weighing machine and pyramids of stacked Sunlight soap.

Hukutaia Domain, seven kilometers (just over four miles) away is a must. This magnificent forest park has many beautiful walks, with identified native trees and plants. Within the park is the sacred 1,000 year-old puriri tree, named Taketakerau by the local Maori tribe of this area, who used it as their burial tree. In forested areas, the use of burial trees was common. The skeletons of important tribe members — after being exhumed, scraped and painted with preservative paint — were placed in caves or hollow trees to protect against their desecration by enemy tribes. When first found by Europeans, this tree contained many bones and skulls, since removed for safe-keeping.

Accommodation in Opotiki includes the moderate **Magnolia Court Motel**, ((07) 315-8490, at the corner of Bridge and Nelson streets. **Patiti Lodge**, ((07) 315-6834, 112 Ford Street, is inexpensive and comfortable.

AROUND THE CAPE

From Opotiki, State Highway 35 winds past tranquil estuaries, through dramatic gorges and around majestic headlands, from which ever-more distant beaches beckon. There's an excellent camping ground at **Opape Beach**, 17 km (10.5 miles) from Opotiki, while at nearby **Torere**, look out for the richly-carved marae and lovely picnic area on the western side of the bay, sheltered by pohutakawa trees.

At the small settlement of **Te Kaha**, stop for a drink at the **Te Kaha Hotel**, overlooking the sea, full of old salts and true East Cape atmosphere, and look at the beautifully-ornate marae. Further on, **Whanarua Bay** is considered by many to be the prettiest bay on the coast, with several beaches ideal for picnics, swimming and fishing, with bush walks up the Whanarua Creek to a series of waterfalls. Locals go eeling down here at night, when the creek banks shine eerily with glow-worms. From here, **Raukokere** is easily recognized by the Anglican Church on the promontory, in the shade of a huge Monkey-Puzzle tree, overlooking another sandy bay.

Waihau Bay is a rock-strewn beach, with scenery reminiscent of the Isle of Skye, the site of the **Waihau Bay Lodge**, ((07) 325-

3804, 107 km (66 miles) from Opotiki and the nicest place to stay on the East Cape unless you are camping. Crayfish and deepsea fishing expeditions go out from the hotel's ramp, which you are welcome to join. Camp sites are available here too. Close by the **Waihau Bay Holiday Park**, ((07) 325-3844, is a fully equipped camping ground. At the cape's tip, **Cape Runaway**, **Lottin Point** and **Hick's Bay** all have dramatic lookout spots. There's a gruesome story attached to Hick's Bay. In 1830, the settlers here were celebrating the marriage between a *pakeha* and a Maori girl when an enemy tribe attacked and ate the wedding guests! InterCity buses run to this point, but no further.

At the settlement of **Te Araroa**, the road descends to sea level and runs along the narrow bay to the far end, where a worthwhile detour leads you out to the East Cape lighthouse. In Te Araroa, look out for the world's largest *pohutakawa* tree. The next main settlement before entering Gisborne District is **Ruatoria**, the center of the *Ngati Porou* tribe, whose ancestors struck fear into the hearts of their enemies. It has a reputation in New Zealand as a belligerent cowboy town, with recent spates of machete and arson attacks. Don't let this put you off, though! There are hot springs at **Te Puia**. Further down, **Anaura Bay** has a nice camping ground. **Tolaga Bay**, 55 km (34 miles) from Gisborne, with its very long jetty, is a curiosity piece. All its streets are named after Captain Cook's men, as the *Endeavour* cast anchor here in 1769. The **Tolaga Bay Inn**, ((06) 862-6856, is a lovely English-style place, with a tavern and inexpensive to moderately priced rooms, in either the house, or self-contained chalets. A popular fishing base, the **Tolaga Bay Motor Camp**, ((06) 862-6716 has one of the cape's best located camping grounds, right on the beach line.

THE TONGARIRO NATIONAL PARK

Sacred to the Maori, full of desolate, supernatural beauty, this vast 76,698 hectare (191,745 acre) park is studded with three colossal active volcanoes that dominate the

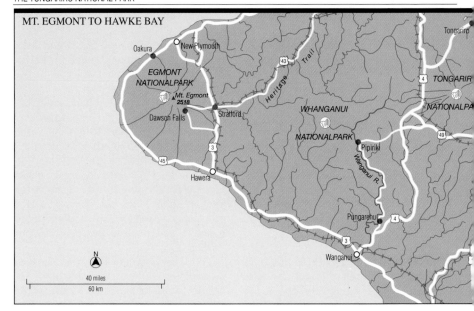

central North Island plateau, Mt. Tongariro, Mt. Ruapehu and Mt. Ngauruhoe.

Even driving through the park's landscape offers unforgettable vistas, as the road dips and climbs through the deep gorges and over high rolling hills of the Kaimanawa Ranges. You can stop at pristine streams for gulps of delicious icy water and fresh air that feels super-oxygenated to starved city-lungs. In spring, bright heather and yellow broom burst into flower across the desert-like camel-hued tussock grasslands. Great strands of totara, matai and rimu trees stand within pockets of beech forest.

Constantly in view are the giant snow-crusted volcanic peaks, whose eerie magnificence are at their most spectacular at first sunlight, when the roseate snows radiate alpine serenity. You will often glimpse the peaks on scheduled flights that cross the North Island, but scenic flights across their craters are far more rewarding. Popular with skiers, these mountains offer tough challenges for hikers, trampers and climbers. The crater summits of Ruapehu and Tongariro also offer the intense pleasure of an outdoor sauna: plunges in hot lakes alternated with rolls in the snow. **Ngauruhoe**, 2,291 m (7,196 ft), with its dramatic pumice slopes, is the most active of the three volcanoes and occasionally erupts murky clouds of smoke and ash. **Ruapehu**, 2,797 m (9,177 ft)

which means "exploding hole" in Maori, has several craters in its three kilometer- (nearly two mile)-wide multi-peaked summit, and its warm, acidic green Crater Lake has a natural amphitheater of perpetual snow, and six small glaciers. Experienced trekkers can climb up to Crater Lake, following the Whakapapa Glacier for part of the way. **Tongariro**, 1,968 m (6,457 ft), is one of the most popular mountains in the North Island for trekkers, who can follow the two to three day Ketetahai Trail up to hot springs on its northern slopes and reach the stunning Blue Lake that occupies a 9,000-year old explosion crater on the volcano's eastern flank. No superlatives can convey the magic beauty of glimpsing the azure brilliance of the lake for the first time, which on a cloudless hot day, seems like a vast circle of captured sky.

The mountain-tops are considered sacred by the Maori, whose legends tell how they were created when a stranded, frozen Maori *tohunga* (tribal priest), called the gods for help. His prayers were answered by the fire demons of Hawaiki, who sent torrents of fire via White Island and Rotorua to burst out through the mountain-tops to warm him up! To thank the fire demons, the priest decided to throw his unfortunate nubile slave, Auruhoe, into the Ngauruhoe volcano as a thank-you present. What the fire

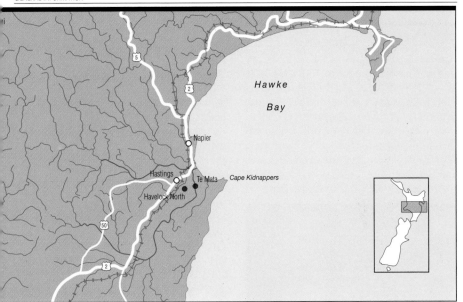

demons thought of her charred remains was never recorded, but she is immortalized in the volcano's name.

ACCESS

The *Silver Fern* train shuttles between Auckland and Wellington, stopping at National Park and Ohakune in the southwest of the park, twice daily each way on weekdays and once daily on weekends.

InterCity has a service three times a week from Rotorua, which stops at Taupo, Turangi, Whakapapa, Tongariro National Park and Ohakune, and then returns along the same route back to Rotorua. The daily Auckland-Wellington bus also stops at the park, but not at Whakapapa. Alpine Scenic Tours, ((07) 386-8392 runs a cheaply priced private bus which shuttles between Taupo, Turangi, Ketehai, Whakapapa and various other points within the park.

If you're driving, the park is encircled and easily reached by a choice of roads, depending on which direction you are coming from. The Desert Road, as this section of State Highway 1 is known, passes down the park's eastern rim from Turangi. The Desert Road is one of New Zealand's highlights, passing a stark landscape of sepia tussockland, etched with blackened trees and low shrubs and framed by constantly-changing vistas of the snow-topped mountains, offering a remarkable contrast to the rest of the region's lush forests and pasture-land. Along The Desert Road, the **Army Memorial Museum** at Waiouru, is a good place to break the journey. It's open daily and has tearooms. State Highway 4 tracks the western side of the park from Te Kuiti, while State Highway 47 crosses the northern side and State Highway 49 the southern side. The main road up into the park is State Highway 48, which reaches Whakapapa village, the location of the Visitor's Information Centre and the Chateau lodge.

GENERAL INFORMATION

At the park's headquarters in Whakapapa village on Mt. Ruapehu, the **Whakapapa Visitor's Centre**, ((07) 892-3729, is the place to consult on all activities whatever the season. They can organize accommodation and book for the ski season. There's a fascinating display on the region's geology, flora and fauna, and lots of detailed pamphlets about walks and treks from Whakapapa and many other points in the park.

In Ohakune, the **Information Centre**, ((06) 385-8427, the **Turoa Ski Field Information Centre**, ((06) 385-8426, and the **Ohakune Ranger Station**, ((06) 385-8578 are all excellent sources of local information.

WHERE TO STAY

Amidst the raw beauty of the park, the imposing **Chateau Tongariro**, ((07) 892-3809, fax: (07) 892-3704, on Mt. Ruapehu is, along with Mt. Cook's The Hermitage, the ultimate in mountaintop elegance. As well as luxury facilities and a superb restaurant, this mid-priced resort has a swimming pool (heated in winter), a nearby golf course and is a good base for the ski-field, six kilometers (nearly four miles) away. There's a

heli-pad. Close by, **Mt. Ruapehu Skotel**, ((07) 892-3719, has a variety of accommodation, ranging from the special summer share rates of $18 per person in the standard twin rooms, through inexpensive rooms to moderately-priced chalets. For apres-ski relaxation there's a sauna, spa pool and a gym for unfolding tight muscles.

The **Whakapapa Motor Camp**, ((07) 892-3897, right opposite the Visitor's Centre, has inexpensive tourist flats, camping and caravan sites. Dotted along the park's tramping trails are nine huts, which can be reached on foot only. Full details of the huts and their location are supplied by the Visitor's Center.

In National Park, the small settlement 15 km (just over nine miles) from Whakapapa and the base for several walks and treks, there are several places to stay. Both **Discovery Best Western Hotel**, ((07) 892-2744, halfway between National Park and

Whakapapa, and **Buttercup Alpine Resort**, ((07) 892-2702, at National Park offers comfortable moderately-priced rooms. The **National Park Hotel**, ((07) 892-2805, near the railway station, is a backpacker's ski hostel with a communal dining room, kitchen and shower area. You need to bring your own bedding and blankets.

Ohakune, located within half an hour's driving distance in the southwest of the park, is the main base for the Turoa Ski Field, six kilometers (nearly four miles) away. There are four excellent moderately-priced options. The **Alpine Motel**, ((06) 385-8758, at 7 Miro Street, has spacious chalets with mountain views. Located close to each other, **Ohakune Court Motel**, ((06) 385-8183, is at 101 Goldfinch Street, while **The Hobbit**, ((06) 385-8248, is on the corner of Goldfinch and Wye Streets. **Mount Ruapehu Homestead**, ((06) 385-8799, at 1 Piwari Street, is a lovely Bed and Breakfast, set in a large private estate. Backpackers will find the **Ohakune Youth Hostel**, ((06) 385-8724, on Clyde Street, offers very good value and a warm atmosphere. It tends to get heavily-booked during the ski-season.

DOWN TO CAPE KIDNAPPERS

Gisborne is the prosperous center of balmy **Poverty Bay**, which got its distinctly misleading name from Captain Cook, when he found little to feed his crew on here, the first place he set foot in New Zealand on October 10th, 1769. A major wine-producing area, Gisborne prides itself on being the most easterly place in the world, closest to the international dateline which is 900 km (558 miles) away. Aside from its pleasant beaches, and a museum with a good collection of Maori art, Gisborne is not really a place to linger.

However, near Gisborne, the sublime beauty of **Eastwoodhill Valley** looks straight out of a Canadian landscape with its russet, amber and silvery trees bathed in soft light. The arboretum was founded by Douglas Cook after he returned to New Zealand from the horrors of World War I's trench warfare, and is home to over 3,000 exotic species. For more details, consult the

ABOVE: Chateau Tongariro, New Zealand's famous luxury lodge. OPPOSITE: Two views of the gannet colony at Cape Kidnappers.

Eastland Information Centre, ((06) 798-6139, at 209 Grey Street.

NAPIER

It is a further 216 km (134 miles) to Napier, New Zealand's Art Deco city and a twin city with **Hastings** on **Hawke Bay**, a gentrified coastal bowl of market gardens, rich orchards and vineyards. Vines were first planted in Hawke Bay in 1850 by a French Catholic mission, and the climate is similar to that in the best grape-growing

As you walk the streets of this small city, look out in particular for the **Masonic, Provincial** and **Central hotels**, the **Rothman's Building** and the **Municipal Theatre**. Along its seafront is the two kilometers (one-and-a-quarter miles) **Marine Parade**, edged with tall Norfolk pines and palm trees. The highlights here are an aquarium, oceanarium, marineland with performing dolphins, roller-skating rink, gardens, an illuminated fountain and a kiwi house. Also on Marine Parade, you'll find the **Staples Complex**, which includes a waxworks

areas of Europe. It has 17 major vineyards, among which produce are some of the country's finest wines, notably Esk Valley Estate, Ngatarawa, Stonecroft and Te Mata Estate.

Napier owes its distinctive Art Deco appearance to a disastrous earthquake that shook the area in 1931 and almost completely destroyed the city and killed 162 people. Rebuilt in the Art Deco and Spanish Mission style, and nicknamed "Riviera City," Napier is a startlingly attractive pastel-hued tribute to the thirties, with some parts almost like a Hollywood movie set.

museum and "Earthquake 31," a simulated earthquake experience, with displays on Napier before and after.

The **Napier Information Centre**, ((06) 835-7182, is also on Marine Parade. They can book accommodation and arrange "Art Deco" and vineyard tours.

If you're going to stay in Napier, why not book into one of its Art Deco treasures? The **Masonic Establishment,** ((06) 835-8689 on Marine Parade and the **Provincial Hotel,** ((06) 835-6934, on Emerson Street, are both classics and inexpensive, as is the **Criterion Backpackers Inn**, ((06) 835-2059, also on Emerson Street. Another inexpensive place to stay is the cozy **Waterfront Lodge,** ((06) 835-3429, on Marine Parade. **Beaches,** ((06)

ABOVE: Art Deco architecture characteristic of Napier.

835-8180, in the War Memorial Building on Marine Parade is "the" place to dine, with gorgeous views, excellent seafood specialities and a very good selection of the region's wines.

Don't leave Napier without walking around **Napier Hill**, with its gracious two-storied mansions, stubborn survivors of the earthquakeof 1931, and views across the Cape Kidnappers.

The road out of Napier leads through Havelock North and up to Te Mata Bay for a dramatic view of Hawke Bay, where the hill sweeps up above a river valley, 1,310 m (4,297 ft) high.

At Cape Kidnappers, at the tip of the bay, is the world's only mainland gannet colony, where about 15,000 birds gather from late July to February. Access can only be made by walking along the beach (which takes about five hours), horse-riding, or riding the beach-route by tractor-pulled trailer. There are details of horse-hire places and tours at the Napier Information Centre. Whatever way you see it, the cape is supremely dramatic, with sheer barren cliffs dropping into the ocean, full of remote grandeur.

CENTRAL AND WESTERN NORTH ISLAND

WAIKATO AND TARANAKI

As you drive south of Auckland, you enter the verdant, richly fertile agricultural belt of Waikato, with its stately homesteads, prosperous towns and endless vistas of cud-chewing, plump cattle grazing on greener-than-green pasture-land.

It's almost inconceivable that last century Waikato district was the scene of some of the country's bloodiest conflicts during the Land Wars of the 1860's. It took nearly 20 years for the British and colonial forces to defeat the rebellious Maori tribes who were intent on keeping what was left of their land. With the rebels driven out or dead, the Waikato supporters of the Maori nationalist King pushed south and Waikato and Taranaki were gradually developed into the intensively farmed lands they are today.

Hamilton

Waikato's main industrial and business center, Hamilton is sniffed at by Aucklanders for its peaceful blandness, but has some compensations. Through it flows the **Waikato River**, the country's longest, full of plump trout and perfect for canoeing. Certainly it's possible to enjoy a day or two in Hamilton, especially if you like designer gardens. Don't miss seeing two of them: the **Eion Scarrow Willow Glenand Gail's of Tamahere**, off State Highway 1, which has two nineteenth century churches within its grounds, with beautifully dried flowers hanging from the rafters. The 58-hectare (145-acre) **Hamilton Gardens**, set alongside the Waikato River, have attractive scenic walks, dramatic river views and pleasant spots. There is also an old-fashioned English garden, a herb garden, a rose garden and a Chinese garden. Another tranquil activity is to take the *M.V. Waipa Delta Paddlesteamer* down the Waikato River. Four daily cruises depart from Memorial Park on Memorial Drive, and there's a licensed restaurant aboard. Other Hamilton high-points include walking through the wildlife sanctuary that borders Lake Rotoroa, more commonly known as **Hamilton Lake**, and the **Waikato Museum of Art and History** at 1 Grantham Street, with its giant carved 140 year-old Maori canoe. You can inquire about accommodation, farmstays and tours at the **Visitor's Information Centre**, ((07) 839-3360, at the Municipal Building, Garden Place.

Downstream from Hamilton, **Ngaruawahia** was closely linked with the mid-nineteenth century Maori King movement and is the spiritual heartland for the Maori Waikato tribes. The royal Maori residence is at **Turangawaewae** on the northern bank of the Waikato River and is the venue for many Maori gatherings. On the nearest Saturday to the 17th March each year, the Ngaruwahia Regatta is held, a great opportunity to see Maori pomp with traditionally dressed, fearsome-looking "warriors" racing in superbly carved war canoes.

The Waitomo Caves

As you drive through the area known as the "King Country," past the center of **Te Awa-**

mutu with its pretty rose gardens and historic St. John's Church, you'll begin to notice many queerly-contorted limestone cliffs and canyons. Beneath such landscape lie one of the country's most famous attractions, the Waitomo Caves, a wondrous underground warren of limestone gorges, bluffs, archways and tunnels, in some parts drenched by spectacular tumbling torrents.

For many centuries, local Maoris did not dare enter the caves, and put a "*tapu*" on them. Certainly the giant eels they fished from rivers flowing out of the caves suggested even more awesome creatures lurked within, and they feared this was the home of the "*taniwha*," a mythical giant sea monster. Legends tell of ghastly echoing cries echoing from the deep caverns. In 1887, a European surveyor's assistant and his Maori friend set out on a raft and floated into the caves on an underground river, with only a candle to provide light. Much to their amazement, they found themselves drifting under shimmering arches into places that resembled nature's version of medieval banqueting halls and cathedrals.

The caves have been amazing visitors ever since.

The most popular guided trip is through the Waitomo Cave, shimmering with thousands of glow-worms, where you boat silently through on an underground river. Tours leave every hour from 9 am to 4 pm as well as 4:30 pm and 5:30 pm over summer. In contrast, Aranui Cave has chambers draped with colorful stalactites and stalagmites, a simply stunning sight. It's open daily at 10, 11, and hourly from 1 pm to 3 pm. Both caves are well-lit and have stairways with handrails; normal street clothing and flat-heeled shoes are fine to wear whilst exploring them.

There are more adventurous tours through undeveloped caves. Black Water Rafting guides dress you in a weighty helmet and a headlight to go "rafting" through dramatic Rookery Cave, wearing an inflatable tube around your middle; this is a journey through underground glow-worm tunnels and small waterfalls on a fairly rapidly flowing river. Lost World Adventure Tours runs a range of tours in the Lost World Cave, a vast subterranean cavern, fringed with forest. To enter its limestone shaft, you have to make

a 100 m (330 ft) abseil descent, and then the surrealistic beauty of the cave is revealed in a soft, ghostly light. Within the cave are constellations of glow worms, waterfalls, fossilized oysters the size of dinner plates and huge golden stalactites. There's an even more startling caving expedition to get back to the surface. You're given careful coaching and build up with a 24 m (80 ft) trial run abseil. The tour price includes all equipment and you need to be "moderately" fit.

Located eight kilometers (five miles) west of Highway 3, the Waitomo Caves can be seen in a day, although the region's many walks and horse-trekking tracks deserve an overnight stay. It's a good idea to visit the Waitomo Museum of Caves as an appetizer before visiting the caves, to learn something of the geology, archaeology and fossils you are about to see. It also has information about bush walks at Opapaka Pa and Piripiri, the unique limestone natural bridges at Ruakuri and Mangapohue, and the magnificent Marokopa Falls and can book tours. They can be reached at ((07) 878-7640. In the area, on the road from the main highway to the caves, the Ohaki Maori Village, a relic of a pre-European Maori *pa* with a weaving demonstration center, and the Mountain View Stud Farm, which breeds giant fluffy lovable Angora rabbits and has a "shearing season," are both worth a visit. In Otorotanga, there's a native bird park, where kiwi eggs have been successfully "artificially" hatched.

Where to Stay and Eat
Nearby Waitomo Resort Hotel, ((07) 878-8289, fax: (07) 878-8289, 59 Main North Road, Otorohanga, is a moderate range, country-club style hotel of great rural charm close to the caves. Backpackers might prefer the Hamilton Tomo Group Lodge, ((07) 878-7442 on the Te Anga Road. Within the region is the luxury Puketawai Lodge, ((07) 878-7292, fax: (07) 878-7272, on Puektawai Road, set within private native bush. Mid-price rates cover all meals.

Over a beer at the Roadside Bar, you'll probably meet local cavers who work as guides in the caves. This together with a post office and a few shops, is the Waitomo township. The Merrowvale Tearooms, ((07) 878-7361, two kilometers (one-and-a-quarter miles) from the Waitomo Caves, offer hot lunches, cakes and filter coffee on their verandah. Another place it's good to know about, is **Roselands Restaurant, (** (07) 878-7611, which specializes in gourmet barbecue dishes and has outdoor tables in its tranquil garden.

Access

The Waitomo Caves lie 76 km (47 miles) south-west of Hamilton. InterCity operates daily return tours from Auckland and Rotorua, but this means you are extremely limited for time. The driving distance is roughly three hours from Auckland and two hours from Rotorua.

The Taranaki Route

From the Waitomo Caves, a further 19 km (12 miles) south, **Te Kuiti** is worth stopping at to see "*Tokanganui-o-Noho,*" one of the finest carved Maori maraes still in daily use. It was built by the followers of the Maori resistance fighter, Te Kooti, to thank the local Ngati Maniapoto tribe for protecting their leader when he sought refuge here during the Land Wars.

From Te Kuiti, the road follows a 169 km (105 miles) scenic route to **New Plymouth**, passing rich dairy pasture-land, the Awakino River gorge, and a beautiful coastal headland with cliffs and peaceful bays. After climbing **Mt. Messenger**, the Taranaki countryside, dominated by the extinct volcanic snow peaks of Mt. Egmont, often compared favorably with Mt Fuji, comes into view.

NEW PLYMOUTH

Mt. Egmont itself is worth the trip to New Plymouth, the coastal center of Taranaki, but the hiking and fishing in the area are also inviting. So are the gardens, and many New Zealanders make an annual trip just to visit them in flower.

General Information

The **Tourism Taranaki** office, **(** (06) 757-9909, at 10 Leach Street, can help with all inquiries about accommodation, garden and adventure tours, transport to Mt. Egmont National Park, as well as scenic flights across its summit, coastal walks, Maori *pa* sites, and places to visit. Another useful contact is the **New Plymouth Public Relations Office, (** (06) 758-6086, at 81 Liardet Street. They can put you in touch with farm hosts, private gardens and crafts people and are friendly and helpful.

Access

Air New Zealand has several direct flights daily from Auckland and Wellington, with connections to other centers. The Air New Zealand Travel Centre, **(** (06) 757-9057, is in the Norwich Union Building, at 12–14 Devon Street East. The InterCity depot is on St Aubyn Street, near Egmont Street, **(** (06) 758-7729, while Newmans operate from 32 Queen's Street, **(** (06) 757-5482. Both companies run frequent services between Hamilton and Auckland, Wanganui and Wellington. By road it takes six and a half to seven hours to drive to Auckland or Wellington, and three hours to Wanganui.

What to See

New Plymouth is renowned for its many beautiful gardens, almost all open daily. Close to the town center, **Pukekura Park** lies in a natural valley, landscaped with shaded bush walks, lakes for boating, an underground fernery and waterfall, with many gardens of lavish begonias, azaleas, rhododendrons and orchids. It also has a flying fox. The adjacent **Brooklands Park** has majestic trees and more formal flower beds.

Another lure is the **Pukeiti Rhododendron Trust**, set in 360 hectares (890 acres) nestled against the lower slopes of the mountain. Located 29 km (18 miles) away on Carrington Road, it flowers into an ocean of blossoms between September and November, woven with hybrid rhododendrons, azaleas and primroses. Further up the road at N° 827, visit **Hurworth Homestead**, an idyllic colonial cottage built in 1855 which is a rare survivor of this region's Land Wars when many surrounding towns began as stockades, and is open as a museum from Wednesday to Sunday.

One of the finest landscaped gardens in the country, **Tuapere**, 8 km (5 miles) away at 487 Mangorei Road, was formerly a private home and garden, now a New Zealand Trust Garden. Around its grand Tudor-style house are woodland walks, a marsh garden, streams, lawns, arches, pergolas and varied plant gardens. **Holland Gardens**, on Manaia Road, Kaponga, on the other side of Mt. Egmont, about 15 km (just over nine miles) from Stratford, is another National Trust Garden. All of these gardens in the shadow of Mt. Egmont can be visited easily in a day. But if you have to choose just two, make them Pukeiti and Tuapere.

Back in town, seek out **St. Mary's Church**, on Leach Street, built in 1845, a Gothic-style stone church that was used a lot by early European settlers as they prayed for their safety during the vicious Land Wars. As well as being one of the loveliest churches in the country, it has interesting gravestones of early settlers and soldiers, as well as of one or two Maori chiefs. **The Gables**, in Brooklands Park, is New Zealand's oldest hospital, while **Richmond House**, in Brougham Street, is a tree-fringed furnished colonial homestead

New Plymouth has two exceptional museums. The more traditional **Taranaki Museum** on the corner of Brougham and King streets, has fascinating Maori artifacts of the region's early moa-hunting period and war trophies from the Land Wars, as well as imaginative displays of colonial life. The **Govett-Brewster Art Gallery**, on Queen Street, has the country's best collection of works by the late renowned New Zealand artist Len Lye. Both museums are open from 10:30 am to 5 pm, Tuesday to Friday and 1 pm to 5 pm at weekends.

Where to Stay

There are two particularly nice moderate range hotels. Set within large forested grounds, the **Taranaki Country Lodge**, ((06) 757-7039, fax: (06) 757-1616, at the corner of Devon Street and Henwood Road, has lavishly comfortable rooms, a swimming pool, a fine restaurant, transport into town and excellent facilities for handicapped people. **The Devon**, ((06) 759-9099, fax: (06) 758-2229, at 390 Devon Street, is another fine hotel, and its Governors Restaurant is one of New Plymouth's best.

Farmlodge Taranaki, ((06) 752-3798, on Hickman Road, Urenui, offers luxurious farm-stay accommodation, including exceptional meals and wine for mid-price rates. You can ask for details for less expensive farm-stay places at the Public Relations Office.

Aotea Private Hotel, ((06) 758-2438, at 26 Weymouth Street, is a pleasant inexpensive bed and breakfast inn.

There's a **Backpacker's Hostel**, ((06) 758-7153, at 69 Mill Road, and a good well-serviced camping ground at the **Aaron Court Motel and Caravan Park**, ((06) 758-8712, at 57 Junction Road, State Highway 3.

Where to Eat

New Plymouth's bountiful produce of coastal seafood and rich dairy products means that this is a good region for sampling squid and orange roughy dishes, as well as New Zealand cheeses. One of the most enjoyable places to dine is the **Ratanui Restaurant**, a restored colonial homestead within a large garden, ((06) 753-2800, at 498 Carrington

Road. Open only for dinner, with blazing log fires in winter, the restaurant specializes in venison, wild pork, baby salmon, rabbit and lamb dishes. Reservations are required.

Within the town center, **Bellissimo,** ((06) 758-0398, at 38 Currie Street is open from 5 pm until late for casual suppers, desserts and coffee.

EGMONT NATIONAL PARK

With its massive snowy bulk, Mt. Egmont is the unmistakable emblem of the region. Dormant for the past three centuries, its solitary cone can be reached after a day's relatively easy 2,518 m (8,309 ft) ascent. Encircling the lower slopes of the mountain, Egmont National Park has lush rain forest,

alpine streams and other challenging high altitude slopes for serious climbers. Although not as developed as Mt. Ruapehu, the island's main ski-field, Mt. Egmont attracts skiers to its small field during winter and has good facilities.

Your first stop should be the **National Park Interpretation Centre,** ((06) 765-5457 situated close to the beautiful **Dawson Falls**, reached from the turnoff from the township of Stratford, (where streets are named after William Shakespeare's characters) and is the park's main center. They have details on all walks and longer treks, and can offer guides. This is also the location of the **Dawson Falls Lodge,** ((06) 765-5457, estab-

The crisp, snow-capped vision of Mt. Egmont rises from the lush pasturelands of Taranaki.

lished in 1896, with lovely alpine chalet-style accommodation. Rooms are decorated in a "Swiss" style, with painted wooden four-poster beds, carved natural wood and stag's heads. Views are spectacular — especially when winter carpets fresh, powder-fine snow across the landscape. There's a gymnasium to build up stamina for the slopes and a sauna for when you return. Lodge meals are simple but good. Rates are moderate.

Another place to stay, further down the mountain, is the **Mountain House Motor Lodge**, ((06) 765-6100, fax: (06) 765-6100, on Pembroke Road, 10 km (just over six miles) north of Eltham, near Stratford. It's also moderately priced, with chalet-style rooms and a fine Swiss chef. It's located close to the Plateau car-park which is the starting point for tramping, skiing and summit climbs. The nearby **Manganui Gorge**, which has wooden walkways through moss and herb fields, is one of the mountain's most beautiful short walks.

From **Oakura**, site of a thousand-year old *pa*, Highway 45 traces the spectacularly lonely route around the coast to **Cape Egmont**, with its lighthouse battered by the elements above chalky-white cliffs. You can stay on this road for an hour's journey or so until you reach **Hawera** and the State Highway 3 to Wanganui.

HAWERA

Although it's not an exciting place to stay, Hawera has some rather interesting places to stop and see. The **Tawhiti Museum** on 47 Ohangi Road, is the most extraordinary privately-created museum in the country. Dreamed up by Nigel and Teresa Ogle, and housed in an old cheese factory, the museum features carefully constructed wax models — many of them life-size — that bring to life the history of Taranaki with painstaking accuracy, an enormous achievement. Displays include models of the nearby fourteenth century Turuturu Mokai Pa, complete with miniature tattooed Maoris, and of bloody battles that occurred between the Taranaki Maori tribes and British imperial troops, as well as many vignettes of the daily lives of early settlers. There's also a bush railway that takes passengers on a dramatic recon-

struction of the logging railways that used to operate in Taranaki, complete with life-size figures, colonial-era buildings and an interpretation center set in an old sawmill. A "Bushman's Kitchen" serves great barbecue meals on railway operating days. Ranking with Mt. Egmont as one of Taranaki's highlights, this museum should not be missed. You might want to call and check which days the railway is operating on ((06) 278-6837. They are open every Friday to Monday from 10am to 4 pm.

The other museum is the **Elvis Presley Record Room**, on Argyle Street, a must for Elvis fans, collected by a dedicated "Elvist," Kevin Wasley.

As you drive out of Hawera, drive up to see the impressive site of the pre-European **Turuturu Mokai Pa**, two kilometers (one-and-a-quarter miles) north on Turuturu Road. You see its deeply-carved trenches and underground tunnels, designed for hand-to-hand combat, where many a head has been claimed as a shrunken trophy. In Maori, the name of this pa means literally "heads on sticks."

WANGANUI

Peaceful, wealthy Wanganui lies on the mouth of the country's longest, and many say, most beautiful, river. Before the country was serviced with roads, the Wanganui River was a watery highway. Navigable for 234 km (145 miles) from the coast to Taumaranui, it was a major thoroughfare into the central North Island, and is steeped in both Maori and pioneer history. In the **Wanganui Regional Museum**, you can see the magnificent carved Maori war canoe *Te Mata-o-Hoturoa,* used by fearsome warriors to spring surprise attacks on the British troops during the Land Wars.

Today, the river remains the city's most picturesque feature, able to be explored by jet boat, guided canoe trips, white-water river rafting or by paddleboat steamer. It also provides access to the magical environment of the **Whanganui National Park**, located deep in the forest. Its many walks — from 20 minutes to three days — take you into a paradise of pristine native bush, where streams with brown and rainbow trout run, and there are trails everywhere of wild pigs, goats and fallow deer. Fishing and hunting permits are issued at Department of Conservation offices in Wanganui, Pipiriki and Raethi.

General Information

The **Information Centre**, ((06) 385-3286, at the corner of Guyton and St. Hill streets, can provide all details about seasonal boat trips, excursions, access to Whanganui National Park and accommodation. The **Department of Conservation** office, ((06) 385-2402, is at the corner of Victoria Avenue and Dublin Street. At Pipiriki, the **Whanganui National Park Office**, ((06) 385-4631 has details of forest walks, guided tours and boat tours.

Access

Air New Zealand operates direct daily connections with Auckland, Wellington, Taupo and Whakatane. You can contact their head office, ((06) 385-4089, on the corner of Taupo Quay and Victoria Avenue. The InterCity depot, ((06) 385-4439, is on Taupo Quay, while Newmans, ((06) 385-5566, is located at 156 Ridgeway Street. Both operate services from Auckland and have connections with Palmerston North, Napier and Wellington. There are services north to Rotorua, Tongariro and Taupo, although this requires a transfer at Bulls, on the way to Palmerston North. By road, Wanganui is about two to three hours distance from New Plymouth, Tongariro or Wellington, and about one and a quarter hours from Palmerston North.

What to See

In town, the **Wanganui Regional Museum** on Wicksteed Street, is a fascinating repository of Maori artifacts, with the country's best display of meres, the greenstone clubs used for scalping, and Moa skeletons. Next to the museum, the **Sargeant Gallery** has many water-colors dating from early colonial times. Close to the pretty **Virginia Lake**, **Puketi Church**, a Maori church, looks plain enough from the outside, but the inside is magnificent with carved wood and woven panels. If you have a yearning to see how wealthy early settlers lived, visit the **Waireka Estate** on Papaiti Road, a private museum only open in summer.

River Tours

The best way to enjoy the river is to do as the old-timers did: ride the river. Boats can take visitors into the spectacular upper reaches of the river which can not be accessed from the road. Jet-boat tours operate from Wanganui, Pipiriki and Pungarehu.

Certainly the most sedate way of enjoying the Wanganui River is a cruise aboard the *M.V. Waireka* which makes summer cruises to the Holly Estate Winery, the Waireka Estate and the Upokongaro Country Village. It also offers moonlight cruises which are as lovely as they sound, and rapids adventure trips, which may appeal to those who saw the movie *Fitzcarraldo*. Another river boat, the *Wakapai* offers a 5-day trip from Wanganui to Taumaranui, stopping at several historic river settlements.

Last but not least, the Wanganui is renowned for its white-water river rapids, something that can be experienced by canoe, kayak, and raft. There are so many tours, some involving several days camping alongside the river, and others venturing into the more challenging, thunderous rapids of the nearby **Rangitike River**, that you should check with the Information Centre, who can suggest trips accredited with the Professional Rafting Association.

Where to Stay and Eat

The Victorian-era **Bushy Park**, ((06) 342-9879, at Ka-Iwi, off State Highway 3, 24 km (15 miles) north of Wanganui, is one of New Zealand's most romantic and inexpensive homesteads. Set within a peaceful native bush reserve, it has charming interiors. Guests need to bring their own provisions but can use the big colonial kitchen to cook for themselves.

The most charming place to stay in Wanganui is the **Riverside Tourist Inn**, ((06) 343-2529, at 2 Plymouth Street, a restored colonial home built in 1885, inexpensive and quaint. The moderately-priced **Burwood Manor**, ((06) 345-2180, fax: (06) 345-8711, at 63, Dublin Street, has more facilities, waterbed suites, a restaurant and a swimming pool.

For an especially good meal, go no further than **Cameron House**, ((06) 345-2690, at 291 Wicksteed Street, located in a Victorian-era house with kauri interiors, two dining rooms and a conservatory. They prepare classic New Zealand cuisine with great finesse. More casual and suitable for lunch, the **Riverside Restaurant**, ((06) 347-8656, at 36 Somme Street, overlooks the water. Both have won Taste New Zealand awards.

THE ROAD TO JERUSALEM

Dotted along the Wanganui River are a string of faintly surreal communities with exotic names — **Koriniti** (Corinth), **Atene** (Athens) and **Jerusalem** — in what is

the 77 km (48 miles) drive between Wanganui and Pipiriki, the riverside township bordering the Whanganui National Park, where the road leaves the river.

THE WAIRARAPA REGION

Buttressed by the Tararua Ranges on one side and Lake Wairarapa on the other, the southernmost region of North Island is one of the country's richest farming areas, with endless vistas of verdant pasture-land.

unmistakably a New Zealand landscape. None of them is larger than five buildings; typically with cow sheds, farm-houses and an attractive meeting house. Jerusalem is the best known, because it was here that the country's best known poet, James K. Baxter founded a utopian community in the 1970's, and where his grave now lies. The road to Jerusalem — and the other tiny settlements along the Wanganui River — is slow, winding and partly unsealed. It is also spectacularly scenic in places.

Travelers without their own transport can take the rural delivery bus which makes

The tiny, sleepy settlement of Koroniti on the banks of the Wanganui River.

MASTERTON

Masterton is the region's main center, the venue for the annual International Golden Shears competition in February, a classic showpiece of macho talent that attracts shearers from all over the world.

Within the Masterton area you can explore **Taranaki Forest Park**, with its western access at the end of Norfolk Road. The resident caretaker can offer you advice on where to camp, bush walk, tramp, fish, hunt and swim.

The **Masterton Information Centre**, ((06) 378-7373, is at 5 Dixon Street. If you need a place to stay, the **Station Hotel**, ((06) 378-9319, at 145 Perry Street is a comfortable

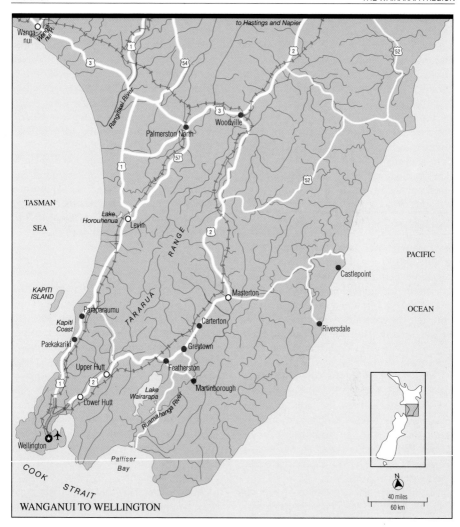

WANGANUI TO WELLINGTON

Victorian-era two-storied lodge with a good restaurant. Or try the **Victoria Guest House**, ((06) 378-0186, at 15 Victoria Street, a restored colonial mansion. Both are inexpensive.

Near Masterton is the **Mt. Bruce National Wildlife Centre**, 28 km (17 miles) north on State Highway 2, where rare and endangered native species are studied and bred. Visual displays tell the intriguing story of New Zealand's isolated varieties of flora and fauna before humans arrived. You'll see kiwis, native bats and such rare native birds as the *takahe, kokako* and the saddleback. Hopefully you will not already have made acquaintance with another species on display: the weta (the world's largest insect), in your camping sleeping bag.

Across to the Pacific coast, **Riverdale** and **Castlepoint** have beautiful beaches for surf-casting and surfing and once a year in March, a beach-race for horses. You can stay slightly inland at **Tinui** at the inexpensively-priced **Tinui Hotel**, ((06) 372-6802. **Carterton** was once a pioneering town but is now an industrial center. **Greytown** has the **Cobble stone's Settler's Museum** where historic buildings, vehicles and farm machinery are on display.

To the south, vineyards flourish in the perfect grape growing conditions of **Martinborough**. This is one of the country's youngest grape growing areas, but the local vineyards have already established an excellent reputation and are delightful to visit.

The road south leads to **Palliser Bay**, an isolated coastal bluff with the eerie mini-Grand Canyon-style rock formations, the **Patangirua Pinnacles** to explore. As you drive out to Cape Palliser, look out for **Ning Nong**, a holiday refuge with dilapidated, bizarre *bachs* or beach homes.

From Featherston, en route to Wellington, you can take a guided kayak tour down the peaceful Ruamahanga River. Call **Kahutara Canoes**, ((06) 308-8453 for details. There is also a distinctly eccentric taxidermy museum slightly out of town.

THE KAPITI COAST

Extending from Foxton to Wellington, the Kapiti Coast is one of the highlights of driving to the capital, with its rugged seacoast backed by mountain forests. If you are taking the *Silver Fern Express*, the train passes through innumerable tunnels strung like beads along the cliffside overlooking crashing surf, with spray splashing against the windows.

Many weekending Wellingtonians head up Highway 1 to the Kapiti Coast's wild, windswept beach resorts, with are dotted with *bachs* or holiday homes and camping grounds. The Cityrail service shuttles between Wellington and has its rail head at Paraparaumu, only 35 minutes drive from Wellington.

From the coast's main town of **Levin**, the lakes **Horowhenua** and **Papaitonga** are only minutes away, with a beautiful bush walk around Lake Papaitonga. Further down the main highway, the **Rangiatea Maori Church** at **Otaki** is worth a stop, with its European exterior and intricately carved Maori interior. A little further on, at Waikanae, the **Nga Manu Sanctuary** on Ngarara Road is an impressive native bird park, with bush walks and picnic areas.

Paraparaumu got its name when a Maori war party found only *parapara* or "scraps" at an *umu* or "earth oven" here. Today the beach town is a popular resort, and deserves a stop to see the **Southward Car Museum** with its giant private collection of vintage cars and vehicles, located off Otaihanga Road. Another place to visit is the **Lindale Farm**, on Main Road North,

to sample its delicious cheeses and ice-cream.

Constantly in view as you drive along the coast, is **Kapiti Island**, about six kilometers (nearly four miles) offshore. Now a bird sanctuary for protected species, the island was once the home of the fierce nineteenth century Maori warrior Te Rauparaha. You can visit the island by arrangement with the Department of Conservation.

The last major halt before entering Upper Hutt, and the fringes of Wellington, is **Paekakariki**, which has a tramway museum in Queen Elizabeth Park. Another treasure-house for rail-buffs is the **Paekakariki Railway Museum** on State Highway 1.

WELLINGTON

Sprawling around a magnificent harbor at the very end of the North Island, New Zealand's capital is framed by a natural amphitheater of steep green hills, dotted with colorful wooden colonial-era houses which perch precariously on narrow zigzag streets. The city's core of gleaming modern skyscrapers is softened by a green belt of bush track walkways that thread upwards to vertiginous hilltop suburbs and vantage points such as Mt. Victoria, which show off breathtaking harbor views by day and a glittering city-scape by night.

Maoris maintain that Kupe, the legendary Polynesian explorer, discovered Wellington harbor. His descendants lived here for centuries before the New Zealand Company decided in 1840 to create a settlement that followed the planned colonization theories of Edward Gibbon Wakefield. In 1865, Wellington was named capital, shifting power from Auckland. Victorian influences live on in the clusters of gracious homes and quirky cottages that cling to bush-clad hillsides in suburbs like Oriental Bay, Thorndon and Eastbourne.

With 350,000 residents, Wellington is a tiny city by international, if not New Zealand standards. Yet it is the country's political and business muscle, and the base for its major corporations and industries. Conservatism and stoicism are strong personality traits of the city, possibly in response to the capital's frequently blustery weather, with winds sweeping straight in from the Roaring Forties. This is why so many of Wellington's bureaucrats seem to have their ties permanently blown around their ears.

ACCESS

Wellington is the hub of the country's domestic air network, and the airport lies eight kilometers (five miles) from the city center. Air New Zealand and Qantas operate flights to Australia, while Air New Zealand, Ansett New Zealand, Mt. Cook Airlines, Eagle Air and Air Nelson link the capital with major destinations throughout the country. An airport bus shuttles between the city and the terminal, with stops along Lampton Quay. For airport inquires, call ((04) 388-9900. The Super Shuttle, ((04) 387-8787, provides door-to-door service, and works out to be much cheaper than a taxi.

Wellington Railway Station, ((04) 472-5409, on Waterloo Quay, is almost right opposite the Beehive. The *Silver Fern* operates between Auckland and Wellington, and the *Endeavour* runs to Napier, a five-and-a-half hour trip.

InterCity, ((04) 472-5399, operates from the railway station, while Newmans, ((04) 385-1149, departs from the main bus station, directly opposite. Mt. Cook, ((04) 388-5020, has a terminal on the corner of Taranaki Street and Courtenay Place, but also stops opposite the railway station. Together they provide a comprehensive link-up with most destinations in the country. There's a free shuttle service from the railway station to the InterIslander passenger ferry link to the South Island, 35 minutes before scheduled departure. More information about transport networks and the Cook Strait Ferry service can be found in TRAVELER'S TIPS under GETTING AROUND.

GENERAL INFORMATION

The **City Information Centre**, ((04) 373-5063, is located at the Town Hall on Wakefield Street, and can take care of all inquires and book tours. They have detailed pamphlets on city bus and train routes, and

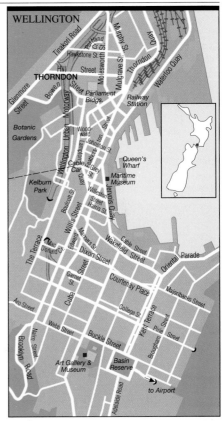

walks and treks within the Wellington region. While there, pick up a copy of the free weekly information broadsheet *Capital Times*, which has listings for restaurants, nightlife, theater and all kinds of activities. The **Department of Conservation**, ((04) 471-0726, at 59 Boulcott Street, has information on walkways and parks in the Wellington region, although much of this is also available at the City Information Centre.

WHAT TO SEE

Before deciding what you want to do in Wellington, why not admire its spectacular harbor setting from the top of **Mt. Victoria**, where there is a windswept lookout 200 m (660 ft) above the city. Ask at the bus terminal for the leaflet about the route up to Mt. Victoria and the walks you can do from the summit down to Courtenay Place, past delightful colonial-era buildings.

The city center is concentrated in a semicircular sweep from Parliament House to Courtenay Place, from Lampton Quay through Willis and Manners Streets, presided over by the corporate towers of The Terrace. You'll notice **Parliament House**, better known as **The Beehive**, as much for its whorl-like shape as for the image it creates of bustling, angrily-buzzing politicians. It's open for guided tours, or you can turn up to attend a 2 pm session when parliament is sitting. This is inclined to be quite raucous, with colorful personal abuse exchanged between government, and opposition members. You can call ((04) 471-9457

for details about the tours. Nearby, the old **Government Buildings** (1867) are especially interesting. Next to the Todjaji Temple in Nara, Japan, they are — with 150 rooms — the largest wooden construction in the world.

From here, **Lampton Quay** has arcades, shops and department stores. Enter **Cable Car Lane**, for a 10 minute, 121 m (440 ft) ascent up a Victorian-era tramway to the **Botanic Gardens**, which has views across the city and the harbor. Once there, you can take a meandering route through the gardens, created in 1869. The Tree Walk contains many native trees and terraced grottoes. At the foot of the hill, are the **Lady Norwood Rose Garden** and the **Begonia House**. Within the gardens, the **Carter Observatory** is open for viewing every clear Tuesday night between March and October between 7:30 pm and 9:30 pm. There are many beautiful walks through the gardens, either back to the city, the Victoria University campus or to the suburb of Thorndon.

Thorndon

The most picturesque colonial suburb of Wellington is Thorndon, a few minutes walk from the Botanic Gardens, with its restored village, many old nineteenth century wooden cottages and beautiful wooded walks. As you walk down from the Botanic Gardens along **Tinakori Road**, you'll enter the tiny shopping village, dotted with interesting galleries, shops and cafes. One of them, the **Millwood Gallery**, sells a fold-out pamphlet *Thorndon Walk* which is a detailed guide to the area.

Historic Buildings

Four buildings in Wellington have museum status and are charming places to visit. Admirers of the New Zealand writer Katherine Mansfield (1888–1923), who spent most of her life as an expatriate in Europe, will be interested to visit the **Katherine Mansfield Birthplace**, (1888) at 25 Tinakori Road, in Thorndon. Many of her finest works draw upon memories of her New Zealand childhood, and this house is mentioned in *The Aloe, Prelude*, and *A Birthday*. It has been faithfully restored as a Victorian family home of the late 1880's. Period furniture, photographs, videos and tapes create a poignant evocation of the writer's life. It's open daily, except Monday, from 10 am to 4 pm. It can be a tiresome place to reach on foot, with blustery winds sweeping across Tinakori Road. Better to take the N° 14 bus from Lampton Quay and stop at Park Street, a minute's walk away.

From here, it's a ten minute walk to **Old St Paul's**, (1866) on Mulgrave Street, probably the best-loved of Wellington's early wooden churches. Designed by the vicar of the parish, the Reverend Frederick Thatcher, it is a fine example of the Early English Gothic style. The church has an atmosphere of peace and stillness, with lovely interiors, stained glass and gleaming brass. Open daily from 10:30 am to 4:30 pm, and on Sundays from 1 pm to 4:30 pm.

Also within the city's heart is **Antrim House** (1905) at 63 Boulcott Street, an impressive Edwardian mansion built for a wealthy shoe manufacturer. Inside you can admire its fine kauri and totara paneling, embossed ceilings and stained glass windows. Visitors are welcome to stroll in the grounds. Open weekdays during office hours, Antrim House is also the base for the New Zealand Historic Places Trust.

In the suburb of Brooklyn, at N°68 Nairn Street, is a restored **pioneer cottage** (1858) which gives an insight into how an artisan's family lived in colonial Wellington. One of the city's oldest cottages, it is completely furnished down to items of clothing and household articles. Open weekdays from 10 am to 4 pm, and weekends 1 pm to 4:30 pm. You can reach it by a N° 7 bus, stopping at Webb Street, just below Nairn Street.

In the inner city, seek out **Plimmer House**, built in the 1870's, a small architectural gem among the high-rise commercial buildings of Boulcott Street.

Around the Bays

Oriental Bay is the city's best-loved seafront promenade, lined with Norfolk pines, old wooden houses and the odd cafe. Its old grandstand has been converted into a bar and restaurant and its beach becomes crowded at the hint of good weather. By car, explore the 30 km (19 miles) **Marine Drive**, which starts from Oriental Bay and continues in an undulating curve around many beaches, bays and little settlements snuggled under rock faces, with **Island Bay** one of the prettiest. As you reach **Miramar Peninsula**, the coast becomes especially wild and rocky, attracting skin-divers. At **Red Rocks** you can see seals basking at their winter colony. From here, a well-marked coastal track leads to **Sinclair Head**, a six kilometer (nearly four mile) windswept but invigorating walk. From here, on fine days, you can see the South Island.

Across the Bay

On a summer's day there's nothing more pleasant than to take a ferry across to **Day's Bay**, the principal beach in **Eastbourne**, an area of small communities along the Eastern Bays otherwise reached by driving through Lower Hutt. Katherine Mansfield describes her childhood home here in her story *At The Bay*. Fringed with Norfolk pines, this is a perfect swimming beach, backed by seafront colonial mansions, which also perch in

dense forest in neighboring hillsides. You can dine in style at **At The Bay**, linger over cappuccino at the **Blue Penguin Cafe**, browse in craft galleries and just enjoy the peaceful outlook. Ferries shuttle between Queen's Wharf and Day's Bay five times daily, and you can check the timetable on ((04) 499-1273. The trip takes about 30 minutes. There are a variety of pleasant walks, including one to Butterfly Creek. Just south of Eastbourne, the road ends and the seven kilometers (just over four miles) track to remote **Pencarrow Lighthouse**, New Zea-

land's oldest, begins. It operated from 1859 to 1935 and was manned for a time by the country's only woman lighthouse keeper.

Museums and Galleries

The **National Museum and Art Gallery** on Buckle Street, near the Basin Reserve, is reached by a short, steep climb. The museum contains many fascinating Maori, Pacific and New Zealand artifacts, and extensive natural history and marine science displays. In the Maori Hall stands a perfectly intact, carved mid-nineteenth century *whare*, or meeting house from Poverty Bay, the finest of its kind. There's also a reconstructed moa and a large pierced stone said to be the anchor used by Kupe, the legendary Maori explorer, while there are also numerous relics of Captain Cook's voyage here. Make sure you see the Bird Hall, the best of its kind in the country. The art gallery concentrates on the

OPPOSITE: Old Government Buildings in Wellington. ABOVE: The Beehive, Wellington's symbol of government.

works of foremost New Zealand painters, such as Colin McCahon and Rita Angus, but has a collection of British paintings, Italian prints and works by Rembrandt and Durer. It's open daily from 10 am to 4: 45 pm.

Down by Queens Wharf, the **Maritime Museum** has an extensive collection of maritime memorabilia, including a step-in hull of a nineteenth century Union Company steam ship's teak captain's cabin. Fans of the game will enjoy the **Cricket Museum**, situated in the Old Grandstand at the Basin Reserve, with its reverential show-

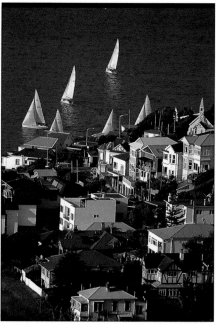

cases, such as the Richard Hadlee Collection, with items of the batsman's clothing and gear. The **New Zealand Crafts Council** has a gallery at 22 The Terrace. The **Petone Settler's Museum**, on The Esplanade, Petone, which is open from 12 noon to 4 pm Tuesdays to Fridays, 1 pm to 5 pm weekends. In the neighborhood, the **Dowse Art Gallery**, on Laings Road in Lower Hutt, has a strong New Zealand decorative arts collection, particularly concentrating on ceramics.

A Park and the Zoo

Otari Native Plant Museum is probably unique — the world's largest open air "collection" of native plants with over 1,200 spe-

cies, hybrids and cultivars. Walking trails through the park cover a distance of 10 km (just over six miles), and the shortest trail takes about 30 minutes, but even so, the experience is just like walking through a secluded forest, and fantails, wood pigeons and kingfishers can been seen from the bush tracks. The main entrance is at the corner of Wilton Road and Gloucester Street, and you can take the N° 14 Wilton bus which takes 20 minutes from the city center.

Wellington Zoo lies off Mansfield Street in Newtown, the first to be established in New Zealand, with a nocturnal kiwi house and a wide variety of native fauna and other wildlife. You can get there on bus N° 11, which leaves from the railway station. Don't forget to check out the *capybaras*, the world's largest rodent! Also at the zoo are miniature train rides, gifts, snacks and an education resource center.

The Hutt Valley

Within 10 minutes drive from Central Wellington, the Hutt Valley extends from the Petone side of Wellington harbor to the Rimutaka Ranges, about 30 km (19 miles) away. Within the valley's boundaries are the outer suburbs of **Lower Hutt**, **Upper Hutt**, **Eastbourne** and **Wainuiomata**, threaded by the Hutt River, where you can go kayaking, jet-boating, rafting and fishing. Lower Hutt is the main shopping center, with the **Dowse Art Gallery**, the **Mitchell Park Rose Gardens**, the **Settler's Museum** and the **Settler's Market** in Petone all within easy reach.

WHERE TO STAY

Mid-price

Parkroyal, ((04) 472-2722, fax: (04) 472-4724, on the corner of Featherston and Grey streets, right in the city center, is Wellington's newest and most impressive international-standard hotel. It has superb facilities, including several bars and restaurants, a health club and board-room. Marginally less flashy, but still vying for top hotel status, the **Plaza International Hotel**, ((04) 473-3900, fax: (04) 473-3929, at 148–176 Wakefield Street, has all the luxury features of an international-standard hotel, and the city's only 24-hour coffee shop. **Wellington Parkroyal**, ((04) 472-2722, fax: (04) 472-4724, at 360 Oriental Parade, another of the New Zealand's prestigious Parkroyal chain, has splendid harbor views. Close by, the **Bay Plaza Hotel**, ((04) 385-7799, fax: (04) 385-2936, also overlooks Oriental Bay, 10 minutes' walk from Courtenay Place.

The following three hotels all have moderate "corporate" rates for business travelers, but are otherwise mid-priced.

Quality Inn Willis Street, ((04) 385-9819, fax: (04) 385-9811, at 355 Willis Street; **Quality Inn Plimmer Towers**, ((04) 473-3750, fax: (04) 473-6329, The Terrace; **Quality Inn Oriental Bay**, ((04) 385-0279, fax: (04) 384-5324, 73 Roxburgh Street, Mt. Victoria.

Moderate

Wellington has a host of hotels that cater especially for business travelers, with excellent facilities, (restaurants, bars, business centers, guest car park, speedy dry-cleaning) and often quite reasonable rates. Here is a selection:

West Plaza Hotel, ((04) 473-1440, fax: (04) 473-1454, right in the city center at 110–116 Wakefield Street. **James Cook Hotel**, ((04) 472-5865, fax: (04) 473-1875, on The Terrace, is considered very swish by Wellingtonians, with its superb Joseph Banks restaurant, located five minutes walk from the Beehive. **Museum Hotel**, ((04) 385-2809, fax: (04) 385-2483, at 51–61 Cable Street, is very cozy, with nice decor and spectacular harbor views. **Terrace Regency Hotel**, ((04) 385-9829, at 345 The Terrace, also has a gymnasium, heated indoor swimming pool and Swedish-style sauna. **St. George Hotel**, at the corner of Willis and Boulcott Streets, ((04) 473-9139 (fax: same number), reduces its rates by almost 50 percent for its weekend "specials:" $68 for a double room from Friday to Sunday nights.

Portland Towers, ((04) 473-2208, fax: (04) 473-3892, at the corner of Hawkestone Street and Portland Crescent. **Airport Hotel**, ((04) 387-2189, Kemp Street, Kilbirnie, has full restaurant and bar, and free airport shuttle bus, as well as a courtesy coach to the city.

At the lower end of the moderate range, **Trekkers**, ((04) 385-2153, fax: (04) 382-8873, at Upper Cuba Street, off Vivian Street, is a

large motel, with a restaurant, spa, sauna and good amenities for handicapped guests.

Bed and Breakfast Lodges and Private Hotels

The following recommendations are all within easy walking distance of the city. **Tinakori Lodge**, ((04) 473-3478, fax: (04) 472-5554, at 182 Tinakori Road, is an outstanding choice, a pretty two-storied colonial house with cozy facilities within historic Thorndon, close to the Botanic Gardens and the former home of an early prime

minister. The moderate rates include lavish breakfasts, daily newspapers and lovely rooms with TV. **Victoria**, ((04) 385-8512, at 58 Pirie Street, **Richmond Guest House**, ((04) 385-8529, at 116 Brougham Street, and **Mansfield Court Hotel**, ((04) 389-9478, at 377 Mansfield Street, are all good quality inexpensive choices. The **Terrace Travel Hotel**, ((04) 382-9506, at 291 The Terrace, is an inexpensive "find," with good amenities and privacy. **Halswell Lodge**, ((04) 385-0196, fax: (04) 385-0503, at 21 Kent Terrace, offers self-contained rooms at inexpensive rates, with a minute's walk from Courtenay

ABOVE: Capital dwellers against a colorful mural backdrop. OPPOSITE: Oriental Bay in Wellington.

Place. The **Rosemere Lodge,** ((04) 384-3041, at 6 MacDonald Crescent, is right in the town center.

Motels

The following recommendations have been selected for their proximity to the city center, and are moderately-priced:

Apollo Motel, ((04) 484-8888, fax: (04) 485-1849, at 49 Majoribanks Street. **Aroha Motel and Cobo Lodge,** ((04) 472-6206, fax: (04) 471-0634, at 222 The Terrace. **Sharella Motor Inn**, ((04) 472-3823, fax: (04) 472-3887, at 20 Glenmore Street, is right opposite the entrance to the Botanic Gardens with its own restaurant and bar. Finally, **The Villa**, ((04) 484-5697, fax: (04) 485-7215, Upper Willis Street, 1 Brooklyn Road, is more like a private residence, with off-street parking.

Backpackers

Rowena's Lodge, ((04) 385-7872, at 115 Brougham Street, is a colonial building close to Mt Victoria and the city center, with a friendly ambience. Another restored colonial building, **Wellington Hostel,** ((04) 373-6271, at 40 Tinakori Road, has a great location, with all basic amenities. The **Beethoven House,** ((04) 384-2226, at 89 Brougham Street, is delightfully eccentric, with the composer's music played non-stop, beginning very early in the morning as a means of beckoning guests to the breakfast table. Run by Allen Goh, the lodge is very characterful and non-smoking, with no prominent sign outside except a tiny "BH."

Camping Grounds

The best choice is the **Rimutaka State Forest Park,** ((04) 564-3066, fax: (04) 564-8551, on the Coast Road at Wainuiomata, has excellent facilities, located close to natural wilderness.

Closer to town is the **Hutt Valley Holiday Park,** ((04) 568-5913, at 95 Hutt Park Road, set amongst *pohutakawa* trees between Eastbourne's beaches and Lower Hutt's shops.

WHERE TO EAT

Wellington has quite a large number of exceptional restaurants, and over recent years, many specializing in ethnic cuisines have opened. Wine bars and open-late cafes are also becoming a much more widespread trend in a city that has traditionally been seen as conservative but is fast matching the pace of Auckland. As the stomping ground of the parliamentarians, diplomats and many influential visitors who oil the country's cogs, the capital has several very select restaurants, where you can expect impeccable food, presentation, service and surroundings.

Expensive

Pierre's, ((04) 472-6238, at 342 Tinakori Road, is one of Wellington's long-standing favorites, with very stylish French-influenced cuisine amidst intimate cozy decor. Another restaurant much favored by parliamentarians is **Joseph Banks,** ((04) 499-9500, at 147 The Terrace, in the James Cook Hotel and named after Captain Cook's botanist colleague. Their innovative, daily menu is complemented by New Zealand's best wines. **Fraser's,** ((04) 473-0342, in the Shamrock Complex, at 230 Tinakori Road, has delightful surroundings in a historic building, with antique lamps and prints of early Wellington. Here, traditional New Zealand cuisine is served with a French influence, and a good selection of wines. **Champerelle,** ((04) 385-0928, at 6 Edward Street, has been rated as Wellington's best French restaurant, with a formal chintzy atmosphere. **Elephant & Castle,** ((04) 385-1974, at the corner of Cambridge and Kent terraces, is much more informal, with a jazz-oriented background. Strange as it may seem, what you are dining in is a converted public convenience, which accounts for its long tram-like shape. Its extensive menu has all sorts of Asian and European influences, matched by the pick of New Zealand's wines, and decadent desserts are a specialty.

Moderate

Top recommendations go to **Tinakori Bistro,** ((04) 499-0567, at 328 Tinakori Road, for its congenial surroundings, creative menu and nice touches like home-baked bread. Some of their best dishes include grilled fish with scallops, mussels with a bernaise sauce and chocolate fudge cake with espresso ice-cream. It's closed on Sundays. **The Settle-**

ment, ((04) 385-8920, at 155 Willis Street, is another Wellington favorite, with a cozy, early colonial atmosphere completed by its cobbled courtyard, kitchen sideboards, dried flowers and wooden tables. You can expect traditional New Zealand cuisine, with particularly good hearty soups, lamb and seafood dishes. Excellent Italian food is served at **Bellissimo Trattoria**, ((04) 499-1154, Dukes Arcade, Willis Street, which makes its own pasta, bread, Italian sausage and gelato ice cream. **Marbles**, ((04) 475-8490, in The Villas at 87 Upland Road, in Kelburn, is set in a lovely restored building and its innovative menu specializes in unusual taste sensations with lots of fruit sauces: rock melon and walnut cream cheese with strawberry dressing, chicken livers with raspberry vinaigrette, for example.

There are plenty of good Asian restaurants. One of the best is **Thiphayathep**, ((04) 499-4488, at 36 Cuba Street, which serves authentic Thai cuisine. **Angkor**, ((04) 384-9423, at 43 Dixon Street, serves Cambodian food, while **Yangtze**, ((04) 472-8802, at the corner of Jervois Quay and Willeston Street, serves good Cantonese cuisine. **Mandalay**, ((04) 384-7389, at 50 Dixon Street, specializes in Burmese dishes, ranging from Volcano Soup — spicy prawns, fish balls and tofu cooked in a clay pot — to the unusual avocado milkshakes.

For a secluded special lunch, try **Grain of Salt**, ((04) 384-8642, at 232 Oriental Parade, or the **Pate Shop**, ((04) 472-1727, in Turnbull House on Bowen Street, which serves daily varieties of pate. **At the Bay**, ((04) 562-6882, at Day's Bay, has an idyllic beachfront setting, especially lovely during the summer with its outdoor balcony. They serve light Mediterranean cuisine and have live jazz on Wednesday nights. If you're coming by ferry, you'll have to come for lunch, since the last ferry back to the city is 6 pm weekdays and 5 pm weekends. Closed Mondays.

Cafe Society

Currently in vogue is the **Aro Street Cafe**, ((04) 384-4970, at 90 Aro Street, Wellington's district of delightful early settler's buildings. It serves all kinds of ethnic food dishes, and has live music Thursday to Saturday nights. It's open until 11 pm every night. At the other end of town, **Cafe Paradiso**, ((04) 384-3887, at 20 Courtenay Place, has a French-influenced menu and stylish interiors. Another popular open-late cafe restaurant is **Alphabet City**, ((04) 384-7544, at 90–92 Dixon Street, which also has a bar section, and serves late night suppers from 11 pm on Thursdays, Fridays and Saturdays. **The Sugar Club**, ((04) 384-6466, at Vivian Street, another open-late cafe, serves some Cajun dishes amongst a varied menu, but desserts are their forte.

Armadillos, ((04) 385-8221, at 129 Willis Street, is another late-night restaurant bar, with a spirited atmosphere and Cajun food.

More sedate, **Konditorei Aida**, ((04) 385-7821, at 181 Cuba Street, serves sumptuous cream-laced Austrian cakes, strudels and coffees, as well as Continental breakfasts and lunches of paprika pork casserole.

Good lunch-time places include **Caffe l'Affare**, ((04) 389-9748, at 27 College Street and the **Courtyard Cafe**, ((04) 372-5251, at 324 Tinakori Road, is a very restful morning-tea and lunch place, set in a grotto-like cobbled courtyard with patio furniture. It's a perfect place to stop after exploring the Botanic Gardens and Thorndon, and they serve very luscious cakes. **City Limits**, ((04) 472-6468, at 122 Wakefield Street, is open from 7am until late, with healthy salads, soups, and cakes.

Another place for coffee and cakes is **Cafe Lido**, ((04) 499-6666, at the corner of Victoria and Wakefield streets, with its fifties style decor, well-thumbed back-copies of the *New Yorker* and dangling papier mache goddess. There are two other open-late coffee bars worth mentioning: **Kahlo's**, ((04) 499-8408, at 103 Willis Street, a little shrine to Mexican artist Frida Kahlo, and **Expressaholic**, ((04) 472-5145, at 85 Willis Street.

Sol, ((04) 801-6068, 1st Floor, Oaks Plaza on Dixon Street, serves Mexican food, *tapas* and all manner of Iberian cocktails. **The Kiwi Rock Cafe**, ((04) 472-1555, at 97 Willis Street, has a fifties juke-box atmosphere, great faddish decor and serves American-style dishes. Next door, **Route 66**, ((04) 473-6688, has the city's widest array of beers, and decor that complements the Kiwi Rock

Cafe: a suspended Harley Davidson motorbike and a model Patriot missile.

Wine Bars

Beaujolais, ((04) 472-1471, at 11 Woodward Street, is the city's liveliest bar, with an extensive wine list that includes New Zealand's top labels, with all except the $100 a bottle variety sold by the glass. Snacks and light meals are served. There's a Mediterranean-feel to its cave-like interior, white parchment walls, polished jarrah (Australian native wood) floors and wrought-iron

chairs. Open from 11:30 am until late. **Aqua Vitae**, ((04) 801-7020, at 156 Willis Street, has over a 100 varieties of wine, with 90 percent of these New Zealand wines, all sold by the glass. Light meals are available.

City Specials

If you find yourself desperately seeking breakfast or good coffee, find **The Buttery**, ((04) 473-0061, at 7 Woodward Street. It opens at 6:30 am. The other contender is **Cafe Cuisine**, ((04) 473-0025, 4 Plimmers Lane, which opens at 7 am to serve waffles

ABOVE LEFT: Wellington's colorful and dichotomous skyline. ABOVE RIGHT: Playing cricket at Andrew Park and OPPOSITE the peaceful Botanic Gardens.

with bacon and maple syrup and other decadent starts to the day.

ENTERTAINMENT AND NIGHTLIFE

Wellington has quite a lively performing art scene. It's the base for the New Zealand Royal Ballet Company and the New Zealand Symphony Orchestra, and there are several venues for live theater. The modernistic glass and metal **Michael Fowler Centre**, in Wakefield Street, is the country's largest and most impressive auditorium. Reper-

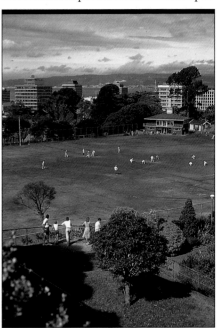

tory theaters include **Downstage Theatre**, at the corner of Courtenay Place and Cambridge Terrace; **Circa Theatre**, at 1 Harris Street; the **Depot Theatre**, at 12 Alpha Street and **Bats Theatre** at 1 Kent Street. Every two years, in March, Wellington holds a three-week International Festival of the Arts, featuring some 30 performances.

A selection of Wellington's best pubs include the **Greta Point Tavern**, at Evans Bay Parade, which has live music on Friday and Saturday nights; **The Caledonian 2**, at 1 Adelaide Road in Newton; **The Featherston Tavern**, at the corner of Featherston and Johnston streets; and the **Brunswick Arms Tavern**, at the corner of Willis and Vivian streets.

Two nightclubs dominate the club scene of Wellington: **Clare's**, on Garnett Street, and **Arena**, on Wakefield Street, worth visiting for its thirties-style design alone.

Late at night, Wellington's Vivian Street area is the city's main red light district, where stoical street-walkers brave the winds.

SHOPPING

The main shopping stretch is found between Lampton Quay and Willis Street, with its highlights being **Kirkcaldies** de-

119 Willis Street is Wellington's best book shop, while the book shop at the foyer level of the **National Library** on Molesworth Street sells prints, antique engravings and old maps.

Wakefield Market, a three-storied warren of stalls, at the corner of Jervois Quay and Taranaki Street, is open every Friday from 11 am to 6 pm and during the weekends from 10 am to 5 pm. Also worth visiting is the **Settler's Village Market**, at the corner of Hutt Road and Railway Avenue in Lower Hutt, which is open Thursday to Sunday from 10 am to 4:30 pm.

partment store and the **Cuba Mall**. Look out for **Tala's South Pacific Centre**, at 106 Victoria Street, which has Polynesian fabrics, beautifully woven baskets, masks and carvings from Papua New Guinea, and Samoan lei necklaces. You can also buy tapes on how to perform Maori action dances! The **David N. White Gallery**, at 149 Willis Street, specializes in Pacific, Asiatic and African ethnic art, and is a good place to browse.

Otherwise, Thorndon has Wellington's best shops. **Mostly Floral**, 324 Tinakori Road, sells delightful Victorian-style gifts, while the **Tinakori Gallery**, next door, sells New Zealand fine art, antique prints and rare maps. **Millwood Gallery**, at N° 291B, is also an excellent book shop. **Unity Books**, at

TOURS

Wally Hammond Tours, ℭ (04) 472-8869, offer one man's characterful, often hilarious personal views on Wellington's foibles, covering the city's main sights in two and a half hours, departing at 10 am and 2 pm. Adults cost $21, children $10.50. At a comparable price and time-frame, **City Scenic Tours**, ℭ (04) 385-9955, departs at 2 pm. Both tours leave from outside the City Information Centre and explore the city's varied attractions, coastline, the harbor and surrounding hills. Ask about tours to the neighboring regions of Martinborough, the Wairarapa, the Rimutaka State Forest and along the Kapiti Coast.

South Island

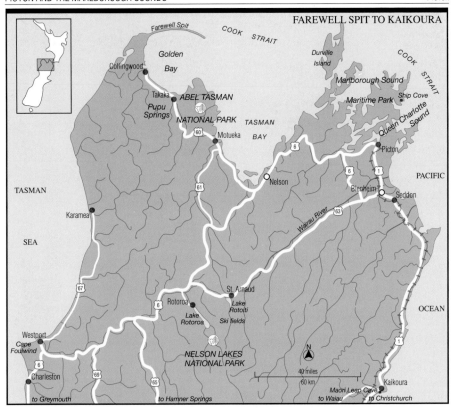

FAREWELL SPIT TO KAIKOURA

SOUTH ISLANDERS call their home "the Mainland." The Maoris named it *"Te Waka a Maui"* or "Maui's canoe," and later *"Te Wahi Pounamu,"* the "place of beautiful greenstone." Larger than the North Island and less populated, the South Island is also crammed with what is arguably more spectacular scenery. The pure variety of its geological repertoire is quite staggering, with mighty glaciers advancing into sub-tropical rain forests, snow-covered mountain peaks towering above coastal beaches, and high alpine passes descending into tranquil lake districts washed in autumnal colors.

Also located in the South Island are the cities of Christchurch and Dunedin. Their Victorian architecture and rich cultural heritage, in the case of the former, English influenced, and the latter, Scottish influenced, is at the root of their appeal. Though they may lack the cosmopolitan feel of Auckland or even Wellington, they are both quite charming and certainly worth a visit.

The South Island is easily reached by the InterIslander ferry and by air from Wellington.

PICTON AND THE MARLBOROUGH SOUNDS

PICTON

Located at the head of Queen Charlotte Sound, the busy little port town of Picton is the southern terminus of the inter-island ferry. Not much has changed since Katherine Mansfield described Picton's cottage-dotted bay as just like "shells on the lid of a box." Although quaint, it's not really a place to linger long, unless you are awaiting a ferry connection to a North Island.

It is worth visiting the **Smith Memorial Museum** on the foreshore, which specializes in whaling relics, and displays items salvaged from the wreck of the Soviet cruise liner *Mikhail Lermontov*, which went down in the Marlborough Sounds in 1986. On each side of Picton harbor is a historic ship: the black hull of the *Edwin Fox*, built in 1853 for the East India Company, later used as a troop transport vessel for the Crimea War and for carrying convicts from England to Australia, now awaiting restoration. On the other side of the harbor is the turn-of-the-century *Echo*, now used as the Marlborough Cruising Club's headquarters.

In Picton, the **Visitors Information Centre**, ((03) 573-7513, is close to the ferry building. It has maps, information on boat cruises and walks in the region. The **Department of Conservation** office, ((03) 573-7582, on the first floor of the Mariners Mall on High Street, has leaflets on the Marlborough Sounds Maritime Park, and walks through nearby Mt. Richmond Forest Park. **Linkwater Lodge**, ((03) 574-2507, on Queen Charlotte Drive, is a pretty, characterful home with delightful moderately-priced rooms, with big fluffy beds, Victorian drapes and lots of windows to let the light stream in. Another good choice is **Admiral's Lodge**, ((03) 573-6590, on Waikawa Road, which is a charming comfortable moderately-priced guest-house.

But better to leave Picton in search of more secluded coves.

Useful Contacts

Skyferry, ((03) 573-7888; Wellington ((04) 388-8380, operates regular alternative flights to and from Wellington. The short flight costs $45 (one way) and operates about six times a day. The Picton airstrip is at Koromiko, eight kilometers (five miles) away, connected by shuttle bus.

Float Air Picton, ((03) 573-6433, also flies to Wellington and costs $46 one way, and operates local and scenic flights around the Marlborough Sounds and to Lake Rotoiti.

THE MARLBOROUGH SOUNDS

The **Marlborough Sounds Maritime Park** is an idyllic, unspoilt playground indented by dozens of secluded bays, pristine beaches and blue inlets. Seen from the air, they form a remarkable jigsaw of green islands and islets against clear crystal sea, a vast drowned valley. These sheltered waterways meander for more than 960 km (595 miles) and many of the perfect spots they contain can only be reached by boat.

The Marlborough Sounds has many associations with early explorers and whalers.

Captain Cook visited the Marlborough Sounds five times, spending a total of about 100 days in and around **Ship Cove**, hoisting the British flag there on January 15, 1770.

General Information

Picton Visitors Information Centre and Department of Conservation office should answer most queries and can supply detailed maps, well marked with beach picnic spots and walkways. If you don't have time to sample the Sounds by leisurely launch, there are a number of roads which run alongside the waterways and give some idea of their beauty, including Queen Charlotte Drive and Kenepuru Road, which goes out to Te Mahia and Portage, and continues on to Waitaria and St Omer, with spider-thin, winding unsealed tracks leading down to the remote areas of Crail Bay, Elsie Bay and Manaroa.

Picton has plenty of charter boats available for cruising, sailing, diving and fishing.

Where to Stay

In Queen Charlotte Sound, 27 km (17 miles) from Picton, on its own private beach, **Punga Cove Tourist Resort**, ((03) 573-4561, fax: (03) 573-7926, in Endeavour Inlet, has natural wood chalets which can accommodate up to eight people, linked to the main lodge by native bush pathways. Meals are excellent, leaning heavily towards fresh scallops, blue cod, crayfish and venison. Rates are inexpensive. They offer a water taxi service to and from Picton, $58 per person return. The **Portage Hotel**, ((03) 573-4309, fax: (03) 573-4309, in Lochmara Bay, has its own private jetty in the tranquil Kenepuru Sounds. This mid-priced resort also has very cheap bunk accommodation, and offers sailing, wind-surfing and fishing activities, as well as a spa pool and gym. It can be reached by road, boat or floatplane from Picton.

Hopewell Cottages, ((03) 573-4300, also in Lochmara Bay, has inexpensive self-contained cottages, while cheaper accommodation is found at the **St. Omer Guest House**, ((03) 573-4086.

OVERLEAF: Tranquil waters and mystical fog envelope a boat in Queen Charlotte Sound.

The more remote, very private **Tia Ora Lodge**, ((03) 573-4253, at Northwest Bay, Pelorus Sound, has moderate-priced rooms and can only be reached by boat.

Useful Contacts

Beachcomber Fun Cruises, ((03) 573-6175, at 8 London Quay, offer a variety of scenic cruises around the Marlborough Sounds in their sleek red passenger catamaran. Their twice-daily "Round the Bays" cruise, departing at 10:15 am and again at 2:15 pm, visits Queen Charlotte Sound's most attractive bays, while another tour originates from Nelson's Momorangi Bay and cruises down the Grove Arm to reach Picton. There are two "Magic Mail Run" cruises, which deliver mail and supplies to remote inlets, and trace historic routes taken by Captain Cook. Another day cruise goes out to the Portage Resort Hotel in Kenepuru Sound.

Marlborough Sounds Charters Limited, ((03) 573-7726, P.O. Box 284, offers fully-equipped "Noelex 25" yachts for "bareboat" hire, complete with dinghies. This is the best company of its kind in the Marlborough Sounds, run by the extremely helpful Shirley and John Flavell, who can keep your car and possessions safe for you if you want.

Sea Kayaking, ((03) 574-2301, R.D.1 Picton, offers guided tours around the Marlborough Sounds as well as rentals of all kinds of kayaks, and tent equipment if you want to strike out on your own.

THE POTTER'S WHEEL AND COASTAL TRACKS

NELSON

The South Island's "Sunshine Capital," summertime Nelson has a Mediterranean climate, inviting golden beaches, lush river valleys, sparkling lakes, fertile fruit orchards and picturesque vineyards. Like the Coromandel Peninsula in the North Island, Nelson province's rural, laid-back, "down under" lifestyle and balmy climate have attracted a large community of artists and craftspeople, especially to the Motueka and Golden Bay area.

The city of Nelson, as it has been entitled to call itself since 1858 by Queen Victoria's decree, retains a strong colonial atmosphere, with its many quaint wooden shops and villas, some converted into craft studios. Not content with naming their city after the one-eyed, one-armed, English seadog, early town-planners went on to commemorate Lord Nelson's ships, cronies and most famous battles in the street names. Hardy Street, named after the captain who received Lord Nelson's famous dying kiss, runs into Collingwood Street, which recalls the admiral who took over when Lord Nelson's lips turned cold. The liveliest nightclub in town (there are four to choose from) is called Horatio's. Nelson also has a Nile West Street and a Trafalgar Square. Nelson is an enjoyable place to be based for a few days, with its lively atmosphere and friendly cafes, either as a prelude to visiting the Abel Tasman National Park or simply for its own sake.

Access

Nelson is located 115 km (71 miles) west of Picton, an easy hour's drive.

Air New Zealand, ((03) 542-8239, has daily direct flights from Wellington, Auckland and Christchurch. Most flights, even those to Auckland and Christchurch, go via Wellington. Air Nelson, ((03) 547-6066, has direct flights to Wellington, Auckland, Christchurch, Motueka, Westport, Palmerston North and Timaru. Mt. Cook, ((03) 546-9300, links with Wellington, Christchurch, Queenstown, Te Anau and Mt. Cook. The Nelson Shuttle Service, ((03) 548-2304 offers a door to door service to and from the airport.

Nelson's bus depot at the corner of Trafalgar and Halifax streets is the hub for all bus services, including InterCity and Newmans, both of which offer scenic routes to the West Coast, stopping at major places of interest. The depot's inquiry number is ((03) 548-2304. There are a variety of alternative bus services which link Nelson with Motueka and Golden Bay, including Collingwood Bus Services, ((03) 524-8188. Nelson Lakes Transport, ((03) 521-6858 runs a shuttle service between Nelson and St. Arnaud daily except Sunday. Wadsworth Motors, ((03) 522-4248, has thrice-weekly buses from Nelson to Lake Rotoiti and Tadmor.

General Information

Your first and only stop can be at the **Nelson Tourist and Activities Centre**, ((03) 546-6228, at 332 Wakefield Street. They can advise on all everything to do with the Nelson and Marlborough region, including accommodation and farm stays. They are also the booking agents for antique, vineyard and craft trails, horse-trekking, guided treks through Abel Tasman National Park, white-water river rafting, caving, gold-panning, fishing, and yacht and launch charters. Their other office is in the Quality Inn hotel.

shop where hand-woven items are made and sold. The **South Street Gallery**, close to the Cathedral, offers an idea of the skill and flair of the community's potters. Within the settlement, you'll find plenty of opportunity to watch artists and craftspeople at work, either in their homes or at combined studios like **Craft Habitat**, at the corner of the Richmond by-pass. The **Mid City Market** at 141 Trafalgar Square, open daily except Sunday, is another craft showcase. The Nelson Potter's Association has a guide leaflet showing where to find the potters in the

Camping gear for walking treks on the Abel Tasman or other tracks can be hired in Nelson from many hostels, or from **Alp Sports**, ((03) 546-8536 at 123 Bridge Street.

What to See

For a place named after a warfaring swashbuckler, Nelson is remarkably peaceful. Protected from gales by surrounding hills, it has a sheltered seafront inlet and tiny, very colonial town center dominated by an English-style **cathedral**. Make sure you visit **Suter Gallery**, near the restful Queen's Gardens on Bridge Road. It houses one of the country's finest collections of craft and colonial paintings. **Seven Weavers** at 36 Collingwood Street is a co-operative weavers work-

Nelson area, and the tourist center has more details of craft trails.

There are two museums worth seeking out. **Founders Park**, at 87 Atawhai Drive, is a collection of restored colonial buildings. In the nearby town of Stoke, the **Nelson Provincial Museum** has a large collection of archive photographs and Maori artifacts. Also in Stoke, is **Broadgreen**, a two-storied cob house built in 1855, surrounded by a pretty rose, lavender and herb garden, and **Isel House**, a colonial homestead from the same era set about with oaks, cypresses,

---

Nelson's architecture has a colonial time-warp atmosphere.

Douglas firs and lofty Corsican pines, open during weekends only from 2 pm to 4 pm.

There are many attractive city walks, especially the riverside bush walk through Queens Gardens. You can pick up a leaflet on city walks from the Tourist Centre. There's a good lookout across Tasman Bay from the summit of **Botanical Hill**. As you stand here, you are at the exact geographical center of New Zealand. From nearby **Matai Valley** there is a particularly scenic bush walk, and the Maungatapu Track leads from here across to the Pelorus River.

Within the Nelson region, the most popular place for swimming is **Tahunanui Beach**, five kilometers (three miles) out of town. **Rabbit Island** is another idyllic beach, 13 km (eight miles) away, with a backdrop of undeveloped forest.

Nearby **Motueka**, an hour's drive from Nelson, is the center of the country's hop and tobacco cultivation; tours offer an interesting look at the industry, while white-water rafting trips down the Buller and Gowan rivers are also popular.

Where to Stay

Unless you really must stay in a conventional hotel, it's much nicer in Nelson to enjoy one of the city's characterful guesthouses. **California House**, ((03) 548-4173, at 29 Collingwood Street, is a charming, non-smoking colonial lodge, and its moderately-priced rooms are very pretty. In the same range, is the 125 year-old restored homestead, **Cambria House**, ((03) 548-4681, at 7 Cambria Street. Breakfasts are a delight here in the lovely beachfront sunroom. In the inexpensive range, you might try **Collingwood House**, ((03) 548-4481, at 174 Collingwood Street, within the town center, or **Palm Grove Guest House**, ((03) 548-4645, at 52 Cambria Street.

If you require international-standard hotel facilities, try the **Quality Inn**, ((03) 548-2299, on Trafalgar Square, with its restaurant and swimming pool, moderately priced, with off-street parking.

Within the Nelson area there are many elegant farmhouses where visitors can stay as guests, paying moderate rates. Contact **Friendly Kiwi Home Hosting**, ((03) 544-5774, fax: (03) 544-5001, at 131A Queen Street,

in Richmond, or **Home Hospitality**, ((03) 548-2424, fax: (03) 546-9519, P.O. Box 309.

Backpackers will enjoy **Tasman Towers**, ((03) 548-7950, at 10 Weka Street, a quirky lodge with self catering facilities. Located 10 minutes from the city, **Alan's Place**, ((03) 548-4854, at 42 Westbrook Terrace, is very friendly and quiet. They have bikes which guests may use free of charge, and may arrange transport to the Abel Tasman National Park.

Campers have excellent choices. The **Tahuna Beach Holiday Park**, ((03) 548-5159, at 70 Beach Road, is set within a huge native park area and has excellent facilities, although it gets extremely crowded in summer. **Richmond Holiday Park**, ((03) 544-7323, on 29 Gladstone Road, is another large complex with a swimming pool, as well as motel rooms.

Where to Eat

Nelson and the adjacent Marlborough region are renowned for their plentiful seafood, especially crayfish, scallops, farmed mussels and salmon, while acres of orchards harvest summertime sun-ripened cherries, apples, pears, peaches, plums and nectarines. Make sure you sample Nelson's scallops, often cooked by the city's restaurants in chowders and in a traditional pernod and cream sauce. Nelson also has many small boutique wineries, and the local "wine trails" make interesting day trips around the district.

For intimate, relaxed dining, **The Brown House**, ((03) 548-9039, at 52 Rutherford Street, has few rivals. Located in a 110 year-old cottage, with candlelit tables and an open fire, this restaurant serves exquisite New Zealand cuisine, specializing in local seafood, wild venison and pork when available. Desserts are eminently more-ish. Also in a restored colonial house, **Junipers**, ((03) 548-8832, at 144 Collingwood Street, is another elegant choice, serving fine cuisine. **The Hitching Post**, ((03) 548-7374, at 145 Bridge Street, is an exceptional, relaxed place for summer dining with its sheltered courtyard, and it has a warm fire inside for winter nights. **City Lights Cafe** ((03) 548-8999, is very lively, with live blues, jazz and Cajun music. Their specialities include Nelson scallops, oysters and Hot Rocks crayfish. Try the wicked double Baileys souffle!

For casual all-day cafe cuisine, **Chez Eelco** is really the only choice, with outside tables shaded by umbrellas. Locally renowned for its Continental breakfasts, lunchtime mussel soup and sticky chocolate cake, it is run by Dutchman Eelco Boswick, a long-time Nelson resident. In the cafe window, signs advertise tramping holidays, horseback riding, farm stays, home-made jewelry, herbal remedies and the local Theravada Buddhist society. There's even one which asks, "Would your daughter make a good marching girl?" Another place to stop for coffee is **Pomeroy's** at 276 Trafalgar Square, which roasts its own specialist beans.

Nightclubs

Aside from **Horatio's** on Halifax Street, you can find plenty of night-time action at **Zhivago's** on the corner of Trafalgar and Hardy streets, or **Limbo's** on Hardy Street. In New Street, look for the **Cactus Club**. Nelson's locally brewed Mac's beer is not at all bad, and it's a staple at these bar counters.

Tours

There are all sorts of inventive and practical tours out of Nelson, covering vineyards and craft studios as well as visits to unusual horticultural operations, including *nashi* pear, green tea, tobacco and hops farms. All details are available from the Tourist Centre. Further afield, **Collingwood Safari Tours**, ((03) 524-8257, offers a five hour drive out to Farewell Spit everyday during summer, from Collingwood and can arrange transport from Nelson. Departure times vary according to the tides.

Discovery Tours, ((03) 548-4431, runs day tours and transport to Abel Tasman National Park, departing at 8:15 am. They visit Ngarua Caves, which have spectacular limestone formations and moa bone skeletons, Pupu Springs, Antoki's tame eel farm and the Wainui Bay winery. Lunch and refreshments are included. You can pick up the tour from Motueka. Call (03) 528-6543.

ABEL TASMAN NATIONAL PARK

From Motueka, over the delightfully-named Marble Mountain, riddled with limestone caves, lies **Golden Bay** and the **Abel Tasman National Park**, a unique coastal park of golden beaches, native bush, limpid rock pools and sand dunes that embrace a sapphire-green pristine ocean. The park's relatively easy main four-day walking track follows the beach and climbs amongst forested headlands of white flowering *manuka* trees, *nikau* palms, with wafting scents of wild oregano, crossing rivers by dramatic swing bridges.

You can join a guided group to walk the Abel Tasman Track or "freedom walk" it, camping where you choose. You can charter a yacht and cruise along the coast, or explore the many isolated, lovely bays by sea kayak.

General Information

Several nearby beach-side villages make ideal setting-off points for exploring Abel Tasman National Park. In Motueka, the **Information Centre**, ((03) 526-9136, on High Street, has useful information about the Abel Tasman, Heaphy and Kaituna tracks, Golden Bay, Farewell Spit, and other regional sights.

Where to Stay and Eat

Rural elegance is the hallmark of the **Motueka River Lodge**, ((03) 526-8668, fax: (03) 526-8668, on Highway 61, Ngatimoti, overlooking the fast-flowing, brown trout-filled Motueka River. Mid-price rates include country-style bedrooms and gourmet meals, featuring the region's superb seafood and game. They offer fishing guides and a package deal of $1,960 for a week's accommodation and five days guided fishing. Also in Motueka, **Doone Cottage**, ((03) 526-8740, on R.D.1, is a lovely 100 year-old home set in its own bush reserve. They offer inexpensive cozily furnished double rooms, and encouraging advice about trout fishing in nearby rivers.

Right next to the park's entrance in Kaiteriteri, **Kia Ora**, ((03) 527-8027, fax: (03) 527-8134, is a lovely wooded retreat with plushly furnished moderately-priced chalets with balconies and beach views. There's an excellent restaurant with a daily changing menu of organically-grown food, a big open-air swimming pool and sauna. The **Kaiteriteri Beach Motor Camp**, ((03) 527-

8010, fax: (03) 527-8031, has idyllic natural surroundings, safe swimming and boating, cabins and good amenities.

Not far away at Little Kaiteriteri, the beach-side **Marahau Camping Ground**, ((03) 527-8176, has cabins, camping sites and full facilities.

Make sure you stop at the **Old Cederman House**, the restored colonial former home of a Swedish seaman who jumped ship, four kilometers (two-and-a-half miles) north of Motueka on the main road to Kaiteriteri. You can dine from 11 am until late in the Victo-

rian dining room or in the courtyard cafe amidst the herb garden. It's also the base for the Abel Tasman National Park Enterprises.

Useful Contacts

Abel Tasman National Park Enterprises ((03) 528-7801, fax: (03) 528-6087, in Old Cederman House, Main Road, Riwaka on R.D.3 Motueka, offers one-day trips and four-day guided treks through the Abel Tasman National Park as well as a daily bus and launch service to various points within the park, with stops at all main settlements from Nelson.

Kaiteriteri Yacht Charters, ((03) 548-6274, on Dehra Doon Road, on R.D. 3 Motueka, invites inquiries about their brisk, pristine

little yachts, perfect for cruising the mild waters around the Abel Tasman National Park.

Ocean River Adventure Company, ((03) 548-8832, runs remarkable four-day guided sea-kayaking trips around the Abel Tasman National Park coastline, often sharing the smooth waters with dolphin schools. The cost, per person, is $220, includes all kayaking equipment, tent and cooking gear. One way trips are also possible, but they don't rent to solo kayakers or one-day trippers.

Abel Tasman Kayaks, ((03) 547-8022, at Marahau, on R.D. 2 Motueka offers one and two-day guided trips, as well as straight kayak rentals at $30 (single berth) and $55 (double) per day.

Water-Taxi Charter, ((03) 528-7497 or Mobile phone (025) 425-401, offers a personalized service to Abel Tasman National Park.

GOLDEN BAY TO FAREWELL SPIT

A winding unsealed road climbs **Takaka Hill**, past **Pupu Springs**, the largest in the Southern Hemisphere, to take in the glorious view of **Golden Bay**, originally called Murderer's Bay by Abel Tasman, where the sand's unusual yellow-orange hue really does look golden and comes from the quartz minerals from Marble Mountain. Stretching in a long crescent, the bay curves as far as the eye can see to Farewell Spit, 35 km (22 miles) away.

Golden Bay has a very seductive appeal for just lazing on the sands, tackling the waves with a windsurfing board and browsing in crafts shops. You can stay at the **Golden Bay Holiday Park**, ((03) 525-9742, Tukurua Beach, Takaka, which has beachfront cabins, tent sites and good amenities.

The beautiful 77 km (48 miles) long four-day **Heaphy Track** starts inland from the little township of **Collingwood**, following the coast and eventually emerging at Karamea on the West Coast. From Collingwood, depending on the tide, you can drive out to Farewell Spit, a 35 km (22 miles) sandspit, beloved by godwits and dotterels, that projects like a beckoning talon from the north-western corner of the South Island.

HEADING SOUTH

Less well-known, the **Nelson Lakes National Park**, about 100 km (62 miles) south of the city, is another scenic reserve. Walking tracks lead to the beech-fringed glacial lakes **Rotoroa** and **Rotoiti**, where deer graze in the deep green forest. The secluded exclusive **Lake Rotoroa Lodge**, ((03) 521-9121, fax: (03) 521-9028, lies in Gowan Valley on the northern shores of the lake, 11 km (nearly seven miles) off State Highway 6, and has its own heli-pad and boat dock for fishing and hunting expeditions. Executive rates include outstanding meals, with inventive game dishes. **St. Arnaud** village, on the shores of Lake Rotoiti offers a range of accommodation, and is a base for two small skifields nearby on **Mt. Robert** and the **Rainbow Mountain** in the Marlborough region.

SOUTH TO THE COAST

A sweeping province of sunshine and wine, **Marlborough** sits in the wide alluvial Wairau River valley. Even if you are just driving through, it offers vistas of remarkably beautiful scenery, with waving summer wheat fields, roadside poppies and undulating hills. It is New Zealand's most successful grape-growing region, producing many deep-flavored wines of international recognition. Muller-Thurgau accounts for over one-third of all vines raised in the area but other varieties include Sauvignon Blanc, Riesling, Pinot Noir, Semillion and Chardonnay. Not surprisingly, one of the region's enchantments is its wineries, recognizable from familiar award-winning labels like Le Brun, Cloudy Bay, Hunter's, Merlen, Te Whare Ra. The strongest presence in the region is Montana, New Zealand's wine giant, which accounts for over 40 percent of the market share. At Riverlands, near Blenheim, you can see the company's six huge 550,000 liter tanks, and inspect the vast operation on a wine-tour.

Encircled by vineyards, the region's main settlement of **Blenheim** sits on the junction of the Taylor and Opawa rivers. **Marlborough**

Promotions, ((03) 578-4480, at the corner of East and Burnett streets, run enjoyable wine tours and tastings to the area's boutique wineries. Otherwise you can visit the town's sights en route to Kaikoura. The **Waterlea Gardens** in Pollard Park and the **Brayshaw Museum** on New Renwick Road are worth visiting. On State Highway 1, five kilometers (three miles) onwards, stop at the delightful **Riverlands Cob Cottage**, restored from the early 1860's period and fringed with hollyhocks. Inside are mocked-up displays showing how its inhabitants would have lived.

A short distance from Blenheim, off Hawkesbury Road, is **Timara Lodge**, ((03) 572-8276, fax: (03) 572-9191 has room for just eight guests. Set next to a lake, this Tudor-style mansion charges executive rates ($245 per person) that include gourmet dinners and lacy, floral, cozy rooms but not lunch. It may be too chintzy for some, but is certainly luxurious.

Stop at **Oak Tree Cottage**, at Dashwood, off State Highway 1 en route to Seddon. This early colonial cottage sells dried flowers, antiques and handicrafts and has a nice picnic area.

ABOVE and OPPOSITE: Two ways of enjoying Abel Tasman National Park. OVERLEAF: Admiring the view in Nelson Lakes National Park.

KAIKOURA

Past the shimmering Lake Grassmere salt flats and in the lee of the towering Kaikoura Ranges, is the wild, wave-thundering Kaikoura coastline. In Maori, *kai* means food and *koura* means crayfish. You'll soon see how the coast got its name. All along the roads are stalls, often manned by freckled eight-year-olds, overflowing with giant lobsters — still wiggling their talons or freshly steaming.

A FLICKER OF THE WHALE'S TALE

Several companies run reconnaissance missions with the whales, most commonly seen between April and August, and dolphins, between August and April, while fur seals and sea-birds can be seen most of the time. Passengers are motored out in inflatable boats, and whales are tracked by hydrophones which pick up the clicking sound of whales communicating. The sight of one of these great creatures lifting itself up from the

But increasingly, Kaikoura has been attracting visitors for other creatures of the deep that lurk near its shores. Rather than being recognized as the *de facto* home of the lobster, it is now becoming known for the schools of huge sperm whales, boisterous, leaping Dusky dolphins and fur seals are regular visitors to the pristine bay. The whales — up to 20 m (66 ft) in length — are seen all year round, but are more common in winter, attracted by the nutrient-rich waters off the continental shelf which plunges to 1,600 m (5,200 ft) within eight kilometers (five miles) of South Bay.

An array of stalactites and stalagmites in Maori Leap Cave, near Kaikoura.

sea, crashing down again with a graceful flip of its massive tail, is unforgettable.

One of the oldest established tours, combining an in-depth commentary on the interesting Maori history of the region, **Kaikoura Tours**, ((03) 319-5045, fax: (03) 319-5045, has its office in the Kaikoura railway station building. **Kaikoura Explorer**, ((03) 319-5641, at Memorial Hall on The Esplanade, has a variety of tours, some leaving from Christchurch, where its office contact is ((03) 389-0835. The **Dolphin Mary Experience**, ((03) 319-6208, offers something different — the chance to swim with Dusky dolphins and fur seals. It supplies wetsuits and hot drinks afterwards. Apparently, it's perfectly safe.

MAORI LEAP CAVE

Kaikoura's other place of interest is the Maori Leap Cave, a sea cave thought to be over two million years old and rich in fossils, with a cavern of eerily beautiful stalactites and stalagmites gnashing their teeth, estimated to be about 3,000 years old. Call (03) 319-5023 to join a guided tour of the Limestone Cave.

GENERAL INFORMATION

The **Information Centre**, ((03) 319-5641, on The Esplanade can help with all inquiries. They will probably suggest that you also have a look at **Fyffe House**, listed by the Historic Places Trust.

There are a number of hotels and motels, but the **Blue Seas Motel**, ((03) 319-5441, at 222 The Esplanade, comes highly recommended. It is moderately priced, has a good restaurant and spacious seafront lawns. **Kaikoura Backpackers**, ((03) 319-6042, known locally as the White House, at 146 The Esplanade, has lots of friendly, colonial charm.

CHRISTCHURCH

A serenely beautiful garden city, Christchurch radiates the understated charm of a small English town with its nineteenth century neo-Gothic architecture. Any resulting severity of atmosphere, however, is softened by well-established parks.

Through the city flows the serpentine **Avon River**, fringed by weeping willows and tall English trees that create a gorgeous autumnal palette. Canterbury's largest city, Christchurch was a planned Anglican settlement almost entirely orchestrated by a devout young English Tory called John Robert Godley. In Britain he canvassed to create the Canterbury Association, citing the New World as a perfect haven for devout and profit-minded souls. Two archbishops, seven bishops, 14 peers, four baronets and 16 members of Parliament sat on the association, which screened hopeful migrants who were to represent "all the ele-

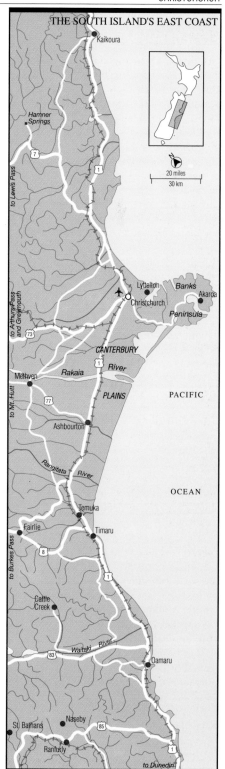

THE SOUTH ISLAND'S EAST COAST

ments, including the very highest, of a good and right state of society."

The first immigrants arrived in 1850. Yet despite the ardently ecclesiastical ideals of the Canterbury Association, the realities of agricultural life in New Zealand demanded a relaxing of standards, and the *"shagoons,"* as the swarthy Australian stock-men were known, were soon let in.

Although loosened, Christchurch's Anglican ideals certainly lived on in the city's many impressive public buildings and homesteads. The boys at the Anglican Christ's College, founded in 1857, are the only pupils in the country to wear straw boaters, even though they are optional. The public-spiritedness bequeathed by Christchurch's founders means that a third of the city is a garden, park or nature reserve. Green-fingered care is evident everywhere, but especially so during the Floral Festival, held from mid-February to mid-March, when there are processions of floral floats down the Avon River, innumerable flower shows and a "Miss Floral" competition.

ACCESS

The International Airport is located 10 km (just over six miles) from the city center, and has connections with Australia, the United States, Asia and Europe, as well as a comprehensive domestic network with most main destinations covered by Air New Zealand, Ansett New Zealand and Mt. Cook. Call (03) 353-7854 for flight information.

The *Southerner Express* links Christchurch with Dunedin and Invercargill, the *Coastal Pacific* connects with the Picton ferry, and the *Trans-Alpine Express* crosses through the high passes of the Southern Alps to Greymouth. All the train services run daily each way, and depart from the railway station, ((03) 379-9020, on Moorhouse Avenue.

InterCity buses, ((03) 379-9020, depart from the Intercity Travel Centre outside the railway station. Newmans, ((03) 379-5641, leave from 347 Moorhouse Avenue, while Mt. Cook, ((03) 348-2099, has a depot at 40 Lichfield Street, near Cathedral Square. All

three services have links to Picton, Queenstown, Dunedin, Mt. Cook and Greymouth.

GENERAL INFORMATION

The **Visitors' Information Centre**, ((03) 379-9629, on Worcester Street, has maps, guide booklets and information on all Christchurch and Canterbury attractions. They can book accommodation and tours. Their *Buses Can Take You Walking,* is a useful map and timetable to getting around Christchurch and the Banks Peninsula by bus. The **Outdoor Recreation Centre**, ((03) 365-5590, is at the corner of Worcester Street and Oxford Terrace, while the **Department of Conservation** office, ((03) 379-9758, is at 133 Victoria Street. **Trailblazers**, ((03) 366-6033, at 86 Worcester Street, can book all kinds of action-adventure tours, from whale-watching along to Kaikoura coast to learning to pilot a small aircraft. You can also hire bicycles and tandems opposite the Botanic Gardens entrance on Rolleston Avenue.

WHAT TO SEE

Christchurch is best explored on foot, on a hire-bicycle, or by canoe on the Avon River. At its nucleus is **Cathedral Square**, dominated by the Gothic **Christchurch Anglican Cathedral** (1864), which has corkscrew stairs to the top for views across the city. The statue opposite is of John Robert Godley, founder of **Christchurch**, the first statue in New Zealand, while to the side of the Cathedral is the **Citizen's War Memorial**. With its lively Friday market, Cathedral Square is where the city's self-appointed "Wizard," a bearded bombastic soothsayer, and other soapbox speakers deliver their messages to bemused onlookers. Nearby the new red-tiled **Victoria Square** has patio cafes beneath tall trees, and a modernistic fountain. From here, you could stop for a swirled cappuccino at **Vesuvio's** on Oxford Terrace. On the Hereford Street Bridge is the Canterbury Information Centre, housed in the **Old Municipal Chambers** building, the city's first official building, built in 1851. Opposite, the marble **Scott Statue** is quite a remarkable achievement when you consider it was created by the talented widow of the great

Cathedral Square in Christchurch.

British Antarctic explorer who was the second man to reach the South Pole. Captain Robert Falcon Scott's expeditions to the Antarctic all departed from Lyttelton port, not far from Christchurch.

Continue across the bridge along Worcester Street to reach the **Arts Centre**, housed in the Gothic stone cloisters of what used to be Christchurch's nineteenth century university buildings. Open all week, the Arts Centre has cafes, craft studios, and shops, and is a focal point for artists, craftspeople, musicians and performers and is the site of a busy

used New Zealand, the closest inhabited land mass, as a supply base before sailing for the seventh continent, and still do. Special items are Scott's sledge, a ski used during his 1904 expedition and Ernest Shackleton's 1914 motor sledge. Scott died on the march back from the South Pole. The museum also has fascinating displays on natural history, and a colonial gallery with mock-up interiors showing the lifestyle of early settlers. Some of the more bizarre exhibits include an early Maori "backpack" and the remains of a cannibal feast in Fiji!

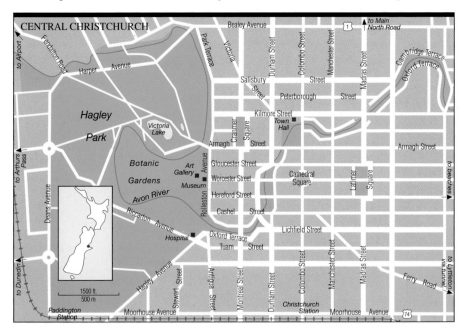

weekend market. The Southern Regional Ballet is based here and the Court Theater offers live theater six nights a week. Tucked away in a turret, you'll find the den used by Ernest Rutherford, the first man to split the atom. As a postgraduate student, this small dark basement room is where he worked in 1893, making some historic early experiments into electromagnetic waves.

Directly across the road, the **Canterbury Museum** is where you can see the finest Antarctic Collection in the world, reflecting Christchurch's position as the base for Antarctic explorations dating back to the time of Captain Cook. Within 70 years of Cook's crossing of the Antarctic Circle, British, French, American and Russian explorers

As you emerge from the museum, you will find yourself at the entrance to **Hagley Park**, a 202 hectare (400 acre), 130 year-old expanse that is a haven for joggers, walkers, golfers, tennis players, picnickers and cyclists, with wooded groves of sycamores and oaks. Within the park, the 30 hectare (75 acre) **Botanic Gardens** is world-class, with spectacular displays of exotic and native plants and trees cast in the English tradition. Within the Botanic Gardens, close to the Rolleston Avenue entrance, near the Canterbury Museum, is the **Robert McDougall Gallery**.

A uniquely Christchurch pursuit is to hire a canoe from the **Antigua Boatsheds** at 2 Cambridge Terrace and paddle through the park, following the tranquil loops of the

26 km (16 miles) river. Or you can be punted by straw-hatted boaters from outside the Information Centre. There are other canoe pick-up points from landings near the Town Hall Restaurant, the Thomas Edmonds Rotunda and **Mona Vale**, departing from the stately Edwardian homestead and meandering through magnificent gardens, located two kilometers (one-and-a-quarter miles) away on Fendalton Road. The weeping willow trees on the river banks have quite a story behind them. Apparently, they grew from specimens planted in Akaroa by

Leisure Centre has Olympic-sized pools, a hydroslide maze, squash courts, bumper boats, mini-golf and bungy-jumping.

The **Air Force Museum** has a comprehensive display of aircraft, exhibits and memorabilia, and lies within Wiggam Aerodrome, where the New Zealand Air Force was established in 1932. It's open from 10 am to 4 pm and on Sundays, 1 pm to 4 pm. At the **Yaldhurst Transport Museum**, you can see many vintage cars, motor-cycles, fire-engines and steam-engines, set in the grounds of a colonial homestead. It's

a French settler last century. A keen Bonapartist, he had sneaked past the guards at St. Helena and pulled a number of slips from the weeping willow over Napolean's grave. These he nursed carefully on a whaling vessel en route for New Zealand before planting them at his new home.

Parks, Museums and Beaches
Within the city's environs, at **Orana Park**, the country's largest open-range wildlife reserve, you can drive through an African style reserve complete with lions, water buffaloes, zebras, oryxes and giraffes. Willowbank **Wildlife Reserve** specializes in showing nocturnal native animals and birds and has a pre-European village. **Queen Elizabeth II**

located 11 km (nearly seven miles) from Christchurch, on School Road, close to the airport. Another excellent transport and technology museum is **Ferrymead Historic Park**, at 269 Bridle Path Road.

Magnificent beaches border the city's suburbs, most spectacularly **New Brighton**, a wild, windswept ribbon of beach that has an endless hazy look whichever stretch of sand you gaze at. Surfers congregate here for the big waves whatever the weather. **Sumner**, 12 km (nearly seven-and-a-half miles) away has an exposed sandy beach, a sheltered marina for wind-surfers and a

School-boys from the Anglican Christ's College enjoying the sun.

curious cave, thought to have been used by early Maori nomads.

Lastly seek out **New Regent Street** in the inner city, for its delightful restored pastel-painted colonial facade.

WHERE TO STAY

Mid-price

At the top of the range, located right on the River Avon, **Noah's**, ((03) 379-4700, fax: (03) 379-5357, is at the corner of Worcester Street and Oxford Terrace. It has plush furnish-

ings, deluxe suites and Christchurch's finest restaurant, the Waitangi, as well as several bars and an all-day brasserie. Locals like to proudly point out that this is where royalty and film stars stay when they pass through. Ask for a room that overlooks the Avon River, which winds past the lobby. Equally flashy, the **Parkroyal**, ((03) 365-7799, fax: (03) 365-0082, at the corner of Kilmore and Durham Streets, also offers international-class facilities, and has a magnificent atrium restaurant. **Vacation Inn**, ((03) 379-5880, fax: (03) 365-4806, on 776 Colombo Street has all

---

ABOVE: The Wizard, Christchurch's well-known and loved eccentric. OPPOSITE: Christchurch's Victoria Square.

the comforts and amenities of a major hotel chain.

George Hotel, ((03) 379-4560, fax: (03) 366-6747, at 50 Park Terrace, has a smaller, more intimate atmosphere and is elegantly furnished. Right next to Hagley Park, **Quality Inn Chateau**, ((03) 348-8999, fax: (03) 348-8990, at 187–189 Deans Avenue, is a modernistic interpretation of a French chateau, with lavish rooms, two licensed restaurants and a heated swimming pool. Its design it is rather impressive, surrounded by a "moat" and inter-linking terraces. If you need a place to stay close to the airport, the best choice is the **Christchurch Airport Travelodge**, ((03) 358-3139, fax: (03) 358-3029, at the corner of Memorial Avenue and Orchard Road.

Moderate

Away from the big hotels the nicest place to stay has to be **Eliza's Manor House**, ((03) 366-8584, fax: (03) 366-4946, at 82 Bealey Avenue. This rather gracious nineteenth century mansion has been lovingly restored as a luxury bed and breakfast. There are 10 rooms, six with en-suite bathrooms, all with brass beds and antique furnishings. **Windsor Hotel**, ((03) 366-1503, fax: (03) 366-9796, at 52 Armagh Street is another luxury bed and breakfast in a pretty colonial house, five minutes walk from town. You can also inquire about Home Hosting at ((03) 351-6672.

There are several other "luxury" moderately-priced options. **Pacific Park**, ((03) 377-3374, fax: (03) 366-9973, at 263 Bealey Avenue, offers pleasant standard accommodation, while the **Cotswold Inn**, ((03) 355-3535, fax: (03) 355-6695, at 88–90 Papanui Road, is the extraordinary product of the owner's vision of a modern sixteenth century Tudor coaching inn. Whether this is supremely kitsch or just very comfortable is a matter of taste. Along the same theme, **Camelot Court Motor Lodge**, ((03) 355-9124, fax: (03) 355-8698, at 28–30 Papanui Road, is within easy walking distance of Christchurch and has mock-period fittings and a spa pool. Its restaurant, Arthur's and Martha's, is a local favorite for its rack of Canterbury lamb and iced layer cake. In town, you can't miss **The Coach-**

man Inn, ((03) 379-3476, fax: (03) 379-1198, at 144 Gloucester Street, with its green and red exterior. This historic tavern with fully-furnished rooms, plush saloon-style restaurant and bar is a good inner-city choice.

Inexpensive
There are several lodge-style accommodations which offer excellent value and comfort. **Turret House**, ((03) 365-3900, fax: (03) 366-3769, at 435 Durham Street, is a nineteenth century mansion, elegantly restored, relaxed haven in the inner city. **Ambassadors Hotel**, ((03) 366-7808, at 19 Manchester Street, is a friendly two-storied converted house lodge, right in the center of town. **Melville Private Hotel**, ((03) 379-8956, at 49 Gloucester Street, three minutes walk from the center, is another, slightly more spartan and cheaper choice. The brand-new **YMCA**, ((03) 365-0502, fax: (03) 365-1386, at 12 Hereford Street is situated next to the Arts Centre and the Botanic Gardens and has spacious, attractive rooms and charges $15 for bunk accommodation. Its impressive facilities include a dining room, self-service laundry, and access to all the "Y" recreation facilities: squash courts, aerobics classes, badminton, table tennis, and a sauna.

Backpackers
Travelers don't really have to rough it at backpacker-priced accommodation in Christchurch. The recommended options offer private spacious rooms, have good amenities for cooking and lounging around. **Rolleston House Hotel**, ((03) 366-6564, at 5 Worcester Street, is a converted nineteenth century house located close to the Arts Centre and has double and family rooms. There is free parking and a lock-up place for valuables. **Charlie Brown's Backpacker's Hostel**, ((03) 379-8429, at 268 Madras Street, is a good choice in the inner city.

Camping Grounds
There are two parks, both with excellent facilities, camping sites, and tourist cabins located on the periphery of the city. You can choose between **Rusley Park Motor Camp**, ((03) 342-7021, at 272 Yaldhurst Road and **Meadow Park**, ((03) 352-9176, at 39 Mea-

dow Street, the larger of the two, which also has a heated pool.

WHERE TO EAT

Aside from Noah's formal, expensive **Waitangi** restaurant, and the Parkroyal's **Yamagen** Japanese restaurant, one of the most delightful places to dine is the **Thomas Edmonds Restaurant**, ((03) 365-2888, at the corner of Cambridge Terrace and Manchester Street. Set in an old band rotunda on the banks of the River Avon, its serene, cano-

pied setting is best enjoyed over a summer lunch. The **Town Hall Restaurant**, ((03) 366-6651, off Victoria Street, is quite formal, with fine New Zealand cuisine. For a variety of delicious seafood dishes, try **Palazzo del Marinario**, ((03) 365-4640, at The Shades, in Hereford Street. More casual and stylish, **Henry Africa's Restaurant and Bar**, ((03) 389-3619, at 325 Stanmore Road, has a regularly changing, eclectic menu, while **Jambalaya**, ((03) 365-0566, in the Arts Centre, serves authentic Louisiana Cajun food, while within the same complex, the open-late **Double D's Bar and Grill**, ((03) 365-0566, has a friendly cafe atmosphere, and its speciality is its manuka wood barbecued meats and fish. **Satay House**, ((03)

365-5766, at Cashell Mall, offers delicious, inexpensive Malaysian food, and their star dish is Rendang Chicken, roasted with coconut, lemon grass and chillis served with rice. They are closed on Mondays. **La Felice**, ((03) 366-7535, at 150 Armagh Street, serves good Italian pasta and gelato. If you are the sort of person who only eats dinner in order to have dessert, then visit **Strawberry Jane**, ((03) 365-4897. It's open for breakfast and its creamy, calorific creations are up for grabs until midnight. Light meals are also served throughout the day.

ENTERTAINMENT AND NIGHTLIFE

Check in the free *Christchurch Tourist Times* for details of concerts and performances in this culturally active city. The mother of all pubs in Christchurch is **Dux de Luxe**, ((03) 366-6919, a Tudor-style building close to the Arts Centre, which has several bars, restaurants and an outdoor garden which often stages live music. Nightclubs include **The Firehouse**, at 293 Colombo Street, and **Bootlegger's** at MacKenzies Hotel, 51 Pages

Christchurch has two outstanding cafes, perfect for ducking into for lunch or a morning coffee. **Vesuvio's Cafe**, ((03) 366-2666, right next to Noah's Hotel on Oxford Terrace, is the more stylish, with good music and open until midnight. **In Italia**, ((03) 365-5349, in Castell Mall, is absolutely the best place to come for lunch. They serve freshly-squeezed juices, real Italian coffee, fresh pasta dishes and heavenly cakes.

Savor a South Island brand beer at the **Oxford Victualing Co.** ((03) 379-7148, at the corner of Oxford Terrace and Colombo Street, a charming riverside pub where you can sit out under the trees. In the heart of the Botanic Gardens, **Gardens Restaurant**, ((03) 366-5076, is a lovely place for lunch or afternoon tea.

Road. Both are open late Wednesday through Saturday nights.

SHOPPING

Christchurch is a good place to find all kinds of fleece-wool and leather products manufactured in craft-rich Canterbury. Use this as a general guideline while browsing in the Arts Centre. Look out for **Dilana Studios**, which creates unique rugs from the designs of leading artists. Also at the center, it's interesting to watch craftsmen at the **Riki Rangi Maori Carving Centre**, where carvings are made from native timbers, shell, jade and bone, then sold in the adjacent gallery. For conservation and natural history items, seek out **Wild Places**, Shop 46 in the Shades Arcade. For books, go no further than **Scorpio Bookshop** at the corner of Oxford Terrace and Hereford Street.

TOURS

Red Bus Scenic Tours, ((03) 379-4600, offers four different daily tours, all departing from Cathedral Square. The two-hour City and Suburbs Tour offers an introduction to Christchurch's gardens, museums and gen-

plores the Banks Peninsula on a high-speed passenger craft, visiting volcanic sea caves, seal and penguin colonies, keeping an eye out for schools of Hector's dolphins. There are three tours of varying length: a one hour tour at $35, a two and a half hour tour ($48) which drifts over shipwrecks and takes tea at Annandale Homestead, and three and a half hours at $65 which also explores Lyttelton Harbour. Tours leave from Sumner, a seaside suburb of Christchurch.

Great Sights, ((03) 379-4268, runs local sightseeing tours and also tours that go to

eral sights and departs at 10 am. The three-hour Hill and Harbour Tour departs at 1:30 pm and wraps up the city's environs and goes for a cruise in Lyttelton Harbour. The full-day Akaroa Tour departs at 9 am all week and 9:30 am on Sunday. The five-hour Wildlife Tour departs 12 noon on Wednesday, Saturday and Sunday and visits Orana Park and Peacock Springs.

Canterbury Garden Tours, ((03) 342-8316 runs daily tours of the city's wonderful private gardens. The cost of $30 covers a morning or afternoon tea, and the tours depart at 9 am and 1:30 pm from outside the Canterbury Information Centre.

Canterbury Sea Tours, (Mobile phone (025) 325-697, after hours (03) 326-6756, ex-

Methven, Mt. Cook, Queenstown, the Milford Sound and Picton, while **InterCity**, ((03) 379-9020, has services out to Akaroa, the Banks Peninsula, Mt. Cook, Lake Tekapo and Hamner Springs.

OVER THE HILLS AND AWAY

Bordering Christchurch to the south, the stark, tussock-grassed **Port Hills** are criss-crossed with vertiginous walkways for adventurous strollers. Up here you can see panoramic views of the city, Lyttelton

OPPOSITE: Punting down the Avon River in Christchurch. ABOVE: Pastoral landscape of the Canterbury Plains.

Harbour and the endless patchwork quilt of the Canterbury Plains. Set within a volcanic skeleton of massive size, now carpeted by green forest and flooded by sea, Lyttelton Harbour is 13 km (eight miles) from Christchurch.

Lyttelton

The South Island's busiest port, Lyttelton has a brusque, maritime atmosphere, dotted with quaint cottages, colonial buildings and the historic castle-like Timeball Station. You'll get salty whiffs of the settlement's history, including its association with Antarctic explorers, in the Lyttelton Museum and in the **Simeon House of Arts and Crafts**, which once belonged to Captain Simeon, a colorful sea-dog who lived here with his wife, five children and assorted servants and surrounded himself with all sorts of marine objets d'art.

One of the most dramatic ways to appreciate Lyttelton's strategic location is to cruise aboard the splendid *S.V. Tradewind*, (1911) the country's oldest square rigger sailing ship, with gleaming brass, varnished woodwork and billowing sails. You may have seen it in the movie, *Return to the Blue Lagoon*, while the other notches on its mast include being a pioneer of Sub-Antarctic expeditions, winner of the 1989 Sydney Tall Ship Regatta, the "Fastest of the Fleet" in the Australian Bicentennial Voyage from Britain to Sydney and the star of three TV documentaries. There are half-day sails ($40 per adult), day sails ($55), and lastly, and most spectacularly, weekend cruises around the Banks Peninsula to Akaroa ($150), with frequent sightings of Hectors' Dolphins. For more details contact Trailblazers in Christchurch.

There are daily launch connections around Diamond Harbour to two islands: **Quail Island**, an early settler's quarantine pen, and **Ripapa Island**. It's also possible to take a cruise on the steam tug *Lyttelton*, built in 1907. At nearby Governor's Bay, visit **Taunton Gardens**, set within a gracious 1853 homestead, and offering an idyllic, jasmine-scented vision of rural Canterbury life. Whether you are returning to Christchurch or continuing onto the Banks Peninsula, make sure you stop at the nineteenth

century Scottish baronial-style **Sign of the Takahe** restaurant, ((03) 332-4052, situated at Dyers Pass Road in the Cashmere Hills, open all day for Devonshire teas, lunch and dinner.

THE BANKS PENINSULA

From the air, the Banks Peninsula juts out from the smooth Canterbury coastline like a great clenched fist. Between its fingers, the Pacific Ocean laps into high-cliffed bays and long deep harbors. Named by Captain Cook after his botanist Joseph Banks, the entire peninsula is within easy driving distance of Christchurch, its main settlement of Akaroa 84 km (52 miles) away. Although it's possible to drive right around the peninsula in a day, try to stay a few days. The Banks Peninsula rivals the Bay of Islands for its pristine scenery, walks, picturesque homesteads and restful, maritime atmosphere.

From Lyttelton, as you wind over its undulating tussock hills, you'll pass the site of an important Maori Ngai Tahu tribe *pa*, and reach the settlement of **Barry's Bay**, the site of a large-scale cannibal feast around 1832 when the formidable North Island chief Te Rauparaha led his Ngati Toa and Te Atiawa warriors on a mission to sack the peninsula. Stop in Barry's Bay at the **Settlers Farmhouse Cheese Factory**, where cheese is made to traditional colonial recipes. Especially good are their Farmhouse Cheddar, Akaroa Mellow and Cheshire cheeses, and their jams and honey. Also look out for **Matthews Protea Nursery** at French Farm, where proteas and other unusual African and Australian plants are grown.

There's a luxurious retreat nearby at **Oihitu Estate**, ((03) 304-5804, a restored French 120 year-old homestead, moderately priced. Another secluded, less expensive choice is **Bayview**, ((03) 304-5875, at Little River, where hosts Martin and Jacqui run a sheep farm homestead, and offer comfortable rooms and delicious farm-produced food. Right on the seaside, the **Des Pecheurs Hotel**, ((03) 304-5803, Main Road, Barry's Bay, is also very appealing and is moderately-priced.

AKAROA

There is no lovelier settlement in New Zealand than this placid, dreamy little harbor village, especially during summer. As you walk along its tree-lined French-named streets, behind white picket fences are charming, wisteria-covered wooden villas with delicate wrought-iron balconies and shuttered windows constructed last century by French settlers. Seagulls wheel above the little pierfront wharf, where you can enjoy a

which you can visit with the help of the *Peninsula Craft Trail* map, available from the Christchurch Visitor's Information Centre.

Access

On Monday, Wednesday and Friday, the **Akaroa Shuttle** bus departs from Akaroa Post Office at 8:20 am, arriving in Christchurch at 9:50 am, and departs from the Christchurch Visitors' Centre at 5 pm, arriving at 6:30 pm. Bookings are essential, call (03) 379-9629 for details of extended services in summer. Aside from hiring a car, the

beer as the sun sets over a harbor renowned for its population of playful dolphins.

The settlement's founder was Jean Langlois, a whaler who had previously founded the Compagnie Nanto-Bordelaise in France. With the permission of King Louis Phillipe he set sail for New Zealand in 1835 with 65 fellow immigrants. Although they intended to found a French colony, the signing of the Treaty of Waitangi whilst they were en route meant that in actuality they became British subjects as soon as they settled here. Many of their descendants still live in Akaroa today.

Like the rest of the Banks Peninsula, Akaroa has many craftspeople and artists, with many galleries and small workshops,

other way to get out to Akaroa is to take the Red Bus Akaroa Tour which departs daily at 9 am from Cathedral Square. If you want to stay a night or two, they will collect you from Akaroa by arrangement.

What to See

Enjoy Akaroa's tranquil setting with a walk around its waterfront, browsing in galleries, craft shops and meeting the locals. The **Langlois-Eteveneaux House and Museum** on Rue Lavaud, displays old costumes, whaling equipment and other relics of Akaroa's settlement and is open daily from 1:30 pm

ABOVE: A pier-side view of Akaroa, Banks Peninsula. OVERLEAF: The glacial beauty of Mt. Cook from Lake Pukaki.

to 4:30 pm. Also see **St. Patrick's Catholic Church**, built by the French settlers in 1864 with native *totara*. It has a lovely stained glass window, filtering soft tones of blue, ruby, gold and purple into the peaceful chapel. Short walks within the town include one up L'Aube Hill to the **Old French Cemetery**, and to the **Herb Farm**, at the end of Rue Grehan, with its beautiful, scented garden. A coastal pathway leads to another Akaroa landmark, a century-old **lighthouse**. Within surrounding native bush reserves, established tracks are perfect for horse-riding and trekking. Or you can ask at the wharf about hiring almost any kind of boat for fishing or just cruising the harbor.

Further afield, explore the beautiful swimming bays of **Port Levy**, **Little Akaroa**, **Okain's Bay**, **Le Bons Bay** and **Pigeon Bay**. Okain's Bay, three kilometers (nearly two miles) from Akaroa, has a **Maori and Colonial Museum**, with many pre-European and Maori art and artifacts, including a replica meeting house and war canoe.

Where to Stay

Akaroa has some of New Zealand's most picturesque mansion bed and breakfasts. First recommendations go to Lavaud House and Glencarrig. **Lavaud House**, ((03) 304-7121, at 83 Rue Lavaud, a stately two-storied home overlooking the main swimming beach. Rooms are airy and comfortable, and the inexpensive rates include breakfast. **Glencarrig**, ((03) 304-7008, at 7 Percy Street, a charming historic home built as the region's first vicarage in 1852, set in its own native bush gardens, and moderately priced. Two other excellent moderately-priced choices are the **White Rose Lodge**, ((03) 304-7501, at 99 Beach Road, a beautiful Victorian French-style mansion, with exceptionally furnished, pretty rooms and the **La Rive Motel**, ((03) 304-7651, Rue Lavaud, with its distinctive cupola, which has self-contained units including kitchens. The **Akaroa Village Inn**, ((03) 304-7421, fax: (03) 304-7423, is the town's most luxurious modern hotel, with 30 cottages, indoor heated swimming pool, licensed restaurant and conference facilities, with moderate rates. Much more down to earth, the quaintly constructed, wooden verandahed, **Ma-deira Motel**, ((03) 304-7009, at 48 Rue Lavaud, built in 1872, is a pub hotel and TAB office. Rooms are on the cheap side of inexpensive and there's a great garden restaurant. **Mt. Vernon's Lodge**, ((03) 304-7180, Rue Balguerie, offer peaceful lodge rooms, cabins and a self-contained flat, with rates that vary accordingly between inexpensive and backpackers. This is a perfect choice if you like horse-riding, as there are guided horse treks. You can bring your pet by arrangement.

There's delightful farmstay accommodation at **Le Bons Bay**, ((03) 304-8529, 20 km (12 miles) from Akaroa, with home cooking and peaceful surroundings. They have two twin rooms and you must book in advance.

Akaroa has good options for backpackers. **Chez la Mer**, ((03) 304-7024, Rue Lavaud, is a friendly non-smoking backpacker's lodge. **Onuku Farm Hostel**, ((03) 304-7612, lies six kilometers (nearly four miles) from Akaroa, and offers free pick-up. **The Barn**, ((03) 304-7671, at Takamatua, Main Road, is a rural bed and breakfast retreat, with a tranquil atmosphere and pretty gardens. You can arrange to go horse-riding. Campers and caravanners can stay at **Akaroa Holiday Park**, ((03) 304-7471, on Morgans Road, which also has tourist cabins. It is set in a large terraced nature reserve overlooking Akaroa harbor.

Where to Eat

The **Old Shipping Office**, ((03) 304-5832, on Church Street, serves superb "Nouvelle Zealandaise" provincial cuisine. It's located in a restored old villa and is open only Wednesday through Monday for lunch and dinner. Make sure you try their chicken liver pate and honeyed scallops. **La Rue Restaurant**, ((03) 304-7658, at 6 Rue Balguerie is another fine choice, located right on the pier-front and open Wednesday through Saturday for lunch and dinner. On the main wharf, the **Pier Cafe**, ((03) 304-7272, is open all day. It is a little exposed and can be windy on a cold night, but is blissful during summer. **Atomic Cafe**, on Rue Lavaud, is very casual and serves fresh wholefood-type meals amidst a very "green" atmosphere. Other staples to know about in town are the **Akaroa Bakery** on Rue Lavaud, for its fluffy bread and cakes and the **Akaroa Fish Shop**, which serves some of the best "fush'n'chups' in the world.

Within driving distance of Akaroa are some very fine restaurants. **Relais Roche-fort Restaurant,** ((03) 304-5832, Ngaio Grove, Duvauchelle, serves fine country cuisine and excellent wines in an exquisite garden villa. It's open for lunch and dinner Wednesday through Sunday and bookings are essential.

Tours

Akaroa Harbour Cruises, ((03) 304-7641. A cruise on the *Canterbury Cat* is a must, especially during November and April, when you're very likely to see schools of dolphins. It departs daily at 1:30 pm all year and also at 11:30 am between November and March, and cruises around the peninsula's volcanic seacliffs, stopping to see a salmon farm and penguin nesting sites. If you don't have your own car, make sure you take InterCity's **Mail Run** which takes you on a 106 km (66 miles) journey around the Banks Peninsula's eastern bays, making many stops at places of interest and taking in the region's wonderful scenery. It departs from Akaroa Post Office at 9:45 pm daily except Sunday, costs $13. You should bring lunch with you.

If you want a walking holiday, the **Banks Peninsula Track** is a four-day guided walkway that winds its way over private land around the dramatic volcanic coast of the peninsula. It costs $80 per person and this includes all accommodation but not food which you'll need to bring along with a sleeping bag, boots and adequate clothing. Book in Akaroa at ((03) 304-7612 or in Christchurch at the Outdoor Recreation Centre, ((03) 379-9629, who can arrange transport to Akaroa.

ACROSS THE ALPS

If there is one train journey in New Zealand not to be missed it is the *Trans-Alpine Express*. This leisurely, coast-to-coast train plies the spectacularly beautiful 250 km (155 miles) route between Christchurch to Greymouth on the West Coast daily. The momentum begins as you chug through the Canterbury Plains watching sheep farms, orchards and the odd horse farm roll by. Snow-capped mountains, silhouetted against a pale blue sky, draw closer. Just before lunch, the train makes a stop at a tiny hill-station, and alert passengers will spy a patiently waiting Golden Labrador on the platform. This is Rosie, who has become the train's mascot, expectant for her daily Great Railway Pie. With the pie dispatched, and Rosie's tail wagging, the train sets off again. As the treatment of Rosie suggests, this is not a posh stuffy train. Although comfortable, it does not pretend to be the Orient Simplon Express. Apart from the Great Railway Pie, its boxed lunch selection consists of Canterbury Lamburger, Goldminer's Lunch (basically a chicken salad) and a selection of New Zealand cheeses.

Trans-Alpine runs a daylight service only. Travelers board in Christchurch at 7:30 am and reach Greymouth less than five hours later. Shortly after lunch, the train begins the return journey, arriving back in Christchurch in the early evening, which is naturally optional for travelers who are taking the scenic route to reach the other side of the coast. The service operates daily, with the exception of Christmas Day and the occasional closure because of flooding, and costs $74 return.

A PATCHWORK OF GREENS

Dramatic scenic contrasts are the hallmark of **Canterbury**, a fertile agricultural region that constitutes a giant eastern chunk of the South Island. Extending from the Pacific coast to the Southern Alps, it nurses the Canterbury Plains, the country's largest flat expanse of pasture-land which looks from the air like a patchwork of many-hued greens.

There are two main routes into North Canterbury from the tip of the South Island, one following the seacoast from Kaikoura, the other driving through the **Lewis Pass**, which links the wet forested valleys of the West Coast with the dry pastoral country of Canterbury. High mountains, braided rivers and silver and red beech forests form the backdrop to the highway, which rises to 886 m (2,857 ft) at the Lewis Pass, which is the starting point for the spectacular high country, St. James Walkway, 65 km (40 miles) long. Within the mountain passes is the spa resort of **Hanmer Springs**, an easy 136 km (84 miles) drive north from Christchurch. Cradled by forested alpine peaks it has hot mineral pools set in gardens of towering conifers. It is a blissful experience to sink into these therapeutic steaming pools, while savoring the alpine scent of pine trees and a view of snow-capped mountains in the outdoor setting of the springs. Nearby, **Hanmer Forest Park** is especially beautiful in autumn, with its colored birch, poplar, sycamore and rowan trees, lining the Forest Walk, one of the prettiest short walks through the park. Explore the park by car, or branch into longer walking trails. It's also possible to hire horses for trail riding. Check with the Department of Conservation office on Jollies Pass Road at Hanmer Springs about forest walks. If this isn't enough outdoor activity, you can jet boat on the **Waiau River** or ski at **Amuri** ski field, 16 km (10 miles) away. In Hanmer Springs, stay at **The Chalets**, ((03) 315-7097, on Jacks Pass Road, which has attractive inexpensive rooms, beautiful views and a good restaurant.

On the other side of Christchurch, South Canterbury's plains offer seemingly endless vistas of prosperous farmland on whose green fields graze fluffy sheep, fat, contented cows and red deer. The giant braided **Rakaia River**, with its alpine gorge, sends gushing tentacles across the landscape that not only provide thrilling jet-boat rides but also some of the best salmon fishing in the country. Westwards, **Methven** comes alive in the ski season with its main Mt. Hutt ski field. The **Hutt Forest** and the **Awa Awa Rata Reserve** have excellent high country walks, while the nearby **Mt. Somers Sub-Alpine Walkway** is a longer tramp, with two huts available on its track and **Peel Forest** is a tranquil reserve with fine walks.

MACKENZIE COUNTRY

As you take the road to **Fairlie**, you enter the evocative sienna tussock grassland vistas of Mackenzie Country, named for James Mackenzie, a long-dead Scottish sheep-thieving

rascal, whose exploits and faithful sheep-dog have become part of the region's folk-lore. As you climb into **Burkes Pass** on State Highway 8, you wind across brown velvety foothills, dancing with purple shadows, to reach the township of **Lake Tekapo**. Overlooking the lake's vivid turquoise waters, the stone **Church of the Good Shepherd** has pretty stained glass windows. A bronze statue of a collie sheep dog stands guard outside, built from a fund by local runholders in the Mackenzie Country. Further on is **Lake Pukaki**, another high alpine lake. Beyond, dominating the landscape, lies the massive bulk of Mt. Cook and the Southern Alps.

MT. COOK NATIONAL PARK

New Zealand's highest mountain at 3,764 m (12,349 ft), **Mt. Cook** and the gigantic 28-km (17-mile) **Tasman Glacier** are within this entirely alpine park set within the Southern Alps. The narrow park extends for only 80 km (50 miles) along the alpine crest, yet contains 140 peaks over 2,134 m (7,000 ft) as well as five of New Zealand's glaciers, comparable only with the Himalayas and Antarctica. Extensive snow-fields lie within the park, crowning the mountain peaks and freezing into pinnacled and crevassed ice-falls and glacial valleys.

Used as a training ground by Sir Edmund Hillary, who went on to make his historic climb of Mt. Everest, Mt. Cook is simply a breathtaking sight as its snowy iridescent bulk looms against an infinitely blue, clear sky above the broad, brown tussock flats of the surrounding alpine basin. The geologist Julius von Haast, later knighted by both Queen Victoria and Emperor Franz Josef of Austria, led the first expedition to the region in 1862. Of Mt. Cook he wrote that it "stood above all, towering into the sky. As far as the eye could reach everywhere snow and ice and rock appeared around us, and in such gigantic proportions that I sometimes thought I was dreaming, and instead of being in New Zealand, I found myself in the Arctic or Antarctic mountain regions." The Maoris call this great mountain *Aorangi*,

OPPOSITE: One of the most exhilarating ways to see the glaciers is by taking a scenic flight.

"Cloud in the Sky." Attempts were made to climb Mt. Cook from the 1860's, but it remained unconquered until 1894, when a trio of young men lead by 24 year-old Tom Fyfe "exultantly stepped onto the highest pinnacle of the monarch of the Southern Alps." Their brilliant climb was not matched for another 61 years — on the 100th attempt. The agile chamois up in the hills, descended from a pair given by Emperor Franz Josef in 1907, may make it look easy. But 140 people have lost their lives on the mountain — it is hardly an easy ascent.

one-way on a scenic flight. Mt. Cook Landline operates daily services between Queenstown, Te Anau, Christchurch and Timaru. Most of its buses connect with longer routes through Twizel, an hour's drive from Mt. Cook. From November to April, there are also special day trips from Christchurch, allowing about three and a half hour stopover time at Mt. Cook. InterCity also makes a 40 minutes stop at Mt. Cook on its daily Queenstown to Christchurch route. Both buses depart from the front door of the Mt. Cook Youth Hostel.

ACCESS

Three main routes converge on Mt. Cook National Park. The main routes are through Burkes Pass from South Canterbury and through the Lindis Pass from Central Otago. The third is from North Otago by the valley of the Waitaki River.

Mt. Cook Airlines has daily direct flights from Queenstown, Christchurch and Rotorua, where you can make connections to other cities. There are fewer regular flights from Te Anau. A bus service connects the airport with the snow-field township. There is no scheduled air service to the Fox and Franz Josef glaciers, but it's possible to fly

GENERAL INFORMATION

The **Park Headquarters Visitors Centre**, ((03) 627-0818, can advise on the numerous walks and tramping routes, and what guided tours are available. At the **Alpine Guides Mountain Shop**, ((03) 627-0834, you can buy or rent skiing and mountaineering equipment. They also run ski-touring and mountaineering courses, but at rather high fees. A one week Mountain Experience course costs $1,075. Private guides usually charge a day rate of about $240, which works out better when you are a group. But if you're determined to walk the difficult Copland Track (see the ADVENTURING

FORTH section) or attempt any difficult ascent, having an experienced guide is essential if you are a novice mountaineer.

SKIING AND SCENIC FLIGHTS

Skiing is the park's main attraction. At Mt. Cook there are glacier skiing, ski planes, heli-skiing, alpine ski-mountaineering, downhill ski touring, and especially in spring, Nordic ski-touring. In short, everything on skis you could possibly want. The main field is located around the incredibly blue waters of **Lake Ohau**.

The **Tekapo** ski-field at the northwest end of the lake are excellent learner's slopes, with heli-skiing from the adjacent Tom Thumb Range for the more adventurous. **Mt. Dobson** is the newest ski-field, and has beautiful views across lakes to Mt. Cook and the Southern Alps. **Fox Peak** has lots of exciting long runs, rewarding for skiers who don't mind rope tows instead of high-speed lifts. Down amongst tussock hills, the tiny settlements of **Tekapo**, **Burkes Pass** and **Kimbell** can be used as bases for these ski-fields, with lodges, hostels and camping sites.

Scenic flights across the Mt. Cook region are, as you might expect, unforgettable. Helicopters and fixed-wing aircraft dip and soar over awesome peaks, high seracs and snow-frozen glaciers. Snow-landings on the glaciers offer miraculous transportation into a magical, hushed panorama of eternal snow. Contact Mt. Cook Airlines, ((03) 627-0849, at the airport for details.

WHERE TO STAY

Although they might not admit it, many visitors to Mt. Cook like to do nothing more than just enjoy the view from **The Hermitage**, ((03) 627-0809, fax: (03) 627-0879, one of New Zealand's most renowned lodges. All rooms have stunning views, the food is exceptional and rates are mid- priced. Also within the same echelon is the **THC Glencoe Lodge**, ((03) 627-0804, fax: (03) 627-0879, although its restaurant is not quite as good. In the moderate-range bracket, **THC Mt. Cook Chalets** ((03) 627-0809, fax: (03) 627-0879, is very cozy. You can experience life on a high sheep station at **Glentanner Park**,

((03) 627-0855, a comfortable old homestead which offers good farm food and magnificent views of Mt. Cook. You can choose between staying in a fully-equipped cabin or use camp-style facilities from your caravan. Rates are inexpensive. The **Youth Hostel,** ((03) 627-0820, has excellent amenities including a sauna, cozy fires and central heating.

THE CANTERBURY COAST TO NORTH OTAGO

If you take the coastal route along State Highway 1 from Christchurch to Timaru, either en route for Mt. Cook or Dunedin, there are quite a few places of interest. Mid-way between Christchurch and Dunedin, the port town of **Timaru**, is a branch off point for Twizel and Mt. Cook on State Highway 8. A detour leads to nearby **Temuka**, a major center for high-quality pottery.

Back on State Highway 1, the route passes into North Otago, where the coastal town of **Oamaru** deserves a browse for its curious ghost-town of Victorian public buildings, constructed from local limestone and left almost completely untouched and largely unused. See Harbour and Tyne Streets, where the original facades are left as they were.

But along this coast, the most remarkable sight is provided by the 60 million-year old **Moeraki Boulders**, located 40 km (25 miles) south of Oamaru and 80 km (50 miles) north of Dunedin. Strewn like giant cannonballs across a sandy bay, dozens of these perfectly spherical boulders — up to three meters wide — were formed by weird freaks of nature that formed secretions around a central limestone core. They look more as though they have been dropped by a passing UFO. The Maori tribes of the region were absolutely fascinated by the boulders and wove many myths around them. The best-known explains how the boulders are the kumaras, gourds, eel baskets and calabashes washed ashore when a group of Maori gods shipwrecked off the Moeraki Coast.

THE WEST COAST

A narrow strip of land wedged between the stormy expanse of the Tasman Sea and the formidable, unbroken chain of the Southern

Alps, the West Coast is never more than 50 km (31 miles) wide. But as it stretches 500 km (310 miles) from Jackson Bay in the south to Karamea in the north, it offers a remarkable journey through a wild, sparsely populated region of magnificent coastline, primeval forests, unruly rivers, mountains and glaciers.

Not only that, New Zealand's "Wild West" — its history steeped in gold-digging, coal-mining and logging — still lives up to its name. Weathered wooden facades of Gold Rush settlements, tiny corrugated iron roofed lean-tos and rusting vintage jalopies are all part of the stoical landscape. West Coasters themselves, known as "Coasters," are hardy individualists, with more than just a whiff of the gritty early settler about them. Stopping in at a roadside tavern down a back-country road is a classic Outback experience. To the rest of New Zealand, they are living "up the boo-ay." But the Coasters know their part of the world is a charmed rarity, no matter how the waves crash like avalanches or the storms rail at darkened, mist-shrouded skies, creating thick pea-soup fog on the coastal roads. Rain here almost literally falls in buckets, transforming stony riverbeds into raging torrents in minutes.

The West Coast has never had a reputation for good weather. In 1642, when Abel Tasman saw its rugged mountain ramparts rising above impenetrable rain forest, he decided to turn north. When he passed this way in 1823, the French voyager Jules de Blossville noted in his logbook that the coast was "one long solitude, with forbidding sky, frequent tempest." His countryman Dumont D'Urville shortly afterwards summed it up in just one word: "Frightful." The first European to explore the West Coast — looking for potential farmland soon after Nelson was settled in 1842 — was Thomas Brunner. After spending 550 days in the wilderness, reduced to a diet of fern root, penguin, rat and finally his own dog, Brunner wrote "For what reason the natives choose to live here I cannot imagine." But for centuries, Maoris had prized the West Coast for its quantities of fine greenstone that lay, easily gathered, in the beds of two great rivers, the Arahura and Taramakau. This is still the best place in New Zealand to buy greenstone, carved or

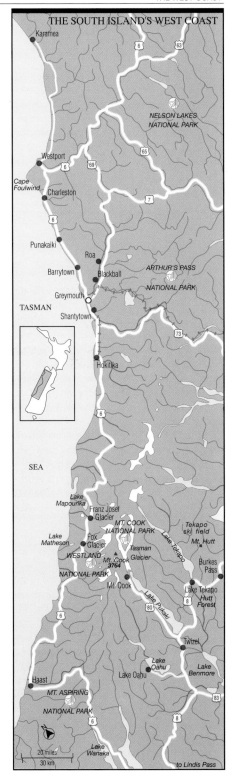

uncarved, and the museums of the region offer exquisite examples of delicately carved pendants, *tiki* and adze.

Soon the earth was plundered for other treasures. The Gold Rush began here in 1866, creating overnight large European settlements, especially at Hokitika. But by the end of the 1870's, the West Coast was losing its golden luster, and the diggers packed up and moved on. With its deserted ghost towns, constantly varying natural wildernesses and profoundly moody beauty, the West Coast should not be left unexplored.

ACCESS

From Christchurch, you can reach the West Coast by three main roads through the Southern Alps. The central route through Arthur's Pass and the surrounding national park of the same name is undeniably majestic, especially when made on the *Trans-Alpine Express.* You can drive via Rangiora and cross the Spenser Mountains to the Reefton Junction. The southernmost and longest route crosses the Lindis Pass, one of New Zealand's most dramatic stretches of scenery, and offers a tour through rugged MacKenzie Country and the Mt. Cook region. This longest route requires a detour to Haast and State Highway 6 along the West Coast.

Regardless of one's point of entry — from Wanaka and the lake district of Central Otago, from Arthur's Pass, or from Nelson on the Murchison road in the north — State Highway 6 is the backbone of the gloriously scenic and remote scenery of the "Wild West."

If you don't have a car, one of the best ways to explore the West Coast is to take a tour. The **West Coast Express** offers six day tours from $89, which stop at all main towns and sights, including the glaciers. They depart Nelson every Sunday and Wednesday, and from Queenstown every Saturday and Tuesday. You can make bookings and inquiries at the Youth Hostel in Nelson, ((03) 548-8817, at 42 Weka Street, or at the Youth Hostel in Queenstown, ((03) 442-8413, Lake Esplanade.

Air Nelson connects Hokitika and Westport with Nelson, Christchurch, Blenheim, Dunedin, Wellington and Auckland.

InterCity and Newmans bus companies operate services to Fox Glacier, Hokitika,

Greymouth, Westport from Queenstown, Picton, and Nelson, while Delta Landline has daily buses between Picton and Greymouth, via St. Arnaud, Murchison and Reefton.

A NATURE RETREAT

One of the best places from which to explore the natural wilderness of the West Coast is **Lake Moeraki Wilderness Lodge,** ((03) 750-0881, fax: (03) 750-0883, an extraordinary place to stay, especially if you like bird-watching. Located 30 km (19 miles) north of Haast, it is an ideal place for people keen on the outdoors, fishing and nature walks. The secluded, natural-wood and comfortable lodge offers moderately-priced rooms, as well as self-contained cottages and backpacker's accommodation. Guests wake up to the sound of tuis, bellbirds and shining cuckoos. The lodge specializes in tours to see Fiordland Crested Penguin and fur seal colonies, as well as fishing salmon and trout in Lake Moeraki. It's run by Anne Saunders and Dr. Gerry McSweeney, director of New Zealand's largest conservation organization, the Forest and Bird Society.

TRAVELING UP THE COAST

Glacier Giants

Of all the sights to be seen on the West Coast, nothing compares to the icy brilliance and eerie magnitude of the **Fox Glacier** and the **Franz Josef Glacier**, which lie 120 km (74 miles) north of Haast. Both are located, 25 km (15.5 miles) apart, in the **Westland National Park**, a vast playground of alpine mountains, snow-fields, forests, lakes and rivers, which, with Mt. Cook National Park on the far side of Main Divide, has been honored as a World Heritage Park. Although only shrunken remnants of their Ice Age ancestors, these glaciers are still stunning spectacles, plunging from high snow cliffs in a vast wall of solid ice down to forested lowland valleys. Nowhere else in the world, except in Chile, is it still possible to find glaciers encroaching like this into temperate forest.

The 13 km (eight miles) long Fox Glacier, is perhaps the grander spectacle of the two, its huge white tongue dominating the valley, dropping 2,600 m (8,580 ft) on its journey. There is easy access by road and you can also walk right onto the glacier — one of the very few opportunities in the world to do this so easily. Pristine white on the surface, except where it has been soiled by footsteps and tracks, the glacier ice radiates a remarkable turquoise color in its hollows and fissures. Glacier ice is not smooth and glassy, but cramped into crisscross fractures and ridges by the grinding weight of its moving mass. The valley is built on a bed of ice more than 300 m (990 ft) deep; rock bottom has never been sounded.

shines from its deep valley. There are better views from the tiny Tudor-style **St. James Church**. To reach the 11 km (nearly seven miles) long glacier, you need to make a two hour return walk through deep forest, and when it comes into view it presents an even more rewarding sight, with its gleaming white and turquoise ice expanse.

Both townships offer guided glacier tours, which are a vigorous and satisfying way of exploring these ice giants. But to really appreciate the magnitude of the glaciers, you do have to see them from the air.

Strictly for the fit, but needing no more equipment than strong footwear, climbs to the 1,337 m (4,412 ft) summit of Mt. Fox rise through sub-tropical forest to steep mountain slopes daubed with summer alpine flowers. Near Fox Glacier settlement is an undemanding nature walk to **Lake Matheson**, which mirrors Mt. Cook and Mt. Tasman, full of picturesque beauty and stillness.

The Franz Josef Glacier township, on the banks of the Waiho River, is surrounded by Westland National Park, for which it is the headquarters. Named after the Austro-Hungarian Emperor by nineteenth century geologist Julius von Haast, not much of the glacier can be seen from the road, but there is no mistaking where it lies, for a pale light

Scenic flights — in helicopters and fixed wing ski planes — provide unforgettable sweeping views across the vast emerald-tinted ice rivers, buckled snow-fields and massive pinnacles glistening like whipped cream. When you alight, you can explore ice tunnels, listen to the creaking ice buttresses and the eternal sound of dripping water.

The park's headquarters at Franz Josef offer detailed information about the many walks in the region. These include the challenging, but rewarding four-day climb over the **Copland Pass** in the Main Divide to The Hermitage at Mt. Cook. The park has over 110 km (68 miles) of walking tracks through

Aerial view of Fox Glacier from Cone Rock.

its varied forest, splashed scarlet with summer *rata* trees and dominated by the high peaks of Mt. Cook, Mt. Tasman and Mt. La Perouse. Easier walks include the four-hour hike to 1,295 m (4,273 ft) **Alex Knob**, up hills bristling with fragrant speargrass, and to Lake Mapourika, which has one of the country's loveliest alpine views.

Within the region you can also go on fishing, canoe and horse-trekking trips. You can take a jet-boat tour to view the secluded White Heron nesting sanctuary at Mt. Hercules on the coast, near Okarito. Alluding to its rarity there is a Maori saying: *"Te Kotuku rerenga tahu,"* the flight of the White Heron is seen only once. Its beautiful dorsal plumage was sought after by Maoris as a symbol of chiefly status.

Useful Contacts

The main **Visitor Information Centre**, ((03) 751-0807, Main Road is the headquarters for Westland National Park, and can help with all inquiries, notably with booking for scenic flights and adventure tours.

White Heron Sanctuary Tours, ((03) 753-4120, offers free transport from Franz Josef for their tours of the White Heron sanctuary near Whatoroa which take place during this rare bird's breeding season from November to February.

Stan Peterson operates **Westland Guiding Service**, ((03) 752-0750, which has a variety of nature walks, including the Fox Glacier and Lake Matheson (35 minutes), Franz Josef Glacier (35 minutes), and both glaciers (three and a half hours), plus hunting and fishing safaris.

Where to Stay

In the little settlement around Fox Glacier, a comfortable choice is the **Golden Glacier Motor Inn**, ((03) 751-0848, fax: (03) 751-0822, a member of Flag Inns, located on State Highway 6. Its well-furnished rooms are moderately priced, and there is a good restaurant. They also have backpacker shares and double rooms with showers and televisions. **Ivory Towers**, ((03) 652-0830, on Sullivans Road, offers cozy backpacker accommodation, excellent amenities and a large verandah for watching dramatic sunsets across the glacier.

Around Franz Josef Glacier, the moderately-priced **Westland Motor Inn**, ((03) 752-0729, fax: (03) 752-0709, nestled amongst the lush native bush of Westland National Park on State Highway 6, is also a Flag Inns member. The lounge area has a roaring log fire, there are spa pools to soak in in a garden of native bush, and the rooms have a very tranquil atmosphere with early morning bird song. Campers can seek out the **Franz Josef Holiday Park**, ((03) 652-0766, on Main Road, which has magnificent forest views, modern kitchen facilities and all amenities, as well as tourist cabins. In town, the cheapest lodges are the **Pavlova Backpackers**, ((03) 652-0738 and the **Youth Hostel**, ((03) 652-0754, both on Cron Street.

THE ROAD TO HOKITIKA

A short detour west from Fox Glacier leads to **Gillespies Beach**, a wild coastal stretch that is interesting to visit for its miner's cemetery and fur seal colony, a three hour return walk. In the early nineteenth century, sealing gangs from Sydney were dumped here, sometimes to starve, to send tens of thousands of seal skins back to their employers. A further 67 km (42 miles) north on Highway 6, lies **Okarito**, a ramshackle, abandoned miner's town on a tranquil shag-dotted lagoon. Keri Hulme, winner of the Booker Prize for her book, *The Bone People*, is a permanent resident here and says she wouldn't swap it for anywhere in the world. Northwards, pretty **Lake Ianthe** was once a prospering gold-field; now there's just a small museum in a wooden shed.

HOKITIKA

Once raunchy, now desolate, Hokitika typified the West Coast's wildest years. It mushroomed overnight in Gold Rush of 1866, growing from a miserable rain-soaked collection of tents to a bustling settlement of some 15,000 complete with a hastily-erected 1,400-seat opera house and some hundred hotels. Many New Zealanders are descended from the Irish miners who began their immigrant lives in Hokitika, fleeing the ravages of the potato famine and hoping for better prospects with gold. In those days, it was renowned as a difficult port: its seafront had too many wrecks to count, and the flotsam sailed up the main street at high tide. Walking through sleepy Hokitika today one wonders where it all went: the opera house, the gambling halls and the dancing girls. These days you couldn't pay money to have your back scratched in Hokitika.

But you could spend it on greenstone. In Hokitika, greenstone is the main fascination. Craft shops and skilled Maori carvers abound, and this is the place to find the country's finest work. You can visit the nearby **Arahura River**, eight kilometers (five miles) away, with its high swinging footbridge, owned by the only surviving local Maori tribe, who still find large amounts of greenstone on its bed.

Two places of interest to visit are the **West Coast Historical Museum** and the **Hokitika Craft Gallery**, both on Tancred Street.

General Information

Expect a warm welcome at the **Visitor Information Centre**, ((03) 755-8101, in Regent Theater on the corner of Weld and Tancred streets. They don't see many tourists, and like to make sure the ones they do are well-informed about the West Coast's attractions. They have pamphlets on nature walks, treks to Mahinapua and Kaniere lakes, adventure activities, tours, and greenstone craft trails in Hokitika's environs.

Where to Stay and Eat

The most pleasant place to stay in town is **Central Guest House**, ((03) 755-8232, at 20 Hamilton Street, which has inexpensive bed and breakfast accommodation. Also inexpensive, **Tudor Motel**, ((03) 755-8193, at 121 Tudor Street, which has a restaurant and good fishing in a nearby river. **Southland Hotel**, ((03) 755-8344, fax: (03) 755-8258, at 11 Revell Street, is slightly more expensive, with rooms that look out across the romantic, forbidding Tasman Sea, usually full of great mist clouds.

Hokitika is not really on New Zealand's culinary map. You can stick with the sea-views at **Tasman View Restaurant**, in the Southland Hotel, or try **Millie's Place**, ((03) 755-8128, a cheerful BYO in New World Mall. The **P.R.'s Bistro and Coffee**

Shop serves the township's best coffee and home-baked excellent cakes.

SHANTYTOWN AND WOODS CREEK TRACK

Continuing up the coast, head inland from Paroa for Shantytown, a delightfully authentic replica mining town nestled in lush, forested hills, straight out of the pages of Tom Sawyer with wooden houses, water-wheels, white picket fences and steam train station. You can take rides on the train, horse-drawn buggy and Cobb & Co. coach and go gold-

panning at a nearby gold claim.It's open from 8:30 am to 5pm daily.

A further 17 km (10.5 miles) away into the forest is the beginning of the **Woods Creek Track**, a superb 45-minute walk dotted with old mining tunnels, water races and wooded bridges through mysterious dense bush. Bring a torch to explore the dark tunnels.

GREYMOUTH

With its "large" population of 8,000, Greymouth is the unchallenged capital of the West Coast. Squeezed between hills, sea and river, once the site of a Maori *pa*, the town

ABOVE: A greenstone carver at work in Hokitika.

began as a government depot for surveyors, developing into a river port as gold, coal and then timber were bought down from the hills. It's a functional town, but lies close to dramatic scenery inland — near the beautiful fern-fringed Lake Brunner, along the riverbanks of the thunderous Grey River, and further north, at Punakaiki. It's a place to stay a night, then keep traveling up the coast.

General Information

The **Information Centre**, ((03) 769-5101, at the corner of Mackay and Herbert streets, assists with all inquiries and can arrange wilderness tours and treks through forest and deserted mining sites that are the feature of the region.

Where to Stay and Eat

In town, **Ardwyn House Homestay**, ((03) 769-6107, at 48 Chapel Street, is a small, friendly guest-house, inexpensive and cozy.

Another good choice is the **Golden Coast Guest House**, ((03) 768-7839, at 10 Smith Street, similarly priced. The **Pavlova Backpackers**, ((03) 768-4848, at 16 Chapel Street, was originally used as a monastery for the St. Patrick's Catholic Church next door. Its bucolic atmosphere might appeal to you just as much as the hallmark evening slice of creamy Pavlova.

For lunch or an casual evening meal, **Cafe Collage**, ((03) 769-5497, at 115 Mackay Street serves New Zealand specialities, with oysters, scallops and whitebait fritters in season. It serves the best food on the West Coast. It is closed Sundays and Mondays.

Tours

Off-beat Tours (Audrey and Charles Fulford), (Ngahere (03) 762-6466, offers jeep tours of the West Coast's highlights, including gold and coal-mining sites, ghost-towns, scenic rafting, nature trails, sailing on Lake Brunner, and stopping at some of the region's more characterful old pubs. Full day tours cost $68.

A Lodge Hideaway

Nestled within Greymouth's high country, with a backdrop of emerald mountains and a dramatic waterfall, the exclusive **Lake Brunner Sporting Lodge**, ((03) 738-0163, fax: (03) 738-0163, lies off Highway 73, 47 km

(29 miles) from Greymouth at Inchbonnie, on Kumara Road. It specializes in hunting and fishing — notably chamois, thar, red deer and brown trout — and charges deluxe rates. This is a restful retreat, with a lakeside setting amidst native forest, with wonderful cuisine. Guided hunting and fishing involve extra charges.

Moana

The *Trans-Alpine Express* pulls into the nearby township of Moana on the northern shore of Lake Brunner, but its tranquil

beauty is worth a longer stay. Located off Highway 73, it can also be used as a staging post to or from the winding forested back road that emerges at Kumara, from which to take the road south to Hokitika. The **Moana Hotel**, ((03) 866-5609, is an appealing place to stay, and you can hire a dingy for cruises on the lake, which locals say is the only one in the world where the fish die of old age.

GHOST-TOWNS AND PANCAKE ROCKS

As you swing onto Highway 6 again, watch out for the turnoff to **Blackball**, 25 km

OPPOSITE: Dramatic rock formations fringe the rugged West Coast. ABOVE: The wondrously shaped Pancake Rocks at Punakaiki.

(15.5 miles) down an unsealed road, surrounded by deserted gold and coal mining relics. As curiously idiosyncratic a place as you could hope to find, Blackball has ramshackle colonial homes with over-grown gardens, creaking gates, barking dogs, and fearless sheep grazing on grass growing in the dilapidated hulks of old cars. Stay at the nineteenth century **Blackball Hilton**, ((03) 732-4705, on Hart Road, which looks like it is straight out of a John Ford western. But remember to bring your candles. There is an eccentric little museum with equally eccentric opening hours for which it can't be blamed since visitors are few.

Close by at **Roa**, the **Croesus Track** begins, a two-day mountain trek gold-mining relics, with an overnight hut to break the journey, before crossing the Paparoa Range to emerge at Barrytown on the coast.

By car, you have to take the long route, looping back onto Highway 6. There's not an awful lot to stop for at **Barrytown**, another seen-better-days mining town, although you can stay at the **All Nations Tavern**, ((03) 731-1812, a characterful, if not salubrious tavern which has bunkroom accommodation.

Punakaiki, 16 km (10 miles) up the coast, located within the **Paparoa National Park** is one of the West Coast's most compelling sights. The curious chalk formations of the **Pancake Rocks**, so-called because of their astonishing resemblance to stacks of giant pancakes, trap the spray in blow holes and funnel it explosively; water squirts high into the air. The **Truman Track** winds down to the beach where you can investigate the coastal reefs and rock pools at low tide. The quaint coastal settlement of Punakaiki has a camping ground nearby, the **Punakaiki Motor Camp**, ((03) 731-1894, fax: (03) 731-1888; while good swimming can be had in the nearby Pororari River or at Pororari Beach, two kilometers (one-and-a-quarter miles) away.

Further on, the aptly-named **Cape Foulwind**, has a four kilometer (two-and-a-half mile), spray-splashed walkway out to a colony of Fur Seals, where you can watch these ruddy-pelted creatures gambol in the surf and seaweed. The road to Westport passes

through **Charleston**, once a gold-mining town, where you can see an operating mine in action at Mitchell's Gully.

WESTPORT

A rather bleak coal export township on the estuary of the mighty Buller River, Westport has one important redeeming feature for visitors: it is the adventure center of the West Coast. The options include white-water river rafting on rapids or through glow-worm lit caves, jet-boating through the Buller River's awesome gorges, caving, tramping or horse-trekking through dense forest studded with nikau palms and going out to see the Fur Seal colony at Cape Foulwind. The **Buller Information Centre**, ((03) 789-6658, Brougham Street, has details on all these activities. Make sure you visit **Coal Town**, an open-air museum on Queen Street South, which has walk-through coal-mining displays complete with sound effects of groaning miners and clattering trolleys. East of Westport is the Buller Gorge Scenic Drive, which winds its way through a remote rugged gorge and offers high coastal views. Five kilometers (three miles) north of Westport, Highway 6 follows the Buller River on a scenic 84 km (52 miles) route to Murchison, en route to Nelson and Blenheim.

In Westport, stay at the **Buller Bridge Motel**, ((03) 789-7519, on The Esplanade, which has comfortable, moderately-priced rooms, a restaurant and a peaceful seafront setting. The **Howard Park Holiday Park**, ((03) 789-7043, on Domett Street, set amongst native bush, has A-frame chalets and camping grounds. **Cristy's**, ((03) 789-7640, on Wakefield Street, is the town's best restaurant and requires reservations. They have a great range of liqueur coffees to keep the raging storms and rain at bay.

Tours

West Coast Adventure, ((03) 789-7286, fax: (03) 789-8104, on Buller Gorge Road, operates rafting, jet-boating, horse-trekking and trekking tours.

Norwest Adventures, ((03) 789-6686, at 41 Domett Street, runs spectacular guided rafting, caving and abseiling tours into river and underground caves, rich in stalactites,

---

OPPOSITE ABOVE: A West Coast dweller poised for a splash. OPPOSITE BELOW: Spiky cabbage trees dot the coastline near Karamea.

stalagmites and Glow-Worm displays, some including treks of several days into the forest.

KARAMEA

The northernmost settlement on the West Coast, Karamea's rich farmland is a startling contrast to its backdrop of rugged forests. If you have made it up this far, then don't leave without seeing the **Oparara Basin**, an area of majestic limestone arches and caves, north of Karamea. Within the nearby **Honeycomb Hill Caves** are a treasure-house of

preserved skeletons of moa and other birds. This delicate cave system can only be entered on guided tours arranged from Karamea. The road-end above Karamea takes you to the start of the **Heaphy Track**. Even if you don't want to attempt the full walk, a day trip along the rocky headlands, *nikau* palm groves and golden beaches of the coastal section is spectacular.

The **Visitors Centre**, ((03) 782-6852, can help with accommodation, tours and track information. Between December and February, the best place to stay is the **Punga Lodge Hostel**, ((03) 782-6805, but when it closes,

ABOVE: A potter in his workshop in Karamea.
OPPOSITE: The best panoramic views of Queenstown can be experienced from Bob's Peak.

try the **Karamea Domain Bunkhouse and Campsite**, ((03) 782-6751. You can pick up the keys from the Tea Rooms.

LONELY FIORDS AND MAJESTIC SUMMITS

This is a region renowned for its spell-binding scenery, from Queenstown's steep alpine mountains, schist canyons and billowing rivers to Fiordland's remote jungle-like rain forests, mystical glacier-carved lakes, thundering giant waterfalls and the magnificent deep fiord of **Milford Sound**, one of the most compellingly beautiful places on earth. Much of the region's wilderness remains unexplored, although the early Maoris traversed many of its most difficult passes in search of much-prized *pounamu*, or greenstone, which they used for adzes and war clubs. Much later, the Gold Rush provided the impetus for European settlers painstakingly to build roads and villages in the rugged, treacherous mountain canyons of the Queenstown area.

Within Queenstown and Fiordland are the country's most rewarding walking tracks, including the exceptional four-day **Milford Track**, where organized treks allow otherwise inexperienced trampers to catch a glimmer of the isolated beauty that lies within New Zealand's forested mountains.

QUEENSTOWN

Queenstown is New Zealand's ultimate picture postcard resort town. Mirrored in Lake Wakatipu's placid surface, it has a backdrop of massive sierra-like snow-capped mountain ranges aptly-named The Remarkables on one side, and the Southern Alps on the other, stretching as far as the eye can see. On fine evenings, the rocky jigsaw ridge of the Remarkables glows pink as it reflects the sunset. Queenstown is spectacularly beautiful throughout the year, but especially so in autumn, when russet-colored sycamore and oak trees create a feathery haze of color against rich farmland. In winter it is the country's brashest ski resort with two snow fields, and all year round it draws adventurers to raft and jet boat through its surging rapids, make light aircraft swoops across Fiordland's lakes, glaciers and mountain passes, kayak and fly-fish for trout in placid rivers, horse-ride through alpine gullies and trek through some of the world's most spectacular natural scenery.

For centuries, the Maoris traversed the arduous, densely forested mountain routes through Fiordland's mountain passes to reach Lake Wakatipu in search of greenstone. Then, in 1862, the Gold Rush began here when two sheep shearers, Thomas Ar-

to less then two hundred. As you explore the Shotover Canyon, you'll see the ghost town ruins of many of these settlements.

An intriguing myth surrounds Wakatipu, the third largest lake of New Zealand, which in Maori means "place of the giant." The serpentine 84 km (52 miles) long lake "breathes" every five minutes, or rather its water level swells then falls. No scientific explanation has been found: but a Maori myth relates the saga of an evil giant who abducted a Maori maiden, then was set alight by her rescuer, his burning body

thur and Harry Redfern, panned a large amount of gold from the Shotover River at Arthur's Point, near Queenstown. Swarms of fortune hunters — including many Australians, Americans and Chinese — descended on these towering mountains and unexplored creeks. Soon daily finds were reckoned in pounds weight rather than mere ounces. Makeshift canvas towns of miners tents, stores and grog shops sprang up overnight, quickly establishing Queenstown, nearby Arrowtown and many smaller camp towns on the lower reaches of the swift-flowing Shotover River, the second-richest gold-bearing river in the world. Then the gold petered out and by 1900 the population had dropped from several thousand

melting the surrounding glaciers to form a huge water-filled crater. Only the giant's beating heart survived, said to account for the lake's regular fluctuation.

Queenstown is an ideal location to sample almost every kind of outdoor activity. Although highly commercialized, action and adventure tours here are so well-organized and infectiously fun that they are an ideal way to experiment with activities that you might otherwise never try. Expert advice and encouragement is on hand for beginners and equipment can be easily hired for a reasonable price. There's enough to keep even the most hyperactive sports addict happy. After all, where else in the world can you go river rafting, bungy-jumping, jet-boating and helicopter flying all in an afternoon, and still be ready for more?

ACCESS

Mount Cook Airlines and Ansett New Zealand both fly to Queenstown: the airport is located at Frankton, a suburb on the town's outskirts. Mt Cook has daily flights from Auckland, Rotorua, Christchurch, Dunedin, Te Anau, Milford Sound, Wanaka, Mt Cook, Nelson and Alexandra, while Ansett New Zealand has daily flights from Christchurch with connections to Wellington, Auckland and Rotorua. Six major bus companies, including InterCity, Mt. Cook, Landline and Newmans, ply daily between Queenstown and most major towns in the South Island. For driving, allow half a day from Invercargill or Dunedin, a full day from Christchurch.

GENERAL INFORMATION

At every step in Queenstown you will be deluged with information on adventure activities, excursions and attractions: the town is pamphlet mad. For one-stop advice on accommodation, bookings, tours and the best up-to-date local information, make a beeline for the **Queenstown Information Centre**, ((03) 442-7318, at the corner of Shotover and Camp streets. Also on Shotover Street, are the helpful **NZTP Tourist Information Centre**, ((03) 442-8238, and the **Information and Track Walking Centre**, ((03) 442-7867. The **Department of Conservation** (DOC) office, ((03) 442-7933, is on the corner of Ballarat and Stanley streets. It has guides and maps explaining the natural attractions, drives and walking tracks, including Milford, Kepler, Routeburn and other walks. **Fiordland Travel**, ((03) 442-7500, at the Steamer Wharf, operates the *TSS Earnslaw* vintage steamer cruises on Lake Wakatipu, launch cruises through the Milford and Doubtful sounds, scenic flights and other excursion trips within Fiorldland.

The **Backpacker Express** runs a useful service to and from the start of the main tramping tracks in the region, originating close to Glenorchy: the Routeburn, Greenstone/Caples and Rees tracks. For information and booking, call (03) 442-9939.

Lastly, Queenstown traders are unique in the country for being allowed to open seven days a week, and the usual shopping hours are 9 am to 5:30 pm and 7:30 pm to 9 pm, except on weekends when shops close for the afternoon.

WHAT TO SEE

Unless you suffer from vertigo, the most memorable way to get your bearings in Queenstown is to take the **Skyline Gondola** to **Bob's Peak**, the summit that towers some 450 m (1,116ft) above the town. At the observation deck you can take in deep breaths of fresh alpine air and panoramic views across Queenstown, Lake Wakatipu, the Remarkables and the Southern Alps. The gondola car operates from 10 am to 10 pm daily. If you are more energetic you can walk all the way up instead on a well-marked track from Lomond Crescent — a steep two-hour climb with plenty of scenic stops along the way.

While you're still taking things easy, another of Queenstown's highlights is to get out onto Lake Wakatipu. You can arrange hydrofoil, hovercraft and jet-boat rides from the main pier, or take a pew on the *TSS Earnslaw*, a gleamingly restored vintage steamer, complete with an elegant dining saloon, which chugs out daily at 12:30 pm (boarding from 12 noon) for an hour's lunch-time cruise around the Frankton Arm, creating a thick black plume that is probably the only pollution you'll ever see in Queenstown. You can opt for longer three-hour cruise out to the remote **Mount Nicholas Sheep Station**, only accessible by boat, which departs at 2 pm. As you cruise, hot pikelets are served off the griddle, topped with jam and cream — a traditional New Zealand afternoon tea. At the station, you'll be shown around by burly, wise-cracking farmers on horseback, with well-trained sheep dogs who demonstrate their authority over swarms of fluffy sheep. The sing-along with the resident pianist on the return journey may cause you to flee to the deck. There's also an hour-long dinner cruise which boards at 6 pm.

Queenstown itself — with its prettified mall of shops, restaurants, cafes and a few tourist-orientated museums — doesn't offer much in the way of sightseeing. The **Sound**

and Light Museum on Beach Street has regular showings of a 20-minute program that recounts the history of the early settlers, interspliced with interesting old footage. You can hop aboard a red London double-decker bus for a three hour excursion to **Arrowtown** that also stops off to watch bungy jumpers at **Kawarau Bridge**. It departs from the top of the mall at 10 am and 2 pm daily.

Other tourist-orientated "attractions" are recommended if you are in a leisurely frame of mind — although they are hardly worth visiting if your time is precious on the

ski slopes or out in the rapids. On the pier, **Water World**'s submarine-like glass window beneath the lake's surface allows you to admire giant trout, shudder-inducing eels and diving ducks as they compete for bread crumbs. If you follow the pierfront, past the small crescent-shaped beach, you'll reach the **Government Gardens**, with its rose gardens, lily ponds, skating rink and tennis courts. Before or after a ride on the gondola to Bob's Peak, you can make a detour to the **Kiwi and Birdlife Park**, an ornithological park within a reserve planted with over 6,000 native trees, open daily from 9 am to 5 pm. Nearby, the **Motor Museum** has a collection of vintage cars, open from 9 am to 5:30 pm daily.

It's worth making a detour to see the preserved prospector's village within the **Goldfields Museum Park**, three kilometers (nearly two miles) from Queenstown on the road to Frankton.

ABOVE: Red deer are a common sight on farms in the Queenstown area.

WHERE TO STAY

As one of New Zealand's most popular destinations, Queenstown offers many sophisticated resorts and hotels as well as every other style of accommodation. The only thing that doesn't vary is the panoramic views of the lake and surrounding mountains. On fine evenings the rocky, snow-powdered ridge of The Remarkables glows pink as it reflects the setting sun. If you book from the Tourist Center, most hotels or lodges can arrange a pick-up service.

Exclusive
Nugget Point Club, ((03) 442-7630, fax: (03) 442-7308, on Arthur's Point Road, is one of the best luxury retreats in New Zealand, located 15 km (just over nine miles) from Queenstown. The apartment-sized suites have everything from marble bathrooms to impressive kitchens and overlook either the Shotover Canyon or the beautifully landscaped grounds. The amenities include the superb Nugget Point Restaurant and club-style bar, a swimming pool with impressive views, well-equipped health club, sauna and a tennis court. You can also make bookings to hire helicopters or hot-air balloons.

Deluxe
Queenstown Parkroyal, ((03) 442-7800, fax: (03) 442-8895, at Beach Street, is the most luxurious place to stay in town. It has lovely gardens, a swimming pool and balconies overlooking the Lake Wakatipu waterfront. The hotel's restaurant, Bentley's Brasserie, is much acclaimed. The **Lakeland Queenstown**, ((03) 442-7600, fax: (03) 442-9653, on the Lake Esplanade, has an equally pleasant ambience with similar facilities, as does the **Terraces Hotel**, ((03) 442-7950, fax: (03) 442-8066 at the corner of Frankton Road and Suburb Street.

Moderate
Two other classy choices are the **Pacific Park**, ((03) 442-6500, fax: ((03) 442-7898, on Frankton Road; and the **Country Lodge Hotel**, ((03) 442-7688, fax: (03) 442-7677, on Fernhill Road, the latter set within a little forest of lush native bush. The **THC Queens-**

town Hotel, ((03) 442-7750, fax: (03) 442-7469, on the corner of Marine Parade and Earl Street, is another plush refuge, right on the waterfront.

Vacation Inn, ((03) 442-8123, fax: (03) 442-7472, on the corner of Adelaide and Frankton Road and the Quality Inn, ((03) 442-6600, fax: (03) 442-7354, on Sainsbury Road, are of a high-quality. The Shotover Resort Hotel, ((03) 442-7850, fax: (03) 442-6127, on Arthurs Point Road some 15 km (nine miles) away from Queenstown, is an excellent base during the ski season. It has an indoor sports center, spa, swimming pools and restaurant.

Inexpensive
There are two exceptional bed and breakfast establishments in Queenstown, both nicer than staying in a conventional hotel. Hulbert House, ((03) 442-8767 at 68 Ballarat Street is a Victorian villa, beautifully restored with five rooms, all with private bathrooms, lake and mountain views and a quiet garden. Located four kilometers (two-and-a-half miles) from Queenstown, Trelawn Place, ((03) 442-9160, at Nery Howard, is a pretty cottage with a tranquil setting on the edge of the Shotover River.

In the center of town, right on the waterfront, Hotel Walters, ((03) 442-7180, fax: (03) 442-8095, at 50 Beach Street, is a convenient choice. The Hotel Esplanade, ((03) 442-8611 at 32 Peninsula Street is one of Queenstown's bargains, and offers the best value you're likely to find. Rooms are spacious, complete with bathrooms and thoughtful touches like extra towels. This hotel is tucked on a peaceful lakeside street behind the Government Gardens. Also recommended is the Queenstown Lodge, ((03) 442-7117, fax: (03) 442-6498, on Sainsbury Road. Queenstown House, ((03) 442-9043, at 69 Hallenstein Street is a good choice for bed and breakfast accommodation.

For Campers and Backpackers
The Queenstown Hostel, ((03) 442-8413, at 80 Lake Esplanade has a booking service for most trips and activities, and is always popular, so book well in advance. Pavlova Backpackers, ((03) 442-8725, at 15 Sydney Street and Bumbles, ((03) 442-6298, at 2 Brunswick Street also offer good value for money.

Campers should investigate the Creeksyde Camper Van Park, ((03) 442-9447, fax: (03) 442-6571, at 54 Robins Road, which won a tourism design award for its unique concept of luxury camping, which extends to kitchens with microwave ovens and private spa bathrooms. Close to Coronet Peak, Arthur's Point Camping Ground, ((03) 442-9306 (fax: same number), located five kilometers (three miles) from Queenstown at Arthur's Point, has a scenic setting and excellent facilities, including a pool and shop.

WHERE TO EAT

Queenstown has a lively nightlife with more than 50 restaurants and dozens of bars, music dens and pubs. Here is a selection:

The Nugget Point Restaurant, ((03) 442-7630, already mentioned, is the place to go. Within its plush dining hall, warmed by an open fire, the restaurant serves distinctive New Zealand cuisine which you can enjoy while looking at the spectacular view of the Shotover Canyon, and it has the best array of local wines to be found anywhere in the region. Another choice for elegant dining is Bentley's Brasserie, ((03) 442-7860, at the Parkroyal Hotel. It's open all day, so you could come here for a sumptuous breakfast. At other meals, dine on innovatively prepared fresh seafood, lamb and game dishes, or try their "Hot Rocks" speciality — a kind of New Zealand Mongolian Hot-Pot. Treetops, ((03) 442-7238, on Arawata Terrace in Sunshine Bay, is renowned for its extensive menu of seafood dishes, which includes Bluff oysters and Stewart Island mussels. Upstairs Downstairs, ((03) 442-8290, at 66 Shotover Street, serves classic New Zealand dishes amidst a chintzy Victorian atmosphere.

The overwhelming attraction of dining at the Skyline, ((03) 442-7860, is clinched firstly by the fun of taking a gondola ride up there, and secondly by the panoramic views from its glassed-in dining hall. Roaring Meg's, ((03) 442-9676, at 57 Shotover Street, is a cozy, candlelit restaurant in a renovated goldmining cottage with a lovingly-prepared array of dishes. It's named after one of Queenstown's legendary characters — an irrepressible hussy with a scarlet reputation. Westy's, ((03) 442-8635, The Mall, is the most fashionable of Queenstown's restaurants, with typically satisfying New Zealand food, live entertainment and an upstairs balcony.

Also in The Mall, the **Stonewall Cafe**, ((03) 442-6429, has a rustic atmosphere, with old stonewalls and an open fire. Particularly good to try are the *kumara* cakes, green-lipped mussels in garlic and char-grilled grouper steaks. **Millies**, ((03) 442-7309, at 24 Beach Street, is a good place to take a family, with its casual outside dining during summer, and has an imaginative variety of soups, salads, seafoods and steak dishes to choose from.

ment food hall great for grabbing lunch or a quick snack. The historic lakefront **Eichardt's Tavern** is best known locally for its stock of beers on tap and wines, but it also deserves mention for cooking the most basic food well.

OUTDOOR ACTIVITIES IN AND AROUND QUEENSTOWN

If the ski slopes are shut, there are plenty of other things to do to in and around Queenstown to keep even the most hyperactive sports fanatic happy. Jet-boating on moun-

Located on the banks of the Kawarau River, the **Gibbston Valley Vineyard** lies 25 km (15.5 miles) from Queenstown, and offers tastings, meals, vineyard and winery tours. Dining is in the elegant cellar restaurant or outdoors in a sunny courtyard surrounded by vines. It's open daily from 10 am to 6:30 pm, and is located on the main Cromwell-Queenstown highway, ((03) 442-6910.

For unpretentious Italian cooking, go to **Avanti** ((03) 442-8503, at N° 20 The Mall. Steak lovers can make a beeline for the **Beefeater Steak House,** ((03) 442-9149, at 40 Shotover Street, where all main dishes are served with a baked potato and salad from a self-service bar. The **Pavilion Mall**, at the corner of Beach and Camp streets has a base-

tain rivers, wild white -water rafting, golf, horse-trekking, alpine walking, fishing, hunting and bungy jumping are all easily arranged. Those with a special yearning for an adrenalin rush can do an "Awesome Foursome" package: jet boating, a helicopter ride over ridges, rafting and a 43 m (141 ft) bungy jump off the Kawarau River bridge, all in a day.

On the Water
Speeding up rivers in jet boats and negotiating rapid-churning water in inflatable rafts are two of the most irresistibly fun activities in Queenstown. The most popular trip, the **Shotover Jet**, ((03) 442-8570, is a fast spin through Queenstown's rocky Shotover Canyon, almost tickling jagged cliffs,

swerving into shallows and executing sudden 180-degree turns with a second's warning to hold tight. It's reassuring to recall, especially as the jetboat spins on its tail for a close encounter with rock canyon walls, that the operators have never yet had an accident and have years of experience at controlling these machines. Another company, **Danes Shotover Rafts, (** (03) 442-7318, make trips on the Kawarau and Shotover rivers, or you can book a Heli-Jet package for a triple thrill ride in a helicopter, jet-boating or white-water rafting.

Peak ski-field which is considered by many to be more challenging.

Both are easily accessible from Queenstown. It takes 30 minutes by car on a tarmac road to reach Coronet Peak; the journey to The Remarkables along a winding gravel road with spectacular views is about 15 minutes longer.

Coronet Peak, which has 280 hectares (610 acres) of slopes with 454 vertical meters (1,500 ft) of skiing available, is somewhat lower, and in recent years has suffered from lack of snow. The recent installation of snow-

You may wish to escape the crowds and enjoy the river's scenery on the **Dart River Jetboat Safari, (** (03) 442-9992, with very enjoyable, tailor-made tours up the Dart River, forging rapids, then purring through pristine waters into the region's deepest, darkest, and most magical scenery. Trips last five hours, costing $95 for two adults.

Skiing in the Alps

One of Queenstown's main attractions in winter is its easy access to some of the Southern Hemisphere's most impressive ski-fields.

The Remarkables were developed in the mid-1980's for beginner and intermediate skiers to complement the nearby Coronet

making machines now enables Coronet Peak to guarantee top-to-bottom skiing on four-and-a-half kilometers (nearly three miles) of trails. Dry powder snow covers the slopes from June to September, while sophisticated facilities are available on the mountains, including helicopters to whisk more experienced skiers to higher and even more difficult terrain.

The Remarkables are about 2,000 m (6,600 ft) above sea level, which ensures

OPPOSITE: White water rafting prepare to launch into the rapids of Queenstown's Shotover River. ABOVE: The aptly-named Remarkables dominate the lakeside settlement of Queenstown. OVERLEAF: The rugged scenery of Skippers Canyon recalls the days of the Gold Rush.

adequate snow in most years, and its highest point is Double Cone, at 2,343 m (7,731 ft) high. It offers runs for every level of ability with three chair-lifts operating. These slopes are open from June to October, and are well-served with good facilities, including a restaurant. Both fields have ski schools.

Other fields include **Cardrona**, 45 km (28 miles) away on the road to Wanaka, less developed but full of pristine beauty, with only cross-country skis for hire and rope-tows for downhill skiers, and **Treble Cone**, 120 km (74 miles) away, which has two T-bars and rope-tows, plus light meals available on the fields, both perfect playgrounds for cross-country skiing. In good weather, adventurous skiers can arrange to go with a guide by helicopter or ski plane for a day of skiing in powder snow on remote mountains and glaciers.

Don't Look Before You Leap

Probably Queenstown's ultimate craze — and certainly the zaniest — is opting to bungy jump, in other words, to throw yourself off a bridge with only a long, thick rubber cord attached to your ankles to save you from the perilous drop into an apocalyptic chasm. There are two jump sites here, one at **Skipper's Canyon Bridge** and the other at the **Kawarau Suspension Bridge** — both look equally daunting. Orchestrated by AJ Hackett, whose feats have included jumping off the Eiffel Tower in 1986, bungy jumping is a well-organized non-stop industry here with an impeccable safety record, although it's unlikely to be covered by your insurance policy! The faint-hearted may find encouragement in the following bungy jumping statistics: the youngest to jump was an eight year-old boy, the oldest an 84 year-old man and the fattest, 220 kilos (488 lbs). Even blind people have tried it. Once you've paid up — $85 for Kawarau Gorge and $129 for Skipper's Canyon — you're weighed to assess how much cord you'll be allotted, then your ankles are secured to the bungy cord. Standing on a tiny platform, you can contemplate your lunacy as the crew yell out the countdown before you plunge head-first into an uncertain future. Within seconds, you'll probably dunk head-first into the river below, before soaring up again on the

bungy, bouncing like a human yo-yo. Finally, once all the bouncing has subsided, you grab the pole held out to you by crew waiting to rescue you in a rubber dingy, and came be pulled onto shore for a towel-down, weak-kneed and shuddering, and sometimes, determined to do it all over again! Or you can re-live it by watching yourself on video — an "extra" that costs $45. For more details, contact the **AJ Hackett Queenstown Bungy Centre**, ((03) 442-7100, beside the Information Centre on the corner of Shotover and Camp streets.

Up in the Air

Helicopter trips includes a climb up the sheer rock face of The Remarkables and teetering at the summit before swooping down to the valley below. A short touchdown at the highest peak is rounded off with a circuit encompassing the lake and Queenstown itself. For excursions further afield, there are range of scenic flights in small aircraft which offer magnificent overviews of the area otherwise never seen from the ground. The flight to Milford Sound is among the most popular. Snow-capped ridges and glassy lakes crowd together, as you fly over forests honeycombed with waterfalls gushing from crevices to streams below. Pilots at the helm like to joke that you are flying into a world convention of mountains.

Golf

One of New Zealand's most outstanding golf courses is the 18-hole **Kelvin Heights**, ((03) 442-9169, set right on Lake Wakatipu in the sheltered bay of the Frankton Arm, with full hire facilities. It can be reached from Queenstown's Lake Esplanade pier-front by a water taxi which operates on demand. Call (03) 442-7956 for details.

EXCURSIONS FROM QUEENSTOWN

Arrowtown

However limited your time in Queenstown, be sure to include an excursion to Arrowtown. This peaceful, almost perfectly preserved gold-rush settlement lies 20 km (12 miles) from Queenstown, reached by driving either past the Coronet Peak skifield past Arthur's Point or via the outer suburb of **Frankton**, past the exquisite mirror-like **Lake Hayes**. By browsing along Arrowtown's one main boulevard — Buckingham Street — with its charming row of pioneer schist-stone cottages, shops, pubs and restaurants, you'll gain an idea of what life must have been like during the pioneering days of the gold rush era. Make sure you see the excellent **Lakes District Museum**, which outlines the goldmining history of the area, where you can pick up the *Historic Arrowtown* map to take with you as you stroll. **Ah Lum's Store**, one of the few Chinese stores to remain intact, the **old stone jail** and **St. John's Church** are worth going out of your way to see, but you'll notice there's a mania for promoting anything remotely historical: whether you really want to see **Ah Wak's Lavatory**, for instance, is up to you!

Arrowtown has several very pleasant places to eat, all on Buckingham Street. Try **The Courtyard** or **The Stables** both with pretty cottage gardens. The **Stone Cottage Restaurant** opens early to serve breakfast, and Devonshire teas until late afternoon. The **Royal Oak Hotel** is a classic goldmining pub that still has much of its original atmosphere enshrined in its motto above the fireplace: "Be happy in this place. Who knows if there is anything to drink in heaven." The **New Orleans Hotel**, offers good Never-Ending Sandwiches and Fisherman's Baskets.

From Arrowtown, you can venture by jeep, horseback or on a six-hour round walk to **Macetown**, a derelict mining town, via a track that crosses the Arrow River 44 times. If you come by tour, the guide is equipped with gold pans so that everyone gets his chance to strike it lucky.

Skipper's Canyon

From Arrowtown, make sure you make the detour to see Skipper's Canyon, New Zealand's equivalent of the Grand Canyon, reached by Skipper's Road, which snakes through tortuous, glacier-formed terrain high above the Shotover River. With terrifying plunges on either side, the road twists along an old bridle path used by miners as they carved through this wilderness of jagged schist outcrops in the scramble to pan for gold. In winter, this tussock country is even more dramatic, blanketed with snow. Ruins of nineteenth century cottages and echoes of a once raucous Wild-West-style lie in rubble along the way. Horses and buggies were the first to use the road built in 1883. Today mainly tour buses use the road, which ends down at the Shotover River, to which jet boats and rafting trips are organized from Queenstown. Along with Ninety Mile Beach in Northland, the Skipper's Road is not covered by travel insurance. Drive *very* carefully and very slowly.

At the old Skipper's township, on the other side of the Skipper's Bridge, all that is left is the graveyard, where tombstones tell the tale of men who lost their battle for gold through misadventure, flash floods and hardship.

If you don't have a car, and would like to join a tour through the canyon, call **Nomad Safaris**, ((03) 442-6699.

The *Kingston Flyer*

The suburb of **Kingston** lies at the very end of Lake Wakatipu, and its attraction is the vintage *Kingston Flyer* train that chugs cross-country to Fairlight, a half-hour journey, serving tea and scones en route. There are daily excursions from Queenstown, departing 10:30 am, and you can ask for details at Kingston Station, ((03) 442-8683.

Glenorchy

As you enter Glenorchy, a sign says, "Welcome to Paradise." Nestled at the head of Lake Wakatipu, at the foot of the Richardson Mountains, Glenorchy lies at the end of an unsealed 50 km (31 miles) scenic drive from Queenstown which curves alongside the lake, fringed by spiky cabbage trees. Muscling in around the lakeside settlement, the surrounding snow-capped peaks offer some of the country's most renowned walking trails. The Routeburn, Greenstone, Caples, and Dart-Rees tracks all start within Glenorchy's environs. Fiordland Travel and InterCity have buses to and fro from the track's entrances. The Backpacker Express in Queenstown, runs transport packages that can also include a night's stay at the **Glenorchy Holiday Park**, at 2 Oban Street, which offers inexpensive accommodation, ((03) 442-9939.

Even if you're not planning a major trek, Glenorchy is a good base for canoeing up the Diamond River with **Adventure Safaris**, ((03) 442-9968. Nearby, the tiny hamlet of **Paradise** is reached by a lovely drive through wooded beech forest, passing a turreted Victorian homestead called **Arcadia**. A young Scotsman who lived here in 1862 became enamored of a local Maori maiden, who asked him, "By what name do you know this place, *pakeha*?" And he replied, "It is Paradise so long as you are by my side." And Paradise is the name it bears to this day.

FIORDLAND

Far away from civilization, Fiordland covers such a huge area that much of it remains unexplored. It is an isolated, beautiful, mysterious and serene wilderness of vast lordly mountains, forested hills, high hanging valleys, sapphire-colored glacial lakes and mystic fiords, with few settlements. It contains many of New Zealand's most famous walking and trekking trails, as well as offering rewards for hunters and mountaineers. **Fiordland National Park** is a 7,607 sq km (2,937 sq miles) area that from the air looks almost Himayalan. Not only does it have one of the world's highest waterfalls, the Sutherland Falls — 580 m (1,914 ft) high — but also one of the world's highest rainfalls — up to 7,600 mm (300 in) a year. As rain drenches forests and mountains, the steep and often sheer flanks of the valleys come alive with water that cascades and streams from every crack, fissure and hanging valley, creating an unforgettable drama of nature that is missed during fine weather, when the vista is merely startlingly fresh and lovely.

With this rain come giant forests — totara, rimu, matai, and red and silver beech trees which grow in precarious places, clinging to humus gathered on rocks. Ferns, mosses and vines engulf the trees and lichens hang in primeval drifts. Glow worms flicker from damp mossy banks.

Fiordland's coast is serrated with immense, wondrously sculpted gashes gouged

ABOVE: Rushing water and rugged peaks in Fiordland National Park.

out by glaciers which finally disappeared after the last Ice Age between 15,000 and 20,000 years ago, leaving behind sheer granite walls that drop hundreds of meters into dark-green sea. Inland, submerged fiords flooded by melted glaciers are called sounds, Milford Sound being the best known.

The European era began in 1770 when on his first voyage, Captain Cook sailed the *Endeavour* past the western coast but could not discern a harbor because the entrance through its mountains was wreathed by mist. Describing the sounds, his words,

"dusk," "doubtful," and "mistake" have become part of Fiordland's folklore. He also noted of the region's notorious sand flies that they were, "so troublesome, they exceed everything of a kind I ever met with." This, from a man who battled sea storms, scurvy and belligerent man-eating tribes, was really something. Bring lots of insect repellent.

ACCESS

Mt. Cook Airlines (((03) 249-7516) links Te Anau with Queenstown and Mt. Cook. Waterwings, ((03) 249-7405, an agent for Ansett, has flights to Queenstown and Milford, while Air Fiordland (((03) 249-7505) links the town to Queenstown, Milford and Mt. Cook. If you are traveling by bus, Inter-City (℄ (03) 249-7559) has a daily service from Queenstown that stops through Te Anau en route to Milford, a mid-way halt on the five hour journey. Mt. Cook Landline (℄ (03) 249-7516) also runs a similar daily service, and a weekday bus from Te Anau to Invercargill.

Backpacker Alternatives, ℄ (03) 249-7419, offers a range of cheap bus trips, from Queenstown and on to Milford Sound, as well as walking tours and launch cruises. By car, allow two and a half hours from Queenstown and three hours from Invercargill.

GENERAL INFORMATION

The **Fiordland National Park Visitors Centre**, ℄ (03) 249-7921 on Te Anau Drive is the place for advice on the region's tracks and attractions, with up-to-date information on weather and track conditions. **Fiordland Travel Office**, ℄ (03) 473-8652, on the Lake Front, is the booking office for launch cruises out to the glow worm caves, Doubtful and Milford sound, the latter two combined with coach trips for part of the way. They also run scenic flights across Milford Sounds, and offer reasonably priced packages combining flights, coach trips and cruises. Inquire here about times, which vary according to season.

TE ANAU

Situated on the southern shore of Lake Te Anau, the largest — and the purest — lake in the South Island, Te Anau (pronounced te ah-now) is the gateway to the Fiordland National Park and the Milford Track, as well as the Greenstone, Caples/Rees, Routeburn, Hollyford and Kepler tracks. Embraced by forested mountains, Lake Te Anau is dotted with isolated bays, coves and islands; to the west the lake branches into three land-locked fiords.

Where to Stay and Eat
Top of the range is the mid-priced **Te Anau Travelodge**, ℄ (03) 249-7411, fax: (03) 249-7947, opposite the lakefront, which has a restaurant, swimming pool and comfortable, but not extraordinary rooms. It has a lot of traffic because a lot of tours block-book

the Milford Track and stay here at discounted rates. The nearby, more modern, **Vacation Inn**, ℄ (03) 249-7421, fax: (03) 249-8037, has a more intimate luxurious feel for comparable rates and has a restaurant, cocktail bar, spa pools and a choice of luxurious hotel or motel rooms. The moderately-priced **Village Inn**, ℄ (03) 249-7911, fax: (03) 249-7003, at Mokoroa Street, is a mock Gold Rush era colonial village which you will either find delightful or horribly kitsch. But the comfortable rooms and thoughtful facilities (especially for handicapped people) make it a good place to stay. There are two inexpensive bed and breakfast choices, both comfortable and friendly. **Shakespeare House**, ℄ (03) 249-7349, fax: (03) 249-7629, is at 10 Dusky Street, while **Matai Travel Lodge**, ℄ (03) 249-7360, is at the corner of Mokonu and Matai streets.

The **Te Anau Motor Park**, ℄ (03) 249-7457, fax: (03) 249-7536, on Mana-pouri Road, is an excellent camping ground, with includes within its spacious grounds a motel lodge, tourist flats, and caravan and tent sites, with prices ranging from backpackers to moderate. Its many facilities include a good restaurant, shop, sauna, tennis courts and daily shuttle buses to Milford.

In tiny, tranquil Manapouri, you can stay at the lakeside **Murrell's Grand View** guest house, ℄ (03) 249-6642, built in 1889, with charming moderately-priced rooms.

In Te Anau, **Keplers Restaurant**, ℄ (03) 249-7909, on the corner of Milford Road and Mokonu Street, offers traditional New Zealand cuisine, with lots of fresh trout on the menu.

FROM TE ANAU THROUGH FIORDLAND

From Te Anau, take the two and a half hour launch trip to see the **Te Ana-Au Caves**, which the Maori named the "the rushing water caves." Visitors glide on a punt along an underground river in darkness, watch-,ing with delight as their eyes adjust to reveal a subterranean starlit milky way of gleaming glow worm lights. The launch departs from Te Anau at 2 pm and 8:15 pm daily.

Doubtful Sound
The six hour round trip out to Doubtful Sound is a memorable voyage into the heart

of Fiordland. It leaves from Te Anau by coach to reach Manapouri, a tiny hamlet on the banks of **Lake Manapouri**. From here, the *M.V. Friendship* glides through the lake's dark, medieval-looking waters, revealing feathery moss-banked forested islands licked by mist clouds, through which tiny sandy bays appear as a flash of white. Maori myth tells of the creation of this "lake of the sorrowing heart." Koronae, a beautiful chieftain's daughter, was lost and injured in the wilderness. Her younger sister searched and found her after a long journey, but did

not have the strength to carry her home. Beyond the reach of their tribe, they comforted each other as they died, and their mingled tears tore the mountains apart.

Landing at **West Arm**, visitors are taken by bus to see a hydroelectric power house, discreetly tucked 184 m (600ft) deep down in a granite mountain. It's fascinating for people interested in nature-respecting energy production, and certainly dramatic even for those who aren't riveted by the subject because of the dark descent in the two kilometers (one-and-a-quarter miles) spiral access tunnel leading to the underground power station complex. Outside, the sign "Beware of Falling Trucks" is left in memory of the wise guy who placed it there during the station's formidable construction period.

From here, the bus continues up and over the spectacular 670 m (2,211 ft) high **Wilmot Pass**, winding through beech forests that

fascinate naturalists with their 500 varieties of moss and lichen, wreathing the forest in drifts like eerie green spider webs ("old man's beard") and carpeting the undergrowth in miraculously springy clumps like green velvet. The sight of all this profuse vegetation is very inspirational, and may encourage you to tackle the eight to ten day trek through this region from Manapouri, through Dusky Sound back to Lake Manapouri following ancient greenstone trails, one of the country's most challenging and beautiful walks. At the turn of the century, one young woman made a humorous comment on her experience of climbing the Wilmot Pass on foot in the log book at the Doubtful Sound Lodge. She wrote, "Now I know I'm popular. 100,000 sand flies can't be wrong."

At **Deep Cove**, you climb aboard the boat once more and chug into Doubtful Sound, fringed by mountains of rich beech and red-blooming rata forest. Within Hall Arm, the dense sciatia-like rock lining the lake is thought by to be more than 400 million years old, in places extending for more than 13 km (8 miles) beneath the forest. When the engines are turned off, you can listen to the sound of centuries-old silence in one of the world's most remote and beautiful places: the rush of waterfalls misted by clouds and the call of wood-hens.

Other Excursions

From Te Anau, other launch trips offer scheduled excursions to bays and islands for picnics, swimming and bush-walks. There are jet-boats rides, fishing charters and a water taxi service for sightseeing, tramping, hunting and fishing. You can arrange for a boat to drop you at a remote bay and return at a prearranged time or hire a sail-boat, out-board motor boat, pedal boat or row boat to get yourself there. Useful contacts include **Sinbad Cruises**, ((03) 249-7106, at 15 Fergus Square and **Lakeland Boat Hire**, ((03) 249-7125 on the lakefront, who offer everything from pedal boats to a 5 m (17ft) cruiser.

OTHER SOUNDS AND LAKES

Along Fiordland's stormy west coast are many remote fiords, many of which are in-

ABOVE: Windsurfers catch the breeze on Lake Te Anau. OPPOSITE: One of the many picturesque moods of Lake Te Anau.

accessible except by sea or very arduous, determined trekking through impossibly dense forest, which often drops away to reveal stark precipices. Yet this farthest reach of New Zealand has a profound allure in its remote, hushed beauty. **Dusky Sound** is the largest, most picturesque and remote of the fiords, with its vast areas of enclosed waters, secluded inlets and outline of mountains disappearing into the sky, all infused with colors of changing light. **Lake Hauroko Tours**, ((03) 216-9995, based out of Tuatapere, runs a four day trek from Lake Hauroko to Supper Cove in Dusky Sound, from where you can either fly out or tramp on to Lake Manapouri.

Two of the largest and least-visited lakes in Fiordland are **Lake Hauroko** and **Lake Poteriteri**, both set deep in the heart of the national park.

Scenic Flights

Te Anau is a main center for flightseeing. **Air Fiordland**, offers about five options. The most popular trip flies over 250 km (155 miles) of New Zealand's most spectacular alpine scenery. Highlights include the Fox and Franz Josef Glaciers, the Tasman Glacier and Mount Cook. You can also combine a scenic flight to Milford Sound with a launch cruise out to the Tasman Sea. The return flight dips over the Milford Track and Sutherland Falls.

Mt. Cook Airlines, ((03) 249-7516, offers a selection of scenic flights, departing from Queenstown, Te Anau or Milford. **Waterwings Airways**, ((03) 249-7405, is located on the pier behind the Fiordland Travel Office. It offers a Fly'n'Boat experience: you board a floatplane to fly over the Kepler Mountains, land on Lake Manapouri and jetboat up the Waiau River. This hour-long excursion leaves daily at 11am, and costs $84 for adults, $51 for children. Waterwings Airways also has a multitude of options and services for trampers.

THE ROAD TO MILFORD SOUND

The 119 km (74 miles) long Milford Road is one of New Zealand's finest drives, beginning in Te Anau. It passes clear icy alpine lakes and tarns, forests of outstanding vari-

ety, river flats and lupin-fringed meadows, pristine waterfalls, hulking granite peaks and permanent snow-fields. Generally allow about two and a half hours to reach Milford Sound, and take special care during winter, when the road can ice over.

Along the road are numerous side-trips. The Routeburn and Hollyford tracks branch off it, and there are shorter walks to **Lake Gunn, Key Summit** and across the **Gertrude Saddle** as well as many marked picnic and camping spots.

Highlights along the road include **Ten Mile Bush**, with its silver, red and mountain beech forests, **Eglinton Valley**, which is most beautiful in summer when buttercups and lupins create a vivid blaze of color. **Mirror Lake**, so calm and reflective that you may not be able to decide which is the right way up when you examine your photograph later, and the long **Avenue of the Disappearing Mountain**. Past beautiful **Lake Gunn**, enclosed in bush, and the smaller, brooding **Lake Fergus**, the road climbs to **The Divide**, at 532 m (1,755 ft). From The Divide, the road drops abruptly into the **Upper Hollyford Valley,** a sub-alpine realm of conifers and hardy mountain trees. Above stands the giant pyramidal peak of **Mt. Talbot**. Soon the road climbs toward the seamed rock walls above the entrance to the **Homer Tunnel**, which offers a dank downhill passage through the rock until you burst into a breathtaking amphitheater of snow-covered peaks and precipices at the head of the **Cleddau Canyon**. This is where you'll usually find kea parrots, swooping and waddling around, hungry for morsels from visitors. These great green birds, with their garbled language have an enormous sense of mischief. You're asked not to feed them, so that they will keep to the straight and narrow. Below, the road zigzags steeply down the canyon and through rain forest. Just before you enter Milford Sound, a parking area on the left marks the start of a 10 minute walk to **The Chasm**, where the Cleddau River plunges through curiously-shaped rocks which it has eroded to form a natural 22 m (72 ft) chasm.

Along the road, you can stay at **Lake Gunn Motor Inn**, ((03) 249-7335, fax; (03) 249-8151, 77 km (48 miles) from Te Anau, set in the heart of Fiordland National Park. It has moderately-priced luxury cabins, a restaurant and tranquil views.

From Te Anau, you can join **Milford Sound Adventure Tours,** ((03) 249-7227, and experience the wilderness on mountain bikes along some of the spectacular stretches of the road, making a gradual descent of 690 m (2,264 ft) from the other side of the Homer Tunnel. You arrive in time to link with a cruise on the Milford Sound, and cycle through a section of (mainly) downhill beech forest on your return to Te Anau.

unreachable tree outposts. It's a vision that recalls a piece of melodious Tennyson: "The cloud may stoop from heaven and take the shape / From fold to fold, of mountain and of cape."

There are many Maori stories connected with the sound, and the soft, semi-translucent flecked greenstone known as *tangiwai* found here had a kind of Holy Grail attraction. Intriguingly, a mysterious lost tribe are said to have lived within the surrounding forest in peaceful isolation until the nineteenth century, before eventually dying out.

MILFORD SOUND

The only sound in Fiordland that can be reached by road, Milford Sound's mirror-calm deep waters are dominated by **Mitre Peak**, a colossal 1,412 m (4,659 ft) rock monolith. Lashed by moody elements, draped in billowing cloud, it is the centerpiece of an unfolding Turneresque tableau that is simply majestic to watch as the light changes. Sapphire skies become dark and oppressive, the forest lichens cast a rich green light over the sound, and cascading waterfalls send white plumes snaking down mountain ridges. Graceful white herons stand like sentries to the wilderness on high,

In Maori, Milford Sound is known as *Piopiotahi*, or "the place of the thrush." The story of the region's name, like many Maori myths, has rather visceral overtones. Maui, the Maori Adam, kept a thrush whose poignant warblings kept him company on his long solitary wanderings. But one day he was lying on the forest floor with the goddess Hine-nui-te-po, who stirred when she heard the thrush singing, crushing Maui to death between her thighs by mistake. How big she was and how small Maui was is not known, but the thrush lived out its life here grieving over his master's untimely demise.

The entrance to Milford Sound.

Captain Cook passed the entrance to the Milford Sound once in 1770, then again three years later: on both occasions the entrance was shrouded by deep mist. He stopped further south at Dusky Sound, the largest and most accessible of the fiords. In 1822, the Welsh sealing captain John Grono discovered, then named the sound after Milford Haven, his place of birth.

Regardless of whether you have come here to walk the Milford Track or not, take the two hour launch cruises out into Milford Sound on the *Milford Haven* or one of the THC's Red Boats, which chug about 15 km (just over nine miles) out to the mouth of the sound near the Tasman Sea. Highlights of the trip, as well as the unmistakable Mitre Peak, include **Bowen Falls**, **Sinbad Gully**, a classic example of a U-shaped glacial valley, one of the last places where the near-extinct flightless parrot, the *kakapo* still survives and **Stirling Falls**, which drop 146 m (481 ft) from a hanging valley, the liquid equivalent of a crumbling 50 story-building, sending out massive gusts of spray at the foot of the falls. You'll usually see fur seals basking on the rocks close to the shore, and sometimes dolphins. During October and November, Fiordland crested penguins nest in the sound before leaving for Antarctica.

It's worth mentioning that old staple — insect repellent — and that the weather can be very changeable, so even in summer come prepared for cold, possibly gale-force gusts.

Access

You can reach Milford Sound by driving through the Milford Road.

You can fly in on a scenic flight from Te Anau or Queenstown, or make it your welcome haven after completing the Milford Track.

Where to Stay

The best place to stay is the mid-priced **THC Milford Sound Hotel**, ((03) 249-7926, fax: (03) 249-8094, which has remarkable views across Mitre Peak and the Milford Sound. Its Lobster Pot Restaurant is also the best place to get a decent meal. Less salubrious, but very popular and cheap is the **Milford Lodge**, ((03) 249-8071 (fax: same number). During the summer periods, it's absolutely vital to book well in advance.

THE FINEST WALK IN THE WORLD

The Milford Track is an apocalyptic 53 km (33 miles) four day hike through chattering rain forests and blithe meadows, along temperamental rivers and up blustery mountain passes, past hurrying waterfalls — so many landscapes that it is like crossing an entire uninhabited continent. Organized treks starts from the head of Lake Te Anau, stay for a night at Glade House, a gingerbread-style lodge where roast beef dinners are served in a long social room with a fireplace. The walk is nearly a parody of a travel agent's brochure ("A dozen entirely different places in three minutes!') and it makes you wonder at the simple miracle of this beautiful planet, left to its own devices, working its magic in constant surprises. It traverses clear green rivers, torrential rapids crossed by wooden bridges, undulating vistas of silken moss, deep Amazonian rain forest, shaded grottoes of profuse ferns, alpine passes with cliffs sprouting waterfalls. Other highlights include crossing a river over a high swinging bridge, but above all seeing Sutherland Falls, one of the tallest in the world. From the high reservoir of Lake Quill, the falls spill 571 m (1,884 ft) in three great leaps down to the Arthur Valley below.

Keep in mind that the track takes you through one of the rainiest places on earth. Officially classified as "temperate rain forest," it gets an average of almost an inch of rain each day. You will get wet at some point, but it's worth it.

GOLD COUNTRY

During the rip-roaring era of the Gold Rush, gold-mining towns — many now ghost-towns — flourished across the burnished high country of Central Otago.

Leaving Queenstown or Arrowtown, you can follow the **Otago Goldfields Heritage Highway**, a meandering well-signposted circuit with many detours, which preserves mining sites and historic buildings from their heyday. The scenery of the surrounding area is stunning. Perhaps most dramatic of all is the **Lindis Pass**, along

Highway 8, which links the region with Mt. Cook and MacKenzie Country. Carpeted with golden velvety-looking tussock grasslands, beneath constantly changing skies, it is a hauntingly beautiful, lonely vision, fragrant with wild thyme and ribbons of bright lupins. Tucked off the Lindis Pass are the remarkable **Clay Cliffs**, west of Omarama, an eerie natural temple of striated clay funnels. Emblematic of the region are the narrow back-roads that branch off the highway, lined with feathery willow trees, and seem to disappear into nowhere.

Wakatipu, pristine Lake Wanaka is always busy with yachts and water-skiers, and the region's clear waterways, especially the Hawea, Hunter and Clutha are renowned for their sizable rainbow and brown trout.

Sometimes called the "Matterhorn" of New Zealand, Mt. Aspiring stands astride the Main Divide of the Southern Alps. 3,000 m (9,900 ft) high and covered in glaciers, it lies within wild, difficult, intensely beautiful terrain, unchanged from the days when other mountains in the region earned such names as Mt. Awkward, Mt. Awful,

WANAKA AND MT. ASPIRING NATIONAL PARK

From Arrowtown, Highway 89 makes a dramatic winding, vertiginous ascent up into the Cardrona Ranges on the road to Wanaka, a ski resort township nestled between snow-topped mountains on Lake Wanaka. It's a good base for exploring nearby **Mt. Aspiring National Park**, as well as the **Treble Cone**, **Cardrona**, **Waiorau** and **Harris** skifields, the latter boasting the largest heli-ski operation anywhere outside Canada. Since the Cardrona Nordic field opened a few years ago, Wanaka also caters to cross-country skiers as well. Softer and prettier than Lake

Mt. Dreadful and Mt. Defiant. With its high lake basins, moraines and hanging valleys, the park is an unspoilt wilderness with many opportunities for trekking, hunting and fishing.

Access

Aspiring Air, ((03) 443-7943, has flights to Queenstown up to four times daily, connecting there with Mt. Cook Airlines, Air New Zealand and Ansett New Zealand to other destinations. They also make flightseeing trips over Mt. Aspiring and Mt Cook to the West Coast and Fiordland. InterCity and

ABOVE: A lone cyclist on the road to Lake Wanaka. OVERLEAF: An aerial perspective of Mt. Aspiring, the "Matterhorn" of New Zealand.

Mt. Cook Landline have regular services between Queenstown, a two hour journey, stopping as they continue en route to the glaciers via Haast Pass. Other connections include Mt. Cook, Dunedin, and Christchurch.

General Information

Wanaka Lake Services, ((03) 443-7495, next to the lakefront jetty, is the township's unofficial Information Centre, with all the information you could possibly want about adventure tours, skiing packages, guided treks and boat hire. Another place to try is the **Wanaka Booking Office**, ((03) 443-7277, Ardmore Street. The **Mt. Aspiring National Park Visitor's Centre**, ((03) 443-7660, is on the corner of Ballantyne and Main roads, has displays, pamphlets on treks, and an aspirational audio-visual presentation.

What to See

On the lake, it's possible to cruise on all sorts of vessels, ranging from a hovercraft to rowing your own dinghy. One of the loveliest walks around the lake goes out to **Eely Point**, 30 minutes away. Another walk leads up to **Mt. Iron**, an easy 45 minute climb that offers spectacular views across the lake and Clutha River outlet. Pay a visit to the three-dimensional **Wanaka Maze**, 10 minutes drive out of town on the Main Highway. After you've puzzled your way through the maze, you can loiter in the center's shop, a treasure-house of New Zealand-made puzzles, jigsaws, hologram displays and wonky mirrors. It's like watching grown-ups playing at the creche. They also serve very lavish Devonshire teas.

It's worth making the half hour drive out to **Lake Hawea**, although you'll have to loop back the same way. But the scenery deserves it, with the empty, winding unsealed road dipping down beside the narrow, bright blue glacial lake, fringed by poplars, the horizon massed with snow-topped mountains. But if you're tempted to put up a tent close to the idyllic-looking lakefront, take heed. By nightfall, the sand flies start waging war. Three days later, my family and I were still shaking them out of our sleeping bags.

Where to Stay

Energetic adventurers will enjoy staying at **Diamond Lodge**, ((03) 443-8614, fax: (03) 443-8615, corner of Orchard Road and Highway 89. Set within deer farmland, this moderately priced lodge has an array of activities — ranging from ski workshops to hovercrafting, hunting to mountain biking. They also specialize in horse-trekking (on a tribe of fine Appaloosa horses) and all adventure activities are tailored to suit guests.

Also moderately-priced, the **THC Wanaka Resort Hotel**, ((03) 443-7826, fax: (03) 443-9069, at Helwick Street on the shores of Lake Wanaka, is a more sedate choice, with beautiful views as well as top-class facilities; restaurants, cocktail lounge, spa pools and tour desk. A rustic out-of-town Bed and Breakfast is **Rippon Lea**, ((03) 443-7135, at 15 Norman Terrace, inexpensively priced.

Rock-bottom rates are found at **Wanaka Backpacker's**, ((03) 443-7837, at 117 Lakeside Road, with a friendly atmosphere and lake views, as well as a spa pool and mountain bikes for hire.

Penrith Park, ((03) 443-7009, at Beacon Point is a well-equipped, secluded camping ground on the lake shore, ten minutes drive from town.

Where to Eat

Wanaka has several extremely fine restaurants. **Capriccio**, ((03) 443-8579, at 123 Ardmore Street, serves up inventive combinations of traditional high country produce. Their Canterbury lamb in filo served with fresh tamarillo sauce has to be tasted. They are open only for dinner. The **Edgewater Resort Hotel**, ((03) 443-8311, on Sargood Drive, specializes in seafood.

At **Rafters**, ((03) 443-8216, Mt. Aspiring Road, expect a casual atmosphere around a big fire, with good traditional New Zealand cuisine. On the lakefront, **Relishes Cafe**, ((03) 443-9018, at 99 Ardmore Street, is a good place for lunch and has a blackboard menu.

To the Goldfields

From Wanaka, Highway 8 leads to the former gold-mining towns of **Cromwell**, **Alexandra**, **Clyde** and **Roxburgh**, which are now better known as producers of fruit, and all of which are on the mighty Clutha River. In summer, as you drive through, you can stop to buy bags of juicy apples, cherries and nectarines from wayside stalls and orchards.

In Clyde, make **Olivers** your base for exploring the Central Otago back-country. It is a treasure. A restored colonial homestead, Olivers has lovely rooms, decorated in a "Country House" style with wide beds, soft chairs and log fires. Every bedroom in the house opens onto the garden, while baths overlook herbs and climbing roses. Food plays an important part in the lodge. Meals tend to include venison, wild pig and other game, with a small selection of a la carte dishes, accompanied by New Zealand wines. Maintaining its high standards, Olivers also grows its own herbs and produces its own honey. Olivers, ((03) 449-2860, fax: (03) 449-2862, on Sunderland (nicknamed Slumberland) Street is moderately-priced.

Clyde is a good base for fossicking in the hills around tiny settlements where populations have been declining since the turn of the century. Within the Maniototo Plains, you can visit **St. Bathans**, a 30 minute drive away, set between the Dunstan and Hawkdun ranges. It consists of a handful of residents, an historic post office, town hall and stone pub. You can buy a beer or an ice-cream at the 120 year-old **Vulcan Hotel**, the only premises resembling a shop for miles, now a backpacker's lodge. Apparently, it has a ghost in Room 1, thought to be the that of a jilted barmaid. Nearby, the man-made **Blue Lake**, once the site of intensive gold-prospecting, radiates an incredible color from its mineral-charged water. Within the Maniototo, other quaint villages (although not as quaint as St. Bathans) are **Naseby** and **Ranfurly**, all on State Highway 85, known locally as the "Pigroot." From here, take State Highway 87 to Mosgiel, en route to Dunedin. On the way, look out for **Middlemarch**, with its bizarre pillar rocks which look like Lot's poor turned-to-salt wife.

DUNEDIN AND THE OTAGO PENINSULA

An attractive hill and harbor city at the southern end of the Otago Peninsula, Dunedin retains many stately influences from the Scottish migrants who founded the city in 1848, intent on establishing a utopian Presbyterian community in the resource-rich wilds of New Zealand. They called the new settlement after *Din-eiden*, the Gaelic name for Edinburgh. During the euphoria of the gold rush in the 1860's, Dunedin became the commercial capital of New Zealand, celebrating its prosperity with a boom in grand public and private buildings in an ornate Gothic style. Dunedin became a city of firsts — founding the country's first university, medical college, educational institutions, electric tram and cable car system, wool mills and daily newspaper. Much of the wealth gradually drifted to the North Island, but the impressive Victorian buildings, cultural legacy and educational institutions — where one in every ten citizens is a student — make this one of New Zealand's more characterful cities.

ACCESS

Air New Zealand has daily direct connections with Auckland, Christchurch, Invercargill and Wellington, where you can link with other flights. Air New Zealand also serves as the agent in Dunedin for Mt. Cook Airlines, which runs flights from Alexandra and Queenstown, with connections to Te Anau, Milford and Mt. Cook. The Air New Zealand office, ((03) 477-5769, is in John Wickliffe House at 263 Princes Street. Ansett New Zealand, whose head office, ((03) 479-0123, is at 1 George Street, has flights to Auckland, Christchurch and Wellington. Dunedin Airport Shuttle, ((03) 479-2481 and the Airporter Express, ((03) 477-9238 both provide door-to-door transport to the airport, a 40 minute drive away.

The InterCity Travel Centre, ((03) 477-2640, is housed in a thirties-style building on Cumberland Street, and has daily bus services between Invercargill, Christchurch, Queenstown, Te Anau, Milford Sound, Wanaka and the West Coast. Mt. Cook Landline, ((03) 474-0674, at 67 Great King Street, runs daily services that encompass major stops along the east coast from Picton all the way to Invercargill via Christchurch and Dunedin. Newmans, ((03) 477-3476, at 205 Andrew Street, have less regular connections to Dunedin and Christchurch.

The Southerner Christchurch to Invercargill train stops at the railway station on Anzac Avenue daily.

GENERAL INFORMATION

The **Visitors Centre**, ((03) 477-4176, after hours ((03) 487-6067, is at 48 The Octagon. Pick up its excellent booklet, *Dunedin Discovered*, for full listings. Also stocked is a series of excellent *Know Your City* booklets, covering all architectural highlights, driving routes and walking tracks within the

city, Port Chalmers, the Otago Peninsula and the Otago region. The **Department of Conservation** (DOC) office, ((03) 477-0677, is also a good source of information for finding out about walking tracks in the region.

WHAT TO SEE

A good half-day is needed to explore the inner city on foot, and those untroubled by a slightly longer walk can easily reach the University campus, Otago Museum and Botanic Gardens. Further afield, a car or bicycle is required to explore the city's scenic Golden Arrow route and the Otago Peninsula, or it's possible to join one of several tours and combine this with a harbor cruise.

City Strolls

Start with the **Octagon**, Dunedin's historic center, with its statue of poet Robert Burns, one of the city's Scottish forefathers. Facing the Octagon are **St. Paul's Cathedral**, the most impressive in New Zealand with a stone-vaulted nave roof and 3,500 pipes in its four-manual organ, and the **Municipal Chambers**, both grand Gothic Revival-style buildings. From here, follow Stuart Street to Anzac Avenue, and if you're interested, have a look at the grandiose Royal Doulton tiled interior of the **Railway Station** on

Cumberland Street. Glance up towards Moray Place and you'll see the towering spire of **First Church**, built by Dunedin's founding fathers, dedicated in 1873, and well worth a look.

The World's Biggest Ball of String

Also on Cumberland Street is the **Otago Early Settlers Museum**. Quirky and beautifully-presented, this museum presents a patchwork portrait of the social history of Dunedin and Otago settlers and its main interest is its eccentric memorabilia. Some of the more unusual items include what the museum claims is the world's smallest bible, which has Robert Burn's family register in the poet's handwriting and some creepy nineteenth century floral arrangements of human hair woven on wire frames. There are relics from the South Seas exhibition held in 1925, including what is reputedly the biggest ball of string in the world. Don't forget the preserved platypus foot or the ball of chewed hair once found by a farmer in a sheep's stomach!

Olveston

At 42 Royal Terrace, 10 minutes walk from the Octagon is Olveston, one of the city's most extraordinary homes. The 35-room

mansion was built in the Jacobean-style by the wealthy Theomin family in the early 1990s, who decorated their house with an eclectic mix of art and antiques and enjoyed domestic ingenuity well ahead of most New Zealand homes. Hour-long guided tours are given daily and reservations are recommended through the Visitors Centre or Olveston at ((03) 477-3320. It's open Monday to Saturday, the first tour at 9:30 am and the last at 4 pm.

Museum and Art Gallery

The **Otago Museum**, on the corner of Great King and Union streets, is very impressive, particularly in its sections on Maori and Melanesian art. The **Dunedin Public Art**

Gallery, at Logan Park at the end of Anzac Avenue, founded in 1884, has an impressive collection.

The Botanic Gardens

The oldest of its kind in New Zealand, the Botanic Gardens were founded in 1863. Determined walkers and city joggers can take trails up to the upper level, with its gardens of rhododendrons, woodland shrubs and native trees. Late October and November are the best times for the azalea garden and the renowned rhododendron dell with over 2,000 trees. Every third week in October is Rhododendron Week, which no real garden-fan should miss if their stay coincides. In a corner of the upper garden is an aviary which houses all sorts of New Zealand native birds. At The Point there's a good view across the city harbor.

On the Steep Side

Baldwin Street in Dunedin's north-east valley is recognized in The Guinness Book of Records as the steepest street in the world. An AA sign at the bottom says "For

---

OPPOSITE: Distinctive Gothic-style architecture is a feature of Dunedin's Victorian heritage.
ABOVE: Larnach Castle on the Otago Peninsula.

safety reasons sightseers are requested not to drive up this street." Many do, however, and Saturday nights are the noisiest with a revving line-up of clapped-out cars determined to make it to the top. The top-end of this 400 m- (1,300 ft) long street has a 13 percent gradient — for every 3 m in a horizontal direction the incline rises one vertical meter (just over three feet). Fables of misadventures abound. The highlight in Baldwin Street's diary is the annual Otago Hill Runner's *Gut-Buster* run up to the top.

City Gems

Pick up a copy of the *Golden Arrow Scenic Drive* from the Visitors center. It directs you around the so-called town belt, a pretty four-and-a-half kilometers (nearly three miles) long woodland drive dotted with grand homes and native bush reserves. Numerous walking tracks branch off here, resonant with humming cicada, tui and bellbird calls. It passes the **Otago Boys High School**, the huge heated **Moana Swimming Pool** with its hydroslide maze and the **University of Otago**. Another vantage place to seek out is **Signal Hill** with its centennial memorial for great harbor views. You can admire several bizarre, beautiful geological formations close to the city. There are two main walks, one along **Tunnel Beach** and the other to the **Mount Cargill Organ Pipes**, both an hour return, with the starting point an hour's drive away. For these walks and many others, ask for the detailed leaflets at the Visitors Centre.

ST. CLAIR AND ST. KILDA BEACHES

Surfers, sun-bathers, strollers and joggers flock to these two beautiful, creamy-sanded beaches, which merge into each other and seem to stretch as far as the eye can see. Both are just 10 minutes drive from central Dunedin. St. Clair is especially good for year-round surfing, and its choppy waves are patrolled in summer. At the southern end of St. Clair is the **St. Clair Hot Salt Water Pool**, open in summer. At St. Kilda, aside from the beach, the steam-operated vintage *Ocean Beach Railway* shuttles back and forth to St. Clair.

WHERE TO STAY

Mid-price

Cargills, ((03) 477-7983, fax: (03) 477-8098, at 678 George Street is stylish, with a landscaped courtyard and garden restaurant. Luxury suites have spa baths and waterbeds. All units are handsomely furnished. The **Quality Hotel Dunedin**, ((03) 477-6784, Upper Moray Place has very central, well-serviced rooms. Its restaurant, Settler's Brasserie, serves excellent New Zealand cuisine. The **Southern Cross Hotel**, ((03) 477-0752, at 118 High Street, is very central. It is a large refurbished vintage hotel with good facilities, including satellite TV. two restaurants, a 24-hour cafe, four bars and a disco. **Pacific Park**, ((03) 477-3374, 21–22 Wallace Street is a modern hotel set five minutes from the center in peaceful native bush overlooking the city and harbor. It also has a licensed restaurant and bar.

Moderate

The **Leviathan Motel**, ((03) 477-3160, at 65 Lower High Street, is typical of an old-style New Zealand hotel, with a thirties-era feel, refurbished and well-kept.

The following are recommended: **Commodore Motor Lodge**, ((03) 477-7766, 932 Cumberland Street is close to the University campus and Botanic Gardens. **Cable Court Motel**, ((03) 477-3525, is at 833 Cumberland Street, while the **Allan Court Motel**, ((03) 477-7526, is at 590 George Street. **Leisure Lodge**, ((03) 477-5360, is at the corner of Great King and Duke streets, situated amid landscaped gardens with a restaurant and bar.

Bed and Breakfast

Deacons Court, ((03) 477-9053, at 342 High Street, has three rooms, a very friendly atmosphere, delicious breakfasts and is inexpensive. Dinner by arrangement. **Alvand House**, ((03) 477-7379, at 3 Union Street (off George Street), is a lovely colonial house in peaceful part of the city center. **Magnolia House**, ((03) 467-5999, at 18 Grendon Street, Maori Hill, is an attractive Victorian villa situated amongst gracious lawns. Non-smokers only. **Manono**, ((03) 477-8638, at 84 London Street has peaceful single rooms. **Sahara Guest House and Motel**, ((03) 477-6662, 619 George Street is a good choice, close to the University campus.

Backpackers
Elm Lodge, ((03) 474-1872, at 74 Elm Row is a good backpacker's lodge. **Pavlova Backpackers**, ((03) 479-2175, at the corner of Rattray and Vogel streets, is located just across the road from the Intercity Depot and five minutes from the Octagon. It's run with great gusto by manager Fiona Ross, who is a great fund of local lore and knowledge. The **YMCA**, ((03) 477-9555, at 54 Moray Place, is one of the nicest old-style Y's in New Zealand — very central and set in a colonial house with a pretty garden. **Manor House**, ((03) 477-0484, at 28 Manor Place (off Princes Street), is a converted colonial house with good facilities and a garden to relax in.

Staying Outside Dunedin
Larnach Castle, ((03) 476-1302, P.O. Box 1350 Dunedin. Staying here is one of Otago's highlights, and it's only 15 minutes' drive from the city. The Castle Lodge, renovated from a farm building, has a row of view-facing rooms. Rooms are cozy, with brass beds, colonial furniture and little touches like potpourri and fluffy towels. Lodge rates are moderate. The Stables are converted from the old Coach house, divided into spartan backpacker's berth rooms. There's a communal kitchen and bathroom area. It's probably most suitable for families or groups. Guests can request dinner in the castle's candlelit dining room, which requires bookings before 5 pm and costs $40. Breakfasts are served on the verandah.

Also on the Otago Peninsula, **Roselle Farm Motel**, ((03) 478-0826, lies on the corner of Weir and Harington Point roads, and has comfortable self-contained, moderately-priced motel rooms tucked in its secluded bay, near the Otakou Golf Course, two kilometers (one-and-a-quarter miles) from Portobello.

EATING OUT

Fine Dining
95 Filleul, ((03) 477-7233, at 95 Filleul Street, has a devoted following in Dunedin. It's open daily from 6:30 pm onwards, and reservations are essential. **Willoughbys**, ((03) 474-1588, next to the Visitors center in the Octagon serves lunch and dinner. The **Clarendon Hotel**, ((03) 477-9095, at 28 Maclaggan Street, is a refurbished colonial building with weekday lunches under $10, and dinners from 6 pm. **Firenze**, ((03) 477-6647, at 487 George Street, bills itself as "The Great Italian BYO". It's open Wednesday to Sunday from 6 pm.

Cheerful Restaurant, ((03) 479-2452, at 141 Stuart Street, Dunedin's best Chinese restaurant. All dishes are prepared with special care to use only cholesterol-free or cholesterol-low ingredients when possible. Bill Chin is a the friendly and jocular host. It's open for lunch and dinner and reservations are advisable. **Prasad's Place**, ((03) 479-0110, 466 George Street, has North Indian cuisine. The **Mediteran**, ((03) 455-8501 at 14 St. Clair Esplanade is set right on the seafront, with wonderful views across the Pacific Ocean. It serves Greek, Maltese, Spanish and Italian dishes, and is open daily from noon to 2:30 pm and 6 pm to 10 pm.

Baghdad Cafe, ((03) 474-1472, at 401 Moray Place is a licensed jazz cafe, open daily from 11 am until late, with live jazz from Thursday through Sunday. The **Terrace Cafe**, ((03) 474-0686, in Moray Place opposite Fortune Theatre, serves Mediterranean cuisine and is open from Tuesday through Saturday, from 6 pm until late. **Just Desserts**, ((03) 477-5331, at 29–31 Bath Street, specializes in mouth-watering, irresistible desserts that put this place on the map for sweet-tooths.

For lunch, **Parisettes**, ((03) 474-0299, at 368 Moray Place, have made their speciality the home-baked "parisette", a thin baked French bread, which is the base for a sandwich filling of your choice. **Albert Arms**, ((03) 477-8035, on the corner of George and London streets is a historic pub serving very cheap, hearty meals, open daily. **High Tide**, ((03) 477-9784, at 15 Kitchener Street, overlooks the waterfront in the old hovercraft building, and has a pleasant garden location.

Out of Town
1908 Cafe Portobello, ((03) 478-0801, at 7 Harington Point Road, has been converted

from a farmhouse, and has a pleasant colonial atmosphere and fine harbor views. it's open from Tuesday to Friday from 3 pm until 10 pm, and from noon to 10 pm during weekends.

City Specials

Haggis-devotees may be interested in the possibility of joining in a Haggis Ceremony at the Savoy Hotel. Contact the Visitor's center for more details.

Westons Wines is a fascinating place to visit. From their hillside home, Geoff and Jill

Weston make distinctive fruit-based wines and conduct an informative one-hour wine tasting session. Conversation usually flows along with the regularly topped-up glasses so that a good time is had by all. By arrangement only, ((03) 467-5544.

NIGHTLIFE

Dunedin's best-loved pub is **The Empire** on Princes Street. **The Captain Cook** has live bands on Friday and Saturday nights. One of the most lively bars is **Foxy's Cafe**, above the Robbie Burns Hotel, at 370 George Street. It has live bands on Wednesday through Saturday, and a split-level restaurant. If you have dinner before the perform-

ances you don't have to pay the $5 cover charge.

Dunedin also boasts a few nightclubs. Most popular is **Club 118**, in the Southern Cross Hotel, which closes at 3 am. **Club Nouveau** at 131 High Street, closes "early" at 10:30 pm, while **Regine's**, at 27 Timaru Street, is regarded by Dunedinites as slightly adventurous, with its occasional transvestites and other such slightly flamboyant members of society. It often has live bands and closes at 1 am.

SHOPPING

The **Carnegie Centre**, at 110 Moray Place is a vintage warren of shops and stalls where you can browse among wares created by leading craftspeople. During summer there are often courtyard performances. For inquires about the center, call (03) 474-0638. **Upstage Handknits**, at 233 Upper Stuart Street specialize in mohair, cotton and hand-woven wools, and opens at 11 am. The **Scottish Shop** at 187 George Street, sells "exotic" items such as oat-cakes, Edinburgh Rock, tartan kilts and Highland dancing accessories. They stock no less than 500 tartan ties and clan crests for colonial-breed Scots, and you can browse to piped Highland bagpipe music.

THE PENINSULA TRAIL

Within an afternoon, and a 64 km (40 miles) round-trip, you can admire New Zealand's only castle and the beautiful Royal Albatrosses, visit a Maori church, stumble on tribes of seals and penguins or even tie up with a cruise through the Otago Harbour. Be sure to pick up the detailed Otago Peninsula guide and map at the Visitors center.

From Dunedin, follow Portsmouth Drive to Portobello Road, where the coastal road hugs the Otago Harbour, with gently curving bays lined with toi-toi, flax and cabbage trees. Turn off up Castlewood Road for **Larnach Castle**, an imposing crenellated mansion circled by a glassed-in verandah and perched high above the peninsula with suitably Gothic magnificence. Completed in 1886, it was the home of William Larnach, an Australian who arrived to manage the Bank of Otago and later became a Member of Parliament. Larnach's extraordinary mansion was only one chapter in his successful, but trauma-ridden life. After the death of his first wife, a wealthy French heiress, Larnach married her younger half-sister in order to care for his children, but she died five years later. The third wife — Miss Constance — became mistress of the estate (and 44 servants) at 17, and was later rumored to have become romantically entangled with Larnach's son — creating quite a Brightonesque scandal in

walled-off section of the castle with their two grown-up children.

The century-old gardens are superb, lovingly landscaped and re-planted by Margaret Barker, and also includes a nursery section, where visitors can buy a wide variety of seedlings and plants. The leaflet issued at reception has a map of the garden, with its highlights of a little rain forest and a rhododendron dell.

From the tiny town of Pukehiki, back on Highcliff Road, take the turnoff for **Hooper's Inlet**, rich with birdlife. As you drive you

socially staid Otago. This factor, along with a rapidly diminishing fortune, may have lead Larnach to put a gun to his head in the Committee Room of Wellington's Parliamentary Buildings in 1898. For many years, the fate of the castle was no less forlorn. It was used as a mental hospital for shell-shocked soldiers from World War I, abandoned, then as a nun's retreat, and eventually abandoned. When the present owners, Margaret and Barry Barker, purchased it in 1967, the interiors were rotting away and cattle were grazing in the ballroom. Today, splendidly restored, it is a major tourist attraction, with a lodge attached for accommodation, and the Barkers achieve a happy balance by living in a

should (if it's not foggy) be treated to a spectacular view over the peninsula, with drops to the coasts of **Sandfly Bay**, and at **Lover's Leap** and **The Chasm**, drops of 200 m (650 ft) and 130 m (426 ft) sheer to the shore. Further on, you'll get a glimpse of **Port Chalmers**, a charming historic seaport on the north shore.

Use your map to drive up to **Taiaroa Heads**, and keep your eye out for the Mc-Grouther's Farm turnoff if you want to visit **Penguin Place**. You'll pass through **Otakou**, site of the pre-European Maori settlement

OPPOSITE: Impressive blow holes are a feature of the rugged terrain of the Otago Peninsula.
ABOVE: An albatross takes flight at the Otago Peninsula colony.

that gave Otago its name. In the whaling days, this was one giant blubber factory, with vats of slaughtered whales bubbling in huge pots. The **Otakou Maori Memorial Church, Marae** and **Cemetery** are all interesting to visit. In the cemetery are buried three great Maori chiefs — the belligerent Taiaroa, Ngatata and Karatei. Visit by arrangement, ((03) 478-0252 or (03) 478-0466.

Sky Sailors and a Disappearing Gun

The **Royal Albatross Colony** at Taiaroa Heads is the only place in the world to see these majestic birds nesting on a mainland so close to civilization. Although there are three species of albatross in the northern seas, and ten in the south, the majestic Royal is the largest of the species with a wing-span of up to three-and-a-half meters (11 ft).

Each year, a community of albatrosses flies to the headland, once the site of an old Maori pa, attracted by its gusty winds. The strong gulfstreams at Taiaroa Heads create a sort of sky adventure park for these heavy birds, who need a wind speed of at least 15 km (just over nine miles) to take flight.

Groups are taken up to the observatory after an introductory talk in the **Trust Bank Royal Albatross Centre**. It can be blustery, so bring warm clothes. The center is open daily, with restricted hours on Tuesday. The viewing season from the observatory opens on November 24 and closes on the September 16, although these dates fluctuate with the progress of the birds. Booking for the observatory tour can be made at the Visitors center. However, you often get a very spectacular display of the cavorting giants by standing in the car-park.

The headland contains the **Fort Taiaroa** gun batteries, built at the height of fears over Russian expansionism in 1885. The most noteworthy of these is the **Armstrong Disappearing Gun**, a breechloader mounted on a hydro-pneumatic carriage. It's open daily, although Tuesdays have restricted times and prior booking is necessary.

Penguins and Seals

Before visiting **Penguin Place** you'll need to first obtain a road gate key for $4. Obtain this as you drive from Dunedin from the

McGrouther's Farm, reached after turning off the Harington Point just beyond Otakou — there's a big sign and it's difficult to miss. ((03) 478-0286 for Mr. McGrouther if you can't locate it. Binoculars are available on request.

From Taiaroa Heads, retracing from the albatross colony, you'll see a road fork. From here the road leads to a car-park with two tiny trails from which you can see the rare yellow-eyed penguins, southern fur seals and nearby, a colony of spotted shags. The penguins are attracted to this region by the profusion of marine life just off the Otago coast, where the Pacific Plate overlaps with the depths of the Continental shelf. The best time to see them are the last two or three hours of sunlight, when they swim ashore, waddle up the beach, greet each other by standing still and climb into their nests. But the seals bask all day on their rocky islet, loll in drifting seaweed or go surfing on the tide. Be careful of these cuddly-looking creatures — if crossed they have an aggressive nature, and some visitors report being chased by the surprisingly speedy sea-dogs. They're often found sun-bathing virtually in the car-park, so beware of treading on a flopped flipper.

Portobello

Roughly half-way between Dunedin and Taiaroa Heads, this classic little colonial-era settlement tucked beside a pretty bay still has a time-warp feel. Visit the **Otago Peninsula Museum**, a replica pioneer's cottage with mocked-up period displays. It's open on Sundays from 1:30 pm to 4:30 pm, and otherwise by arrangement. Call (03) 478-0255.

Within Portobello, there are several craft shops to explore and two excellent restaurants for stylish dining.

On Portobello Road lies the turnoff to **Glenfalloch Woodland Gardens**. This peaceful, harborside estate is owned by the Otago Peninsula Trust and has beautiful gardens of azalea, camellia, rhododendron, magnolia and fuchia within lawns, native bush and waterfalls. An original colonial kauri homestead has been turned into a pretty restaurant; there's a potter's kiln with a training program and many bush walks clearly marked for post-Devonshire tea strolls.

TOURS

The **Wild Coast Explorer** is undoubtedly one of the best tours of its kind in New Zealand. What makes this tour really special is visiting a private beach where a conservation program for the rare yellow-eyed and little blue penguins is underway. Here, you're shown nesting chicks, and depending on the penguin's whims, you may see them waddle in from the sea and find their nests. The tour costs $29. The same company also runs **Twilight Wildlife Experience**, a specialist wildlife tour for enthusiasts which includes conservation input, **Architectural History and Castle Bus tours**, consecutively $46, $30 and $19 including entrance fees. Book at Wild South, ((03) 477-2486 or 474-3300.

Newtons Coach Tours

This is Dunedin's longest-running tour and crams as much as possible into its time. There are three tour options, and it's possible to do all three in one day, (heavily discounted) or just stick with one. It operates all year around, except major holidays and can be booked on ((03) 477-5577.

Harbour Cruises

M.V. Monarch owner and skipper Colleen Black is a round-the-world sailor and biologist who introduces visitors to the wildlife and history of the Otago Harbour and Peninsula on her cruises. One of the hour's highlights is viewing the albatross colony from the sea, watching the great birds wheeling across the headland. You'll often see seals, shags and sometimes penguins as well. Tours operate from October to April, leaving every day from 1:30 pm. Another possibility is to take the **Monarch Coach and Cruise** tour which combines a bus tour, so you see the Otago Peninsula from all angles and cover most of its sights. It costs adults $39 and children $20 and leaves from the Visitors center at 1 pm.

In the City

Chocolate lovers must include a visit to the **Cadbury Chocolate Factory** in their stay. Located at 280 Cumberland Street, tours run

every Monday to Thursday, and run between 1:30 pm to 2:30 pm and 2:30 pm to 3:30 pm. Children under five are not allowed. Book directly at the factory on ((03) 474-1126.

If you like beer you'll like the **Speights Brewery Tour**. Guided tours run on weekdays starting at 10:30 am, at the factory's headquarters at 200 Rattray Street. The century-old factory still stands on its original site, when it produced Speights for thirsty gold miners out in the Otago hills.

Adventure Tours

There are two star tours on offer — one on land and one on sea. You can go **Surf Rafting**, speed-plunging into the spray in a motorized raft, exploring the beaches of St. Kilda and St. Clair. Among other antics, you shoot through a rock tunnel and zoom beneath huge cliff faces. Make sure you bring a bathing suit to wear under the wetsuit, a towel and a pair of sneakers. Call (03) 455-0066 for details. It costs $36.

An hour's drive from Dunedin, **Ardachy Trail Rides** operate out of Hindon hill country near the Taieri Gorge, with horse trails cutting through mountain streams, stopping for swims and fire-grilled meals. You can arrange to hire out the horses from one and a half hours ($19 per person) to up to a full day ($55). It's possible to stay at the Ardachy homestead, from which you can make walking, fishing and horse-back sorties. Call (03) 489-1499 and speak to Leila or Robin Graham.

All tours can be booked through the Visitors Centre.

On the Right Track

For spectacular scenery and the antiquated charm of a historic railway take the **Taieri Gorge Limited** scenic trip. The 60 km (37 miles) four-hour trip passes through distinctive native grasses and trees of the Taieri plains to the stark schist canyons of the gorge. Old-style wooden carriages have been restored, and there's a plush dining car.

From October to March, the train departs at 3:30 pm, returning at 7:20 pm, and from April to May departs at 2:30 pm, and costs $39 for adults, each with two accompanied children free. Book at the Railway Station at ((03) 477-4449.

THE OYSTER TRAIL

THE CATLINS

Several hours drive from Dunedin, past Balclutha, lies one of New Zealand's least known scenic regions, the Catlins. The district is a wedge of rolling hill country between the Clutha and Mataurua rivers. Within the **Catlins State Forest Park**, a tranquil haven of virgin rain forests and waterfalls, lies a coast backed by towering

clay cliffs, riddled with burrows of blue, and the rarer yellow-eyed, penguins, spotted shags, gannets and sooty shearwaters. There are numerous colonies of fur seals here too.

The region's main settlement is at **Owaka**, close to **Nugget Point**, with its remote light-house standing sentry over a seal colony. You can stay at **Greenwood Farmstays, (** (03) 415-8259, at Tarara on the Catlins Coast, near the Purakanui Falls, which charges inexpensive rates. They also have a beach cottage at Papatowai for hire. The **Visitors Centre, (** (03) 415-8341, is at the corner of Ryley and Campbell streets.

One of the most enjoyable ways of exploring the Catlins is to join the tour run by

Catlins Wildlife Trackers, ((Dunedin) (03) 455-2681. They run two-day tours into the Catlins from Dunedin, exploring its unusual wildlife, meeting locals and staying on a comfortable home-stay. The cost of $250 includes everything, but they ask you to bring walking shoes and a sleeping bag.

From the Catlins National Park, you can head straight for Invercargill along the coastal highway, or reach that town by looping back through Balclutha via Gore. Either way, the scenery is enjoyable.

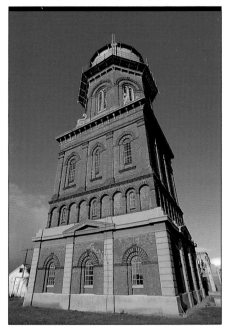

INVERCARGILL

New Zealand's most southernmost city, Invercargill was originally settled by Scots from Dunedin, and its wide tree-lined streets bear the names of Scottish rivers. Aside from its huge pyramid-shaped **Southland Centennial Museum and Art Gallery** on Gala Street with its fascinating sub-antarctic environment displays and *tuatara* house, Invercargill is a sprawling, rather functional service community for the region's many farm, cattle and deer stations. It's a place to stop through en route from the Catlins to make the flight to Stewart Island.

Nearby **Bluff**, 27 km (17 miles) away, is the region's port, a rather stark outpost in the shadow of a massive aluminum smelter massed with fishing fleets. Its real claim to fame are Bluff oysters, lifted from the deep clean waters of Foveaux Strait.

Access

Air New Zealand and Ansett New Zealand link Invercargill with daily direct flights to Dunedin, Christchurch, Wellington, Palmerston North and Auckland. Southern Air has daily flights to Stewart Island from here.

The Southerner Christchurch–Dunedin – Invercargill train service operates daily except Sundays, departing from each end of the line at around 8:50 am and arriving at the other end at about 6:30pm. The journey takes three and a half hours from Dunedin and nine and a half hours from Christchurch.

InterCity and Mt. Cook Landline have daily connections to Te Anau, Queenstown and Christchurch, with more frequent services to Dunedin.

General Information

The **Visitors Centre**, ((03) 218-6090, at 82 Dee Street, should be able to answer any inquires about the region, suggest farm stays and wildlife tours.

Where to Stay and Eat

The **Grand Hotel**, ((03) 218-8059, close to Don Street on Dee Street, is considered to be one of the city's fine old landmarks and has moderately-priced rooms. Another old classic, also moderately-priced, is **Gerrards**, ((03) 214-3406, fax: (03) 214-4567, at the corner of Esk and Leven streets. Built in 1898, this turreted Victorian curiosity has been since renovated and has rather quirky rooms.

The **Ainos Steakhouse and Restaurant**, ((03) 215-9568, in the Waikiwi Shopping Center in Ruru Street, is a casual, friendly BYO. But it also happens to serve the city's best meals, leaning towards inventive seafood dishes, with especially good pan-fried Southland oysters and whitebait dishes. The **Moa's Grillroom** on Dee Street is the best place for travelers to descend if what they need is a non-nonsense meal. It serves meat and fish dishes in a massive trencher. It's not fancy and you don't need to book.

GATEWAY TO ANTARCTICA

STEWART ISLAND

The last outpost of Pacific civilization, Stewart Island is regarded by most New Zealanders as the end of the earth. The legendary gales of the Roaring Forties lash this southernmost island of New Zealand, giving its 500 hardy, amiable Stewart Islanders a character as tough as the climate. Located 27 km (17 miles) from the South Island

across Foveaux Strait, Stewart Island covers a massive area of 1,680 sq km (618 sq miles) and has some 750 km (465 miles) of indented coastline, yet is virtually unexplored. Roads stretch only 20 km (12 miles) from the only settlement of **Oban** in **Halfmoon Bay**, although there are extensive walking tracks cut through the island's dense emerald forest. This is a perfect place if you crave total seclusion, primeval jungle-like forests, rich birdlife and a total escape from civilization, with shores lapped by giant tentacles of kelp.

OPPOSITE LEFT: Purakanui Falls in the Catlins State Forest Park. OPPOSITE RIGHT: A typically stoical civic building in Invercargill. ABOVE: Colonial buildings dot the main port of Oban in Stewart Island.

General Information

In Invercargill, you can make inquiries about tramping, hunting permits and fishing at the **Department of Conservation**, ℓ (03) 214-4589 in the State Insurance Building on Don Street. In Oban, the **D.O.C. Visitors Centre**, ℓ (03) 219-1130, is beside the deer park on Main Road. For cruises and charters contact **Moana Charters**, ℓ (03) 219-1202, **Matangi Charters**, ℓ (03) 219-1444, or **Stewart Island Yacht Charters**, ℓ (03) 219-1126.

Access

You can get there from the mainland from Bluff by boat (two or three times a week) or by air. Southern Air makes the 20 minute flight between Invercargill and Stewart Island twice daily all year round. An adult return fare is $135, children $67, and there are several discounts. Call Invercargill, ℓ (03) 214-4681 for details. One can organise a day trip to Steward Island from Queenstown. InterCity scheduled bus service (adult $50.25 and children $30 roundtrip) which connects with Southern Air. Call (03) 442-8238, Queenstown, for details.

What to See

There is a surprising amount to do in this most remote of all major New Zealand islands, where you are almost literally at the end of the earth. You can explore Oban's snug harbor in Halfmoon Bay, moored with sturdy fishing boats, visit the small, but interesting **Rakiura Museum**, and down some Roaring Forties beer at the bar of the South Seas Hotel, while you contemplate energetic walks into the forest. At Harrold Bay, about three kilometers (nearly two miles) from Oban, is an old stone house built in 1832.

Stewart Island is internationally renowned by keen ornithologists who flock here to witness a variety of birdlife here unmatched in the rest of the country. The focus of their interest goes by the name of *Apteryx australis lavaryi*, to give the Stewart Island brown kiwi its scientific name. This pear-shaped brown and gray strider differs from its cousins on other New Zealand islands, having been cut off from them since the Ice Age. Local guides pick up enthusiasts from the jetty at Halfmoon Bay, and kiwi-seeking parties set out at dusk, cruising

through some of the most enchanting scenery in the entire Pacific, past deep coves, gamboling dolphins, and bush-clad headlands, to **Glory Bay** where the group proceeds to search for the nocturnal birds who snuffle through rotting kelp for insects. Aside from the kiwis, there are hundreds of other native birds, including the rare flightless kakapo parrot, weka, bush birds such as tuis, parakeets, bellbirds, ferbirds, robins, dotterels and numerous sea birds.

A visit is incomplete without a boat trip to **Paterson Inlet** or to the little islands offshore from Halfmoon Bay. Scenic cruises also visit salmon farms, seal colonies and an old whalers base, and there are also fishing cruises for anyone who wants to try their hand at the sea. Inland there are many walks

into deep forest along Department of Conservation tracks, strategically dotted with bush-huts for overnight trips. Dense with ferns, splashed with wild orchids, this virgin forest is breathtakingly lonesome. One of its most spectacular walks reveals the granite dome of **Magog**, nicknamed "Bald Mountain," rising above unbroken forest. Up in the hills are impressively-horned red deer and white-tailed Virginia deer, introduced by European settlers a century ago and now found wild all over the island.

Where to Stay
The **Stewart Island Lodge**, ((03) 219-1085, fax: (03) 219-1681, is a stately turn-of-the-century mansion nestled in an idyllic setting amongst ferns and pines overlooking Half-

moon Bay with luxurious, mid-priced accommodation for up to eight guests, a splendid seafood restaurant (with a roaring fireplace) and atmospheric bar for lingering long into the night. Their launch, *MV Toa Tai* is available for cruises and fishing charters. A moderately priced option is the **South Sea Hotel**, ((03) 219-1059, fax: (03 219-1120, in Halfmoon Bay, which has great charm, home comforts and a charismatic bar. The more modern **Rakiura Motel**, ((03) 219-1096, at Horsehoe Bay, Halfmoon Bay offers all amenities, a decent restaurant and is inexpensive. All hotels have superb sea views and waking at dawn, you'll hear a chorus of bird calls.

Halfmoon Bay in Stewart Island.

Travelers' Tips

GETTING THERE

BY AIR

On the world map, New Zealand inches down towards Antarctica, almost as far away from the rest of the world as you could get. This "farawayness", of course, is part of New Zealand's attraction. But for the same reason, it's not usually a destination travelers visit without a little forethought; after all, it involves many fatigue-inducing flying

matter of shopping around and tireless question-asking. Overall, you'll get the best value for your ticket to New Zealand if you purchase a ticket package that allows you to stop off in other destinations as well, usually within a given time frame stretching from six months to a year. Possible destinations in the so-called Circle Pacific ticket, for instance, include the West Coast of the United States, various islands in the Pacific, New Zealand, Australia, Asia and back to the West Coast.

There are many round the world ticket varieties put together by travel agents at

hours across many thousands of kilometers — as well as a fairly expensive ticket.

The vast majority of visitors fly there. Auckland and Christchurch are the two main international airports, served by 24 international airlines offering either nonstop, direct or in-line services to destinations in North America, South America, Australia, Asia, the United Kingdom and Europe as well as the neighboring Pacific islands. Wellington, the hub of the domestic network, also has a service to Australia.

The best secret to a well-priced ticket is always a good travel agent. Finding one is a

various prices with different stopover options. They usually combine the routes of Air New Zealand with one of the following airlines: Singapore Airlines, British Airways, Cathay Pacific, Lufthansa and Thai International, as well as various other airlines.

Budget-conscious travelers looking for a simple return fare are strongly advised to check out charter flights, as they are often half the price charged by scheduled carriers. Another low-fare ticket is the advance purchase excursion ticket, which must be booked and paid for usually a month in advance and can then only be changed at extra cost.

Another factor is the time of the year. Prices during peak season (mid-December to mid-January) can be as much as 30 per-

The kiwi, New Zealand's most widely recognized symbol.

cent more than at other times in the year. Ask your travel agent about the many discount fares, seasonal and package deals available. Most airlines have at least one, as does New Zealand's Mount Cook Line and other travel companies. In London, two good low-fare specialists are Trailfinders at 42–48 Earls Court Road, London W8 and STA Travel at 74 and 86 Old Brompton Road, London SW7 and 117 Euston Road, London NW1.

Auckland and Christchurch airports charge everyone departing the country a departure tax of NZ$16 and Wellington NZ$20.

ARRIVING

TRAVEL DOCUMENTS

By and large, New Zealand only requires its visitors to hold a valid passport. Australians do not need visas and can stay in the country indefinitely, while British passport holders (with UK residence) do not need visas and can stay in the country for six months. Within this ruling, visas or immigration fees are not required for tourists or business visits up to three months for citizens of Western Europe, Ireland, Canada, Scandinavia, Ireland, Japan, Singapore, Malaysia, Thailand, Indonesia, Kiribati and Nauru. If you do not fall into this category or wish to seek work or study, then you must have a visa. You can check with New Zealand diplomatic or consular offices, or from the New Zealand Immigration Service, P.O. Box 4130, Wellington. There are NZTB (New Zealand Tourism Board) overseas travel offices in the following countries who will answer any visa queries and can also offer advice and book tours, accommodation and transport within New Zealand:

Australia: Downtown Duty Free House, 84 Pitt Street, Sydney NSW 2000, (((00612) 221-7333, fax (00612) 235-0737.

Canada: Suite 1260, IBM Tower, 701 West Georgia Street, Vancouver BC V7Y IB6, ((604) 684-2117.

Hong Kong: 3414 Jardine House, Connaught Road, Central, Hong Kong, ((852) 525-5044.

Japan: Toho Twin Tower Building, 2F 1-5-2 Yurakucho, Chiyoda-ku, Tokyo 100, ((0813) 508-9902.

Singapore: 13 Nassim Road, Singapore 1025, ((65) 235-9966.

United Kingdom: New Zealand House, Haymarket, London SW1Y 4TQ, ((071) 973-0363.

United States: Suite 1530, 10960 Wilshire Boulevard, Los Angeles, California 90024, ((213) 477-8241.

Germany: Friedrichstrasse 10–12, 60323 Frankfurt-am-Main. ((069) 971-2110, fax (069) 97 12 11 13.

CUSTOMS

Visitors over 17 years of age may import duty-free 200 cigarettes or 50 cigars or 250 grams (eight and three quarter ounces) of tobacco, 4.5 liters of wine (the equivalent of six 750 ml bottles) and one bottle containing not more than 1125ml of spirits or liqueur. New Zealand slaps heavy import duties on cameras, cars, TVs and other electronic equipment, but goods of a combined value of NZ$500 can be brought in duty-free.

There are very finicky regulations about the import of animals, plants, seeds, insects and certain foodstuffs. For centuries, by virtue of its geographical isolation, New Zealand has been free from many animal and agricultural diseases and wants to keep itself that way. When you arrive customs officials in their uniform of shorts and long white socks will sternly spray the interior of the aircraft as you remain seated, making you feel a little chastised, as though you're not quite clean enough. It's supposed to be harmless for humans, but cover your mouth and nose anyway.

MONEY

New Zealand uses a decimal system of currency, divided into dollars and cents, and exchanges at approximately NZ$1.70 to the USD$1. There's no import or export limit on foreign cash or traveler's checks, and unused New Zealand currency can be changed into mainstream foreign currencies at any bank.

Credit cards are widely accepted, including Visa, American Express, Diners Club and MasterCard. Traveler's checks can be changed at all banks, and hotels and stores in the main cities and tourist destinations will also be happy to change them for you.

WHEN TO GO

This really depends on what kind of holiday you're anticipating having because New Zealand is a year-round destination. It ranges from sub-tropical in the north to temperate and alpine in the south. Because the country is surrounded by seas, the weather is susceptible to sudden changes. Remem-

ber that the seasons are "upside down" or reversed in the Southern Hemisphere, meaning that it's summer at Christmas. Summer runs from December to March, autumn from March to May, winter from June to August and spring from September to November.

WHAT TO TAKE

New Zealand's climate is never totally predictable. Although the country is very compact, weather varies dramatically in different parts of the country. In general, come prepared for all types of weather, even in the middle of summer. In keeping with New Zealand's relaxed lifestyle, dress is mostly casual, although it's amazing how many restaurants and pubs are sticklers for out-dated dress codes. In the large cities, if you want to dress up for restaurants and nightclubs, that's up to you. Everything you could possibly need or want in the way of outdoor activity equipment and clothing is widely available at hundreds of specialist

shops. For other items, New Zealand is a very modern, well-equipped country with shops that stock most essentials.

TOURIST INFORMATION

New Zealand has information dissemination mania. In the large cities and towns, you'll feel positively besieged with information — brochures, maps and mini-guides — about every attraction and activity you could imagine. Helpful staff can answer queries, book accommodation, transport and tours and offer reliable advice on anything under the sun about New Zealand. There are about 90 government Visitor Information offices nationwide, identified by a green "i" sign.

Added to this, even the smallest, apparently nondescript town usually has some kind of tourist office. Or if you're really off the beaten track, there's nothing wrong with stopping to ask the local farmer. If you're lucky, you'll get a cup of tea and some "bickies" too!

GETTING AROUND

New Zealand has a reliable, well coordinated transport network and distances are short. This makes independent travel in the country fairly straight-forward and hassle-free. The most useful reference for up-to-date services and fares is the readily available Passenger Transport Summary, put out by the New Zealand Tourism Department. It's wise to reserve all services in advance, particularly during the peak season between December and February.

BY AIR

If you're pressed for time, cover the distance by air. Flying in New Zealand has recently become quite a competitive business, keeping prices relatively low. There are three main domestic airlines, Air New Zealand, Ansett New Zealand and Mount Cook Airlines, who fly between the major cities and towns. Air New Zealand also links with the flights of Mount Cook, and the smaller Air

Nelson and Eagle Air, and offer over 400 flights to 31 destinations each day. The main domestic hubs are Auckland, Wellington, Christchurch, Dunedin and Queenstown. All three of the main airlines have special fares available to tourists for travel within New Zealand, well worth investigating before you leave, since these packages can be purchased overseas at a lower price, and in the case of Ansett New Zealand, represent a 30 percent saving on all adult economy fares.

Prices range from NZ$110 (Wellington to Nelson) to NZ$597 (Kerikeri in the Bay of Islands to Queenstown). They also have special weekend and standby discount rates worth finding out about from your travel agent. Reporting time for any flight is 30 minutes prior to departure.

By Train

Not to be outshone by the airlines, InterCity (which runs the bus, rail and ferry network) offers a variety of special fares, and much improved food and service — as well as sheepskin-covered seats — to lure travelers to the "romance" of rail. There are only a handful of main routes: Auckland to Wellington on the *Silver Fern,* Wellington to Napier on the *Bay Express,* Picton to Christchurch on the Coastal Pacific, Christchurch to Dunedin and Invercargill on the *Southerner Express* and the scenic *Trans-Alpine Express* between Christchurch and Greymouth.

Train fares are usually around the same price as bus fares on the same route. InterCity offer a Travelpass which provides unlimited travel on any InterCity bus, rail and Cook Strait Ferry Service, ranging from 8 days (with a fortnight to use it) and 22 days (with a month), which should be booked overseas in order to obtain a significant discount.

By Bus

Some of the best Kiwi wisecracks I've heard have been delivered by a broad-accented bus driver, breaking the monotony of endless sheep, green fields and mountains. In rural areas, drivers often act as mailmen too, accurately aiming newspapers on doorsteps without stepping on the brakes. Coach services range from fairly comfort-

able to exceedingly comfortable and from surprisingly inexpensive to very cheap. Just about every town and city in the country is connected to a network of coach services operated by either InterCity, Mount Cook or Newmans. All three operators offer special discounts. InterCity's Travelpass and Mount Cook's Kiwi Coach Pass are both good bargains.

Less conventional, certainly cheaper and sometimes much more entertaining is a growing number of backpacker's transport buses. There are several options depending

on where you wish to travel. Northcape Shuttle service Northland, departing from Auckland. The East Cape Fun Bus provides a circular trip from Auckland around the East Cape and can arrange continued North Island transport. Kiwi Experience offers a countrywide network and has a combined pass with InterCity. Another national service is provided by Pavlova Experience, which links with the network of Pavlova hostels.

In the South Island, the Magic Bus offers off-beat tours rather than just transport, as does the original backpacker's bus, the West Coast Express, both providing action-packed trips down the West Coast with departures from Nelson and Queenstown. From Christchurch, you can pick up the Shoestring Travel bus and the Flying Kiwi bus, both of which plan varied, comprehensive itineraries.

OPPOSITE: New Zealand is renowned for the diversity and beauty of its skiing fields.
ABOVE: Deer farming has become a mainstay industry in the South Island.

By Car

This is definitely the best way of exploring New Zealand. So much of its most magnificent scenery is found off the main highways, along dirt-track roads, lakeside drives and forested tracks. In fact, the country is made for driving. Distances are short, traffic is light, roads are well-signposted, maps are easy to follow and it's almost impossible to get lost. Rates for rental cars vary between operators and are dependent on the type

Southern Cross. Smaller companies have more competitive rates—as low as NZ$54 per day. My best recommendation for vehicle reliability, price and overall helpfulness is Economy Rental Cars in Auckland ((09) 275-3777 and Christchurch ((03) 356-7410.

In New Zealand, motorists drive on the left-hand side of the road. The speed limit for built-up areas is 50kph (30mph) and the motorway or open road speed limit is 100kph (60mph). The main difference to remember is that unless an intersection is controlled by traffic lights or stop and give way

and size of car, the distance driven and the length of hire. Avis, Hertz and Budget are the leading car rental companies, with outlets at most airports and agents across the country. A deposit is usually requested when picking up the vehicle and the vehicle does not necessarily have to be returned to the place of pick-up. Typical costs for an unlimited distance rental of a small car (Toyota Corolla or Mitsubishi Mirage) are around NZ$125 to NZ$150 a day. There are special deals available for long weekends, extended hire and credit card users. You'll find their offices at all the main airports. Other car rental companies include Thrifty, Dollar or

signs, you must give way to all traffic on your right. Seatbeats are compulsory, as are motorbike helmets.

Lastly, the Automobile Association (AA) provides a road map and breakdown service. Free reciprocal membership privileges are offered to members belonging to equivalent overseas organizations, including free accommodation and camping site directories and excellent regional maps. Check with the telephone directory in each town for the local AA address.

By Camper Van

Regarded by some as the height of suburban travel, this is either a mode of transport that

Traffic jams like these are part of the charm in rural New Zealand.

appeals to you or not. Devotees claim the self-sufficient benefits of combining transport and accommodation far outweigh any self-conscious pretensions to style. After all, you'll hardly be alone — thousands of New Zealand families holiday this way every year. Other than specific "no camping" areas, you can park for up to seven days on any public scenic spot, lakeside, mountain view or seacoast place you want. In addition, there are plenty of camping grounds — or motor camps as they are known in New Zealand.

Hire campervans come in all shapes, up to six berths and are generally equipped with gas cooking, rings, heating, fridge, cold running water, a hot shower, pots, pans, crockery, duvets and linen. All you need to do is get off the plane, collect your vehicle, visit a supermarket and drive away.

Rental based on unlimited kilometers per day varies from NZ$80 in the low season (two-berth) to NZ$205 in the high season (six berth) and it's best to pre-book. Other costs include insurance (usually around NZ$14) and a returnable bond of around NZ$560. Of the campervan and motorhome companies in New Zealand, I would particularly recommend Mount Cook Line, in Auckland, ((09) 377-8389; Wellington (04) 385-4130 and Christchurch, ((03) 348-2099; Newmans, in Auckland, ((09) 303-1149; Maui Campers, in Auckland, ((09) 275-3013 and Christchurch, ((03) 358-4159 and Budget Motorhomes, in Auckland, ((09) 309-6737, and in Christchurch, ((03) 352-2649.

By City Buses and Taxi

Within cities, buses are plentiful, reliable and cover almost anywhere you could want to go. Contact the Visitors Information office for any details and timetables. Taxis are readily available, although quite expensive, with a set amount for the flag fall and then a charge for every part of a kilometer. A surcharge is added for a booked call.

Ferries

Modern Inter-Islander ferries join the two main islands and carry passengers and vehicles. The 84 km (50.4 miles) cruise leaves Wel-lington to cross the Cook Strait and weaves through the Marlborough Sounds to dock at Picton three hours and 20 minutes later. The *Aratika* and *Arahura* ferries both have comfortable lounge and deck areas, bars, restaurants, shops and even a cinema. Morning, early and late afternoon, and evening services operate both ways daily. Reservations are necessary, particularly for vehicles during December to February. You can usually book up to six months ahead of travel time at any InterCity travel agency. You can save up to a third on return fares anytime between the first sailing on Friday and the last on the following Monday for both passengers and vehicles. This does not apply during Christmas and holiday weekends.

A ferry also leaves the South Island at Bluff bound for Stewart Island, a journey of two and a quarter hours.

ACCOMMODATION

The variety of accommodation New Zealand has to offer is impressive. It's possible to take as much pleasure in staying at an exclusive sporting lodge as camping out under the stars. One costs a considerable amount, the other can cost nothing. Between the two, you have a huge range of choices.

Standards are high and prices are not inflated, although expect to pay for quality. While I have attempted to be as precise as possible when quoting prices for hotels, it is virtually impossible to take into account all the variables. For instance the price of the same hotel room could vary substantially depending on the time of year (summer is regarded as peak-season), the number of occupants, the length of stay and whether special discounts are available. I have therefore divided hotels into six categories according to the range of prices you can expect to pay for a double room per night. Exclusive means you can expect to pay NZ$450 upwards to NZ$2,000 a night; deluxe hotels charge between NZ$250 and NZ$450; mid-range between NZ$150 and NZ$250; moderate establishments will cost between NZ$70 and NZ$150; inexpensive (usually motels or Bed and Breakfasts) charge between NZ$30 and NZ$70, while backpackers hostels will ask between NZ$15 to NZ$30 per person.

There are many excellent directories to New Zealand's accommodation, as fat as bibles. Recommended are the free *Where To Stay Guide*, up-dated by the New Zealand Tourism Department (NZTD) and *Jason's* three directories on hotels, resorts and lodges, motels and motor lodges, and lastly, budget accommodation. Any tourist information office will have the useful *Camp and Cabin Association's Holiday Parks Directory*; the *Farm and Home Stay Directory* and the *Blue and White Backpacker's Bible*. One particularly useful book, a comprehensive guide to the country's most charming home stays, is the *New Zealand Bed and Breakfast Book*, compiled by J & J Thomas, published by Moonshine Press. The NZTD also puts out *Access*, a special accommodation guide for disabled travelers.

LUXURY AND SPORTING LODGES

True pampering, even by the most jaded criteria, is best appreciated at New Zealand's exclusive luxury and sporting lodges.

Set in some of the country's most dramatic, beautiful and tranquil locations, each lodge has its own character and many specialize in activities such as trout and salmon fishing and hunting. Some are renowned for absolute luxury; others are more casual and are priced accordingly. Some have chalet or cabin accommodation; others house guests within a single lodge building. You can expect excellent food and personal service, as well as professional guides for the activities in the area. There are some 36 recognized lodges in New Zealand. Some of the most renowned include Huka Lodge near Taupo, Solitaire Lodge and Moose Lodge, both near Rotorua, Puka Park Lodge in Pauanui, north of Thames, the Chateau at Tongariro National Park, the Hermitage at Mt. Cook and the Nugget Point Club at Queenstown.

HOTELS

In the cities and resort destinations you'll find a number of international chain hotels, such as the Regent, Hyatt, Parkroyal, Sheraton, Pan Pacific and Southern Pacific ho-

tels, as well as locally-owned international standard hotels, such as Pacific Park. The most expensive hotel is the Regent in Auckland where a suite costs up to NZ$2,000 a day.

MOTOR INNS AND MOTELS

There are thousands of good quality medium class hotels, motor inns and motels throughout the country. The main difference between motor inns and motels, both of which usually offer parking right outside the room, is that motels often have fully equipped kitchen. If you're planning to cook for yourselves, make sure you request a kitchen when you book ahead. Facilities for both usually include en-suite bathrooms, television, radio, heating and electric blankets. Most have a swimming pool, spa, laundry room and children's play area. Reputable local chains include the Manor Motor Inn, Flag Inn, Best Western, Quality Inn, Mitchell Corp and Autolodge.

SMALL HOTELS AND GUESTHOUSES

Moderately priced options include guesthouses, small private hotels and Bed and Breakfasts which are usually located in comfortable, well-restored older homes. You may have to share bathroom facilities. The classic Kiwi country pub, with its neat, clean rooms and friendly atmosphere offers the lowest-priced hotel accommodation.

FARMSTAYS

Farmstay holidays offer an ideal opportunity to meet New Zealanders on their own ground and experience a slice of New Zealand life. Accommodation is in typical New Zealand rural family homes and you share delicious country meals with your host family. Hosts only accept one reservation each time so you have their full attention. As you join the family as an honored guest, your bedroom will be in the family home and in most cases you'll share bathroom facilities with the family. You'll be welcome to join in the daily activities of the farm — perhaps down in the shearing shed or bringing home the cows to milk, or harvesting kiwifruit and consuming enormous morning teas!

A number of well-established companies arrange home and farm stays around the country, and the over 1,500 rural properties on their books vary from dairy farms and high country sheep stations to horse-studs and orchards. Hosts are paid for each stay but most are in the business for the opportunity to meet people and you'll find their hospitality very genuine. Tariffs usually include dinner and breakfast and range from NZ$70 to NZ$100 per person a night. Payments are made to the host organization either direct or through a travel agent, and

barbecue area and a children's playground. Sites for campers usually cost NZ$8 per day per adult. There are often simple cabins (NZ$5 to NZ$20 for a double, no bedding); tourist cabins and tourist flats (NZ$25 to NZ$70 self-contained with bedding).

Cabins are the perfect option if you're traveling on a budget, are happy to carry some bedding (a sleeping bag) and are happy not be under canvas. Most contain just beds and basic furniture; others are more sophisticated with tourist flats at the top end of the cabin scale offering linen and

you can get details of farm stays from your nearest Visitors Information Office or contact The **New Zealand Association of Farm and Home Hosts**, ((04) 472-8860, fax: (04) 478-1736, P.O. Box 95, Wellington.

MOTOR CAMPS AND CAMPING GROUNDS

New Zealand is a land of endless motorcamps and camping grounds. These usually offer tent and caravan sites which have communal kitchens, power points, clean shower blocks, hot and cold running water, flushing toilets and laundry facilities. Additional facilities may include a store, swimming or mineral pools and or spa pools, TV recreation lounge, dryer or drying rooms, car wash,

equipped kitchens. You'll find motorcamps in cities, in out of the way spots and near beaches and national parks.

If you've got a tent and you're prepared for the big outdoors, you'll find it in any number of popular or wild and beautiful spots, where you can wake to the sun rising over a misty lake or a crystal clear ocean inviting an early morning plunge.

Throughout New Zealand's beautiful parks, forest parks and reserves, the Department of Conservation maintain a network of huts which provide simple, pleasant bunkroom accommodation. Hut fees range from

Scenes of idyllic solitude are part of New Zealand's lure.

nothing to NZ$12. In more popular areas they are equipped with gas for cooking, a toilet, fireplaces and supplies of wood or coal.

BACKPACKERS

If you're traveling on a budget, New Zealand's extensive network of private hostels are great value, clean and tidy and usually well-located. They range from 4 beds to 100, from NZ$5 to NZ$15 per person per night (usually on a share basis) and have all the amenities for self-catering. Such accommodation can be found in cabins, small hotels and bunkrooms of hostels. The Youth Hostel also has hostels throughout the country with nightly dormitory rates from NZ$8 to NZ$14 per person. For further information, prices and lists of hostels, contact the Youth Hostels Association, ((09) 379-4224 in Auckland, 36 Customs Street East, corner of Customs and Gore streets or in Christchurch, ((03) 379-9970, corner of Gloucestor and Manchester streets.

FOOD AND WINE

It's not difficult to eat well in New Zealand, which has an abundance of world-famous lamb and dairy foods, venison, a diverse array of seafood plus organically-farmed vegetables and fine New Zealand wines. The food and wine cult is a fairly new phenomenon. Over the past decade, greater exposure to European and Asian influences has produced a cosmopolitan array of ethnic restaurants, cafes, wine bars and specialist delicatessens in the larger cities.

Eating out-of-doors has been a feature of life in New Zealand for hundreds of years, and summer barbecues are almost obligatory facets to the antipodean lifestyle. Certainly this was the way the Maoris have always cooked, placing food in flax baskets and steaming it in a *hangi* oven over hot stones.

Specialities particular to New Zealand include the bounty of shellfish reaped from its shoreline. It's common, even in cities, to see people thigh-deep in water gathering mussels and *pipis* into large flax bags at low tide. Delicate huge Bluff oysters from the Foveaux Strait are prized, as are scallops and increasingly paua (New Zealand abalone). Maoris traditionally ate the now-protected *toheroa*, a giant clam-sized mollusk, as well as tuatua (lizard-like reptile), and sea eggs, which have a dangerous spiky appearance until cooked and de-husked. Another Maori delicacy is the muttonbird, a greasy, salty cooked sooty shearwater bird. This is definitely an acquired taste, compared to the taste of a dead parrot by one sampler. More reassuringly, crayfish is widely eaten, as are a delicious variety of fish from local waters, such as snapper, orange roughy and tarakihi. Huge brown and rainbow trout are fished from New Zealand's rivers, as are the tiny, translucent whitebait, whose somber fate is to be turned into delicious fritters.

You may be fascinated by some local fruits. New Zealand brims with orchards plentiful in more pedestrian fare like apples and oranges. Kiwifruits have become synonymous with New Zealand, but more unusual are tamarillos, feijoas nashi pears (a cross between an apple and a pear), tangelos, or even the cache of succulent, sweet-tasting fruit in the core of the nikau palm, called "millionaire's fruit salad" because the tree dies when its heart is removed. Reserve this culinary treat only for emergencies if you are lost in the forest and haven't eaten for three days.

As a dessert, Pavlova is more than a national dish, it's an institution. Sweet, airy, and laden with calories, the dish was named after Anna Pavlova who visited New Zealand in 1926, and is better known as plain "Pav". Ironically, the famous dancer kept herself to a rigid diet that excluded potatoes, bread and red meat, let alone a dessert of such sumptuous proportions. Even though Australians contest claims of inventing the "Pav," both nations share it as a national dish, usually topped with kiwifruit slices or fresh strawberries.

New Zealand wines, especially white, are becoming recognized world-wide for their good value and high quality, moving beyond mass-market wines to challenge the French classics and the firmly-entrenched stars of California and Australia. Within the main wine-producing regions of Auckland,

Gisborne, Hawke Bay, Martinborough, Marlborough, Blenheim, Canterbury and Central Otago, you'll find plenty of opportunities to visit vineyards.

Star vineyards include Kumeu River and Goldwater Estate in the Auckland region; Morton Estate from Taurangay, Matawhero from Gisborue, Ngatawara from Hastings and Esk Valley from Napier. Kiwifruit wines and liqueurs are achieving some recognition too.

New Zealand's most famous beer is Steinlager, exported to some acclaim. In the South Island, "mainlanders" are rarely seen with a "Steinie" in their hands, but a Speights instead.

EATING OUT

In this book, restaurants may sometimes be categorized as licensed or BYO (guests may bring their own liquor), and are described as expensive when a meal for one costs more than NZ $60, moderate when between NZ$35 and $60 and inexpensive when under $35, all prices including wine.

EATING IN

If you stay in motels, backpacker lodges or camping grounds, you'll probably want to take advantage of kitchen facilities which allow you to cook your own meals. Even in small towns, supermarkets stock basic supplies, while on the coast, expect to find plenty of cheap, super-fresh seafood in the local fish shop.

TIPPING

Tips are eaccepted for good service. Neither hotel nor restaurant bills include service charges, but there is 12.5 percent Goods and Services Tax (GST).

HEALTH

With all its clean air, pristine water and outdoors activity, New Zealand is the sort of place that makes you feel healthier just by being there. Medical care and emergency facilities are excellent, but services are not free to visitors unless you have taken out travel insurance which covers all medical expenses. Health insurance can be bought on arrival from any number of local companies, if your own health plan does not cover New Zealand. Hotels and motels usually have their own arrangements with duty doctors, and after-hours pharmacists are listed in the local telephone directories.

In general, simple precautions go a long way. The one main health hazard is very rare as well as very easy to avoid. New Zealand's thermal mineral pools contain minuscule quantities of a type of amoeba or micro-organism which can cause fatal amoebic meningitis. But it can only enter through the ears and nose, so if you keep your head well above the water you'll be fine. Make sure children don't jump or dive into thermal pools.

Biologists claim they have found giardia, an intestinal parasite, in the alpine mountain streams that have previously been pure enough to bottle. So far it's not endemic. If you want to take extra care in the outdoors, boil the water for three minutes first.

Like other countries in the southern hemisphere, New Zealand has very strong summer sun, with rising cases of melanoma and other skin cancer. Sunburn and sunstroke are dangers. When you go out into the sun — and especially on the ski slopes where the snow surface reflects the rays — regularly protect all exposed skin with ultra-violet barrier (or filter) cream and use lip salve frequently. Sunglasses, preferably with UV filters, are essential.

Anyone who is about to embark on adventurous outdoor activities, such as tramping or river-rafting, should know about the potentially fatal dangers of hypothermia or exposure.

There are no snakes or dangerous wild animals in New Zealand. The only poisonous creature is the very rare *katipo* spider which hardly anyone ever sees. There are various fish, jelly-fish and other sea creatures which can sting or bite or which are dangerous to eat. Local advice about these is usually the best. Mosquitoes and sand flies are the worst pests, quite capable of driving you to insanity at your tranquil riverside campsite. Insect repellent doesn't always stop them.

TIME

New Zealand is close to the international date line and is 12 hours ahead of Greenwich Mean Time. Daylight Savings — an advance of one hour per day — begins the first Sunday in October (clocks go forward one hour) and finishes the third Sunday in March (clocks go back one hour).

BASICS

ELECTRICITY SUPPLY

The electric current is 230 volts, 50 cycles alternating current, although some hotels and motels also provide 110 volt-20 watt sockets for electric razors.

WEIGHTS AND MEASUREMENTS

All measures are metric. In case you are not used to this method here are a few approximate equivalents: one kilogram to two pounds; four liters to a gallon; a kilometer to five eighths of a mile; 20 °C to 68 °F; a yard to a meter.

OPENING HOURS

Most New Zealand offices and businesses are generally open to the public Monday to Friday between 8 am and 5 pm. Unless otherwise stated, museums, art galleries, and libraries are open from 9am to 4:30 pm. Banks are open Monday to Friday from 10 am to 4 pm, closed on holidays. Post Offices are open from Monday to Friday 9 am to 5 pm, closed weekends and holidays.

Shops and stores generally open between 9 am and 5:30 pm Monday to Thursday and until 9:30 pm Fridays. They are also open from 9:30 am to 1 pm on Saturdays in the main cities. In some tourist areas, such as Parnell and Queenstown, shops are also open on Sundays and most evenings too. Generally only dairies, which sell milk, papers and groceries, are open on Sunday.

WATER

New Zealand towns and cities have excellent public water supplies and tap (faucet) water is fresh and safe to drink.

TOILETS

Public toilets are generally ubiquitous, well-kept and well-supplied with paper and soap. You'll find them in all petrol stations, department stores, bus and train stations, car parks, museums and art galleries. In small towns, look out for the Plunket Rooms, which offer women's toilets and facilities for changing babies' nappies.

COMMUNICATION

MAIL

In some suburbs, rural areas and increasingly in the cities, postal services are available from general stores.

TELEPHONES

Telephone calls made from coin or card-operated public telephones to the local area (free call zone) cost 20 cents per minute. To place a long-distance call within the country, first dial the national access code 0, followed by the area code and finally the local number. Area codes for New Zealand cities and regions can be found in the telephone directory. Or call Telecom directory assistance on 018. For direct dialing of international calls you dial 00, then country code, area code and telephone number. Most hotels have facsimile facilities. The nationwide emergency number to call the police, fire service or ambulance is 111. Elsewhere, instructions are found in front of telephone directories or alongside public telephones.

MEDIA

There is no national newspaper, although Auckland's *New Zealand Herald* and Wellington's *Dominion* both have large circulations. Other regional newspapers range from the reasonably international to the totally parochial, worth reading to get a New Zealand world perspective. The *National Review* is the closest to a serious analytical news-magazine, whilst *The Listener* has weekly listings of radio and TV programs. Glossy publications giving insight into the New Zealand way of life are Auckland's *More, Metro, North and South* and *Fashion Quarterly* magazines.

There are four national radio networks in New Zealand and many local commercial radio stations broadcasting on both AM and FM bands, some with such apt names as Wellington's *Radio Windy* and Rotorua's *Geyserland FM*. Three national television channels broadcast a mixture of local and overseas current affairs, documentary, film and entertainment programs. Some large hotels also have satellite dishes to pick up CNN and Sky. Look for programs in the daily newspapers or in *The Listener*.

SHOPPING

The best advice is always to look for what local craftsmen do best, for what you won't find anywhere else. Depending on how ambitiously you follow this rule, you could take home a house-load of beautifully crafted native kauri furniture or just a pot of kiwi-fruit jam. The main souvenir staples — fluffy sheepskins in every conceivable manifestation, iridescent paua shell (abalone) and carved greenstone (New Zealand jade) — are by no means the only appealing items to buy.

Throughout the country, arts and crafts are very popular items to buy. Look for authentic, intricate wood, bone, and jade carving that reflect New Zealand's long Maori traditions and cottage crafts industries. New Zealand jade, more commonly referred to as greenstone, does not match the sheen of Burmese jade, but is nevertheless a distinctive Kiwi product. Greenstone and bone are worked into jewelry, ornaments, and Maori *tikis* (ancestral figurines). Greenstone is still mined along the West Coast of the South Island, and workshops in Hokitika allow visitors to watch the greenstone being worked.

You could easily spend all your time in New Zealand visiting craft studios of potters, painters, carvers and artisan's studios, particularly in the Bay of Islands, Coromandel, Nelson and the Banks Peninsula, which have large populations of artists and craftspeople.

With more than 100 million sheep, it follows that one of New Zealand's greatest exports is its sheepskin and woolen products, with a vast variety of coats, jackets and floor rugs. Most souvenir stores stock items made with slinkskin, opossum, deerskin,

leather and suede. Woolen goods — hand-knit sweaters and hand-spun yarn — are also good purchases. Outdoor garments and equipment also make excellent purchases. Companies like Canterbury — who make the rugby jerseys worn by the All Blacks — T Ski and Action Downunder produce smart, colorful recreation gear.

Other souvenir treats in New Zealand include vacuum-packed, exportable packages of such specialities as Bluff oysters, venison, honey and kiwifruit. A bottle or two of one of New Zealand's excellent wines is nice to take away with you too.

While not for everyone, the art of defying gravity bungy-style has become a major attraction in Queenstown.

Goods and Services Tax (GST) is a 12.5 percent surcharge applied on all goods and services. The only way to avoid it while shopping is though Duty-Free.

SAFETY

By and large, you will meet with good-natured generosity on your travels.

Hitch-hiking, for instance, is still considered fairly safe in New Zealand. However Auckland, the largest city, seems to have more problems than anywhere else in the country. Racial intolerance, rising unemployment and sheer boredom seem to be the main factors. The usual precautions for personal safety apply, especially in Auckland. Avoid walking empty streets and going into public toilets late at night. Don't flaunt your leather jacket either — there have been cases of them being grabbed off people's backs. Don't advertise a bulging wallet, always lock unattended vehicles and make use of safes at hotels and lodges.

WOMEN ALONE

The same rules for safety apply to women traveling alone. Rapes and violent assaults of women tourists are not unheard of. Women should never hitchhike alone and be attuned to their instincts when it comes to accepting offers of hospitality. It is very easy in New Zealand to find yourself almost completely alone on beaches, mountain trails or even in a bus station, and you may feel justifiably nervous about going to such places on your own.

PUBLIC HOLIDAYS AND FESTIVALS

JANUARY
New Year's Day
Annual Yachting Regatta, Auckland
FEBRUARY
New Zealand Day or Waitangi Day, 6 February, celebrated with Maori pomp and war canoe races at Waitangi in Northland.
New Zealand Open Fishing Contest, Ninety Mile Beach, Bay of Islands.

Martinborough Country Fairs
Marlborough Food and Wine Festival, Blenheim.
Floral Festival, Christchurch.
MARCH
Good Friday and Easter Monday
Fiesta Week, mid-month in Auckland, with fireworks and the Round the Bays Run.
Golden Shears Sheep Shearing Contest, Masterton.
Ngaruawahia Regatta for Maori Canoes, Hamilton.
New Zealand International Festival of the Arts, Wellington.
Dunedin Summer Festival
APRIL
Anzac Day, April 25
Highland Games, Hastings
JUNE
Queen's Birthday (the first Monday in June)
New Zealand Agricultural Field Day, Mystery Creek, Hamilton.
JULY
Queenstown Winter Festival
OCTOBER
Labor Day (the fourth Monday in October)
NOVEMBER
Canterbury Show Week, Christchurch
International Trout Fishing Contest, Rotorua
DECEMBER
Christmas Day and Boxing Day

The following local holidays commemorate provincial anniversaries. When they fall Friday through Sunday the holiday is observed on the Monday immediately afterwards, otherwise it is observed on the preceding Monday.

Northland: January 29; *Auckland*: January 29; *Hawke Bay*: October 17; *Taranaki*: March 8; *Wellington*: January 22; *Marlborough*: November 1; *Canterbury*: December 16; *The West Coast*: December 1; *Otago and Southland*: March 23.

NEW ZEALAND SLANG

Most New Zealanders grow up with English as their only language, although Maori is increasingly smiled upon as an official language too, with some 50,000 fluent speakers. But "New Zildish" — or Kiwi slang — can be both baffling and amusing for outsiders. You'll be asked "Gidday, how ya going?" which doesn't refer to whether you ride a car or a bike, but your general state of health. People say, "Crickey Dick," or "Blimey, mate," instead of "Oh Golly." "Fair dinkum," means "is that so?" New Zealand's raunchy Gold Rush "Wild West" ways created many florid expressions. A local pub is known as "the boozer," while someone who drinks a lot is always "on the piss." If someone is "on the ran-tan," it means they are "out on the town" painting the town red. A "dead marine" is an empty beer bottle, and if someone collapses in a drunken stupor (as is not unheard of in New Zealand), they will be referred to as a "blotto joker." A "wowser" is a kill-joy or a party-pooper. Pub talk is peppered with "just quietly..." which means "between you and me..." and "it's your shout" meaning its your turn to pay for the next round of drinks, while a "bludger" is someone who never pays. When you "shout," you'll find that "she'll be right, mate" is a phrase that trips off the tongue of your drinking companions.

"Townies" are city-dwellers to country people, but "townies," are likely to retort that they have no intention of living in the "back-blocks," which means a remote rural district, "gone bush," or "up the boo-ays," which means the same thing. The expression: "He's up the boo-ays shooting *pukekos* with a long-handled shovel," is a uniquely novel way of implying that someone's disappearance is unaccounted for, and wherever they are, they're probably doing something they shouldn't. People don't depart, they "shoot through," and if someone is tired they'll tell you that they're "right shagged," "buggered," or "puckerooed." Liars are "fibbers," while people who go insane are "crackers" or "gone berko" (berserk) and are sent to the "loony bin" or the mental institution.

You go to the "flics" instead of the movies, and invite people over for "tea" rather than dinner, a manner of speaking that can befuddle visitors, especially if you are asked to "bring a plate," which means bring a plate with something *on it*, not an empty plate!. People are always stopping to "have a cuppa" (of tea) and chew "chutty" not chewing

gum. A "cow cockie" is a dairy farmer, a "Dally" is a Dalmatian immigrant, and "Dally plonk" is the wine made by naturalized Dalmatian immigrants, currently winning international awards. A "dairy" (pronounced dearie) is New Zealand's ubiquitous corner shop, a "bach" (pronounced batch) is a modest holiday home, stemming from the word "bachelor" which has a "dunny," the rather crude word for the lavatory, or even a "long drop," a pit toilet. "Jandels" are flip-flops, while "pikelets" are a kind of scone.

A number of Maori words have entered the language of English-speaking New Zealanders such as "hangi" for earth-oven, "marae" for a Maori meeting house, "pakeha" as a non-offensive term for white people.

THE MAORI LANGUAGE

When pronouncing Maori words, the main thing to keep in mind is the sound of the five vowels:

a ar, as in f*ar*ther
e air, as in m*ea*sure
i ee, as in s*ee*m
o or, as in l*ow*
u oo, as in r*oo*m

Most Maori words, all syllables end in a vowel. Thus "maori" is pronounced ma-o-ree. The most confusing compound consonants are WH and NG. The closest sound in English for WH is F, while NG is a nasal sound, used as the beginning of a syllable. For instance, *Whangarei* is pronounced *Fa-ñga-rei*, while *Ngaruwahia* is pronounced *Ngar-roo-ar-war-hee-ar*. Most bookshops have Maori-English phrasebooks and dictionaries in New Zealand.

Some Maori Words
welcome *haere-mai*
good-bye *haera-ra*
hello, good health, good-luck *kia-ora*
good morning *morena*
how are you? (one person) *kei te pehea kowa*
how are you? (two people) *kei te pehea korua*
I am well *kei te pai*
until we meet again *ka kite ano*
yes *ae*

no *kao*
war dance *haka*
feast *hakari*
oven made by digging a hole and steaming food in baskets over burning embers *hangi*
carved, stylized human figure worn around the neck, usually shortened to "tiki' *hei-tiki*
food *kai*
sweet potato, a Maori staple food *kumara*
psychic power or influence *mana*
Maori culture, things Maori *maoritanga*
chin tattoo on women, only occasionally seen these days and usually on old women *moko*

flat greenstone war club *mere*
fortified village, usually on a hilltop *pa*
European, white person *pakeha*
taboo, forbidden *tapu*
priest, wizard or soothsayer *tohunga*
amulet or figurine, often a carved representation of an ancestor *Maoritiki*
satisfaction for injuries received; payment; revenge *utu*
water, names with "*wai*" in them are usually on a river *wai*
house *whare*
meeting house *whare runanga*

EMBASSIES AND CONSULATES

As New Zealand's capital, Wellington is the base for consulates and embassies of many countries, including the following:

Australian High Commission ((04) 473-6411, 72-76 Hobson Street.

Austrian Embassy ((04) 801-9709, 22 Garret Street.

Belgian Embassy ((04) 472-9558, 1 Willeston Street.

British High Commission ((04) 472-6049, Reserve Bank Building, 2 The Terrace

Canadian High Commission ((04) 473-9577, ICI House, 67 Molesworth Street

Chinese Embassy ((04) 472-1180, 2–6 Glenmore Street

French Embassy ((04) 472-0200, 1–3 Willeston Street

German Embassy ((04) 473-6063, 90–92 Hobson Street.

Indian High Commission ((04) 473-6360, 180 Molesworth Street

Indonesian Embassy ((04) 475-8699, 70 Glen Road, Kelburn

Italian Embassy ((04) 473-5339, 38 Grant Road

Japanese Embassy ((04) 473-1540, Norwich House, 311 Hunter Street

Malaysian High Commission ((04) 385-2439, 10 Washington Ave

Netherlands Embassy ((04) 473-8652, corner of Featherston and Ballance streets.

Norwegian Embassy ((04) 471-2503, 199 Lampton Quay

Philippines Embassy ((04) 471-2455, 50 Hobson Street

Royal Danish Embassy ((04) 472-0020, 105 The Terrace

Singapore High Commission ((04) 479-2076, 17 Kabul Street

Swedish Embassy ((04) 472-0909, 39 The Terrace

Swiss Embassy ((04) 472-1593, 22-24 Panama Street

Thai Embassy ((04) 476-8619, 2 Cook Street, Karori

United States Embassy ((04) 472-2068, 29 Fitzherbert Terrace.

Maori carving at Waitangi Maori meeting house.

Suggested Reading

Collections and Anthologies

Anthology of Twentieth Century New Zealand Poetry, selected with an introduction by Vincent O'Sullivan, Oxford University Press, 1979

Automobile Association Book of New Zealand Walkways, Landsdowne Press

Into the World of Light: An Anthology of Maori Writing, ed. by Witi Ihemaera and D.S. Long, Heineman, 1982.

Oxford Book of Contemporary New Zealand Poetry, chosen by Fleur Adcock, Oxford University Press in association with Auckland University Press, 1982.

Fiction

FRAME, JANET *An Autobiography: To The Is-Land, Angel At My Table, The Envoy From Mirror City; Owls Do Cry*, W.H. Allen, 1961; *A State of Seige*, Pegasus Press, 1967; *Living in the Maniototo*, Braziller (New York) 1979.

GEE, MAURICE *Plumb*, Faber and Faber, (London) 1979; *Meg*, Faber and Faber (London) 1981; *Sole Survivor*, Faber and Faber (London) 1983.

HULME, KERI *The Bone People*, Winner of the Booker Prize in 1985. *Ihimaera*, Whiti, Tangi, Heinemann, 1974; *Whanau*, Heinemann, 1974; *The New Net Goes Fishing*, Heinemann, 1977.

MANSFIELD, KATHERINE *Collected Short Stories*, Sargeson, Frank, Collected Stories, Penguin, 1982.

General

BUCK, SIR P. *The Coming of the Maori*, Whitcombe and Tombs, 1974.

BULLER, SIR W *Birds of New Zealand*, Whitcombe and Tombs, 1967.

COBBS, L., and DUNCAN, J. *New Zealand's National Parks*, Hamlyn, 1980.

DOCKING, G.C. *Two Hundred Years of New Zealand Painting*, A.H. and A.W. Reed, 1971.

HOUGHTON, B.F., *Geyserland: A Guide to the Volcanoes and Geothermal Areas of Rotorua*, Geological Society of New Zealand.

HUNTER, GRANT, *The New Zealand Tramper's Handbook*. Heinemann Reed, Auckland 1989.

KING, MICHAEL *Being Pakeha*, Hodder and Stoughton Ltd. 1985.

LAING, R.M. and BLACKWELL, E.W *Plants of New Zealand*, Whitcombe and Tombs, 1964.

METGE, J. *The Maoris of New Zealand*, Routeledge (London) 1976.

ORANGE, CLAUDIA, *The Treaty of Waitangi* and *The Story of a Treaty*, both published by Allen & Unwin, Wellington, 1989.

PICKERING, MARK, *New Zealand's Top Tracks*, Heinemann Reed, Auckland, 1990.

POPE, DIANA AND JEREMY, The *Mobil Illustrated Guide to New Zealand*, Reed, Wellington, 1982.

POTTON, CRAIG and WOOD, PETER *New Zealand's Geothermal Landscape*, Craig Potton Publishing Ltd, Nelson.

REED, A.W. *A Dictionary of Maori Place Names*, Reed Menthuen, Auckland 1986.

SALMON, J.T., *The Native Trees of New Zealand*, Reed, 1980.

SINCLAIR, KEITH *History of New Zealand*, Penguin and Allen Lane, (London), revised 1988; *A Destiny Apart. New Zealand's Search for National Identity*. Allen and Unwin, London. 1986.

Photo Credits

All photographs by **Robert Holmes** except those listed below:

Trevern and Anna Dawes: Pages 3 to 7, 19 to 21, 34 to 35, 38 to 39 *left*, 59, 62 to 63, 72 to 73, 78 to 79, 84 to 85, 96 to 97, 98 *right*, 99, 104, 105, 118 to 119, 124 *right*, 125 to 127 *left*, 130 to 131, 140, 152 to 153, 157, 161, 166 *top*, 172, 175, 176 to 177, 188 to 189, 192 *right*, 193, 196, 200, 207, 208, and 213.

Nik Wheeler: Pages 12, 15, 22 to 23 *left*, 31, 33, 37, 39 *right*, 54, 56 to 58, 61, 64 to 69, 87, 89, 180, 185, 197, 204 to 205 *left*, and 222.

Quick Reference A–Z Guide
to Places and Topics of Interest with Listed Accommodation, Restaurants and Useful Telephone Numbers